The
Accidental
Startup

The
Accidental
Startup

Danielle Babb, Ph.D., MBA

ALPHA

A member of Penguin Group (USA) Inc.

This book is dedicated to all the men and women so bravely and proudly serving in our armed forces to protect the freedoms we so cherish. You allow us to pursue our dreams by sacrificing for your nation. Thank you.

ALPHA BOOKS

Published by the Penguin Group

Penguin Group (USA) Inc., 375 Hudson Street, New York, New York 10014, USA

Penguin Group (Canada), 90 Eglinton Avenue East, Suite 700, Toronto, Ontario M4P 2Y3, Canada (a division of Pearson Penguin Canada Inc.)

Penguin Books Ltd., 80 Strand, London WC2R 0RL, England

Penguin Ireland, 25 St. Stephen's Green, Dublin 2, Ireland (a division of Penguin Books Ltd.)

Penguin Group (Australia), 250 Camberwell Road, Camberwell, Victoria 3124, Australia (a division of Pearson Australia Group Pty. Ltd.)

Penguin Books India Pvt. Ltd., 11 Community Centre, Panchsheel Park, New Delhi—110 017, India

Penguin Group (NZ), 67 Apollo Drive, Rosedale, North Shore, Auckland 1311, New Zealand (a division of Pearson New Zealand Ltd.)

Penguin Books (South Africa) (Pty.) Ltd., 24 Sturdee Avenue, Rosebank, Johannesburg 2196, South Africa

Penguin Books Ltd., Registered Offices: 80 Strand, London WC2R 0RL, England

International Standard Book Number: 978-1-59257-886-3
Library of Congress Catalog Card Number: 2008939798

12   10   09   8   7   6   5   4   3   2   1

Interpretation of the printing code: The rightmost number of the first series of numbers is the year of the book's printing; the rightmost number of the second series of numbers is the number of the book's printing. For example, a printing code of 09-1 shows that the first printing occurred in 2009.

Printed in the United States of America

Note: This publication contains the opinions and ideas of its author. It is intended to provide helpful and informative material on the subject matter covered. It is sold with the understanding that the author and publisher are not engaged in rendering professional services in the book. If the reader requires personal assistance or advice, a competent professional should be consulted.

The author and publisher specifically disclaim any responsibility for any liability, loss, or risk, personal or otherwise, which is incurred as a consequence, directly or indirectly, of the use and application of any of the contents of this book.

Trademarks: All terms mentioned in this book that are known to be or are suspected of being trademarks or service marks have been appropriately capitalized. Alpha Books and Penguin Group (USA) Inc. cannot attest to the accuracy of this information. Use of a term in this book should not be regarded as affecting the validity of any trademark or service mark.

Most Alpha books are available at special quantity discounts for bulk purchases for sales promotions, premiums, fundraising, or educational use. Special books, or book excerpts, can also be created to fit specific needs.

For details, write: Special Markets, Alpha Books, 375 Hudson Street, New York, NY 10014.

Contents

Appendixes

Letter to the Reader

Welcome to the world of entrepreneurship! My name is Dr. Dani Babb; I am an author, professor, and analyst for the media in the world of business. I write and teach for a living, and it is with great pleasure that I wrote this guide for the budding entrepreneur—designed for the underemployed, the unemployed, and the "just sick and tired of the corporate world" workers in our nation and throughout the world who want to do business in America!

With rising costs of going to work (including the time and money spent commuting), the increasingly overwhelming feeling of being tied to our day jobs 24/7, and electronic gadgets that routinely make us feel completely incapable of leaving work behind, many of us have turned to running our own business as a dream we always wanted to fulfill, but were never quite sure how. Having started (and ended) many companies, and now running a successful one in multiple lines of business, I understand firsthand how it feels to try and fail—try and fail—and then try and *succeed* at owning and running your own business—the best feeling in the world.

A professor by nature, I tend to write to help others—whether through articles or books. This book is designed to help walk a new entrepreneur, step by step, through all the steps needed to own and run your own business. From figuring out what you want to do to quitting that part time job, from planning family time to going through all the legal and financial obligations of owning your own business, all the way through marketing it successfully and exceeding profit expectations, this book is geared toward making you a success!

Throughout the last couple of years, we've seen the face of business change drastically in this country. One thing that hasn't changed is the amazingly resilient entrepreneurial spirit. The thing deep in our gut that keeps us wanting a better life; to be in business for ourselves; to create something and call it our own—to be the masters of our own success.

Success is based on many definitions; I give lots of personal examples throughout this book. My goal is for you to hit the mark of success based on what is important to *you*, the reader—the new entrepreneur. With practical advice, surveys from the trenches (responses from other entrepreneurs living our dream), lots of research, and fantastic resources, you have in your hands a pathway—a guide book—to creating and sustaining your own business. To all of you who want to be your own boss; to all of you who are tired of making "the man" rich instead of yourself; to all of you who are weary of the ups and downs of corporate downsizing, rightsizing, and all those other terms that create personal instability; to all of you who are sick of commuting two hours and taking orders from people who don't understand the business—I say *go for it!* Educate yourself, prepare what you need to so you feel comfortable moving onward, and let's get going!

I'm always open to questions and comments, and many people communicate on my blogs and forums to share ideas. I welcome you to my website and hope to see you in both the virtual community and the traditional seminars—but most importantly, I wish you the best of luck in your new business endeavors.

Sincerely,

Dani Babb, Ph.D., MBA
www.drdaniellebabb.com

Introduction

Entrepreneurs have lots of motivations and reasons for pursuing their dreams. Some are driven by income potential, others are fulfilling a childhood dream or using their expertise to build their own business instead of choosing to go to work for someone else.

Entrepreneurs are risk takers—they realize that the potentially incredible rewards are worth the hard hours and the risks, and they focus on the possibilities, the upsides, and the pride of ownership. They love to build; they have passions and dreams and they don't sit idly by watching others pursue them without acting on their own.

The rising costs of fuel, the increasing commute times, and spending less time with family and more time tied to a BlackBerry are driving the desire for many people to start and run their own businesses. Many face underemployment— in fact, underemployment casts a wide net. Underemployment means not being employed at the rate you want to be—perhaps not using your skills to their fullest or not having as much work as you want. It means having the ability, based on your education level, to get a higher paying job but working in a low-skill, low-wage job instead. Underemployment means working part time when you need and want to work full time. Underemployment has many causes—companies needing part time people to avoid paying costly healthcare means that they may avoid full time workers and create underemployed workers, or businesses seeing an economic slowdown that impacts their bottom line may choose to put people on part time payroll or contractual work because they aren't sure if they will be able to pay the bills of full time workers. Underemployment isn't just an American problem; it is affecting Australia, the UK, and many developing nations. That doesn't solve our problems, though.

Of course, being underemployed is not as financially devastating as being completely unemployed, but many of you picking up this book may be in that situation, too. Unemployment rates were on the rise throughout 2008 and many economists predict this may continue throughout the rest of the decade.

Yet many unemployed and underemployed folks—or even those fully employed but unhappy in their jobs—have alternatives. The alternative is finding and pursuing your passion—and in comes entrepreneurship. Estimates indicate that 80 percent of new jobs today are created by small businesses, and business people—those who are new to the job market right out of college perhaps and Baby Boomers alike—are finding solace, comfort, and satisfaction of all kinds in their own businesses instead.

Running your own business takes perseverance, it takes risk, and it takes planning—and then some! Entrepreneurship isn't for everyone, but it is for many. However, many people just don't know where to begin, and that is what this book will help you do.

From finding your passion to determining how to make money doing it; from creating a company name and logo to nationalizing your brand; from small time to a global company—this book walks you through all the steps of becoming an entrepreneur, and then the challenge of maintaining your status as one.

Be informed, enjoy the journey, read the survey data from the trenches. The survey asked many questions from what kind of technology entrepreneurs use to what they found most difficult, to what they found most useful and whether they met revenue expectations, and when. Most importantly, don't lose your passion while you educate yourself with as many sources as possible—this book being one. Welcome to entrepreneurship!

Acknowledgments

Thanks to Matt for hanging in there through all the ups and downs and crazy changes in life—it is a blast isn't it?

To my dear friend Arlene—we sure do go through some weird stuff together don't we? Partners in crime forever!

A very big thank you to Bob Diforio—the best literary agent there is—for his friendship and as always, his expertise

Hugs to my grandfather, Donald, who is an inspiration and a compass in life.

To my nephew—may you have all in life that you want and persevere to get it.

To my great friend Alex, for his wisdom and humor and teaching me so many terrific things.

To Shane for all of his hard work and dedication and his unwavering friendship.

To my friend and business partner, John, for his wisdom and knowledge and seeing the soul behind the steel.

Does Self Employment Make Sense for You?

The very first thing you need to determine when deciding to go into business for yourself is whether self employment—being your own boss—makes sense for you.

It might seem as though the automatic answer is "yes," but there are some vital things to consider before reaching this paramount decision. For instance, do you work best within a corporate structure? Do you want to be responsible for your own destiny or would you prefer a ladder to climb? Are you willing to put in the hours and commitment it takes to be successful in your own business? Do you have the flexibility required to plan for, launch, and operate your own venture—do you have children, a spouse or significant other, and other important commitments? These are some things to think about as we embark on our discussion of what it takes to be an entrepreneur, what your personal situation is, and why you might just become the next Accidental Tycoon.

Throughout this book, I will refer to a survey that I created and conducted, with a sample rate of greater than 200, specifically for this book. All participants were required to have started a business and be self-employed entrepreneurs. The results will fascinate you, and they begin in this chapter!

You're probably wondering why you're having a difficult time deciding whether going to work for yourself is the right thing for you. In the aforementioned survey, a full quarter of the individuals surveyed said it was a tough decision. On the contrary, though, three quarters of the participants said it was not a tough decision, but most indicated that they could have used more information before taking the plunge.

Your Current Position

Most of you reading this book will have some employment situation you are trying to remedy. There are many, and we will go through what each means and how it may impact your life as an entrepreneur. The key thing is to analyze and acknowledge what your own personal situation is, and what you're trying to get out of becoming your own boss.

Unemployed

The unemployment rate in the United States in 2008 was rising, hovering at a bit over 6 percent. This means that about 6 percent of you are not working, and many of you want to be. There is a phenomenon in economics called the "natural rate of unemployment," which means that a segment of the population doesn't want to work and therefore isn't unemployed by definition. However, economists have argued for years over what the "natural rate" really is, and some even argue that there is no such thing, given ample opportunity and pay.

If you are unemployed, there is probably no better time for you to pursue your own business—unless you are actively looking for a job and have a mortgage payment due next week. If that is the case, you may have to find a corporate job with some flexibility so you can still start your own business on the side, and eventually make "it."

Underemployed

What does it mean to be underemployed? It means you want more work than you have now, and this may very well apply to you. Numbers on underemployment aren't widely collected or considered very accurate because if you have a job you are not unemployed, which is the number economists focus on.

If you are underemployed, you might be working part time but really need to be working full time. You might be a part time administrative assistant wanting full time work, or you might be in a part time job working for an employment agency and looking for a full time position. You may have dreams of owning your own business, but with family obligations and your part time job you're struggling to find the time.

This actually may be the most ideal situation to be in; you are in fact earning something—hopefully enough to pay the bills—and you can use the time you would be spending looking for a job becoming the next great small business owner. All it takes is an idea, a plan, and some courage.

Additionally, lots of workers may have full time jobs, but feel underemployed because the cost of goods and services they purchase, like fuel and clothing, have gone up, so their current job no longer makes ends meet. Having a full time job and not being able to pay the bills is extraordinarily frustrating. The "out" for you may well be becoming your own boss, even starting while you still hold down your day job.

Certainly the costs of getting to work and preparing for that day job are rising. You may be seriously concerned about the rising costs of living or commuting to work—or you may just flat out be tired of wasting one to two hours per day stuck in traffic. Being your own boss means working from wherever you think best—whether that's from your home office in your PJs or from your own corporate skyscraper.

It is very important to note where the survey respondents said they were when they made the switch to self employment:

- 63 percent were employed when they took the leap to their own business
- 26 percent were underemployed and wanting full time work
- 10 percent were unemployed

Worried About Losing a Job and Conflicting Obligations

Still yet, you might be fully employed but seeing your company, well, struggling to maintain its employment level. You may be working for a large financial institution and have a nagging feeling that you'll be losing your job very shortly, or you may just feel insecure with a frustrating boss, cost-cutting, and a business looking to make the company more "efficient"—often by cutting positions.

Often those most at risk are middle management, who are said to add less value than senior leaders or worker bees. You may have time during your day to begin your own business without quitting your job. Try to think of what you do during the day and see if you can carve an hour or two out of it to begin your new business. The goal? Not to rely on "the man" (or "the woman") anymore—but on yourself instead!

You may also be torn between conflicting obligations—family and work—and have a corporate job that is getting more demanding with 24/7 response times, all made possible due to our lovely society driven by BlackBerry devices and cell phones. Perhaps you are just tired of this, and you want to set the rules. Who can blame you? I did the same thing.

SURVEY SAYS

What were some of the reasons our survey participants said that they knew having their own business was right for them? Knowing they would feel better about themselves by working for themselves than by working for someone else, and that the profit and loss would be attributed to their own work. Others noted that it was a natural part of their professional development. Some said they had worked their whole career just to start their own business. Others felt that Corporate America put people into boxes and that running into the glass ceiling was disheartening—they weren't going to hold themselves down in their own business! Still others indicated that the country so badly needed the service they provided that it was a "no brainer." Most mentioned the possibility of earning a good income, and many noted that the ability to spend time with their families and set their own schedules were tops on their priority lists.

Benefits of Working for Yourself

The benefits of working for yourself are phenomenal and potentially endless. There are vastly more benefits, in my view, than drawbacks. Like many of you may decide to do, I quit my day job with a new home and heavy mortgage, less income from my new Accidental Business than anticipated, and a new marriage with additional costs and heavy home obligations. Still, the benefits of working for myself significantly outweighed the downsides. Personally, I was tired of the layoffs in information technology; tired of the constant boss changes that left us all wondering if we would be replaced by the new boss's best friend from his or her former company. This, in many respects, was more stressful than quitting and "going for it" on my own. After careful analysis, you may come to the same conclusion.

So what are some of the benefits?

Stable Income

Did I just say stable income? Yes, stable. Why? Because you are setting your salary, not some random corporate representative from human resources in conjunction with an accountant who wants to cut costs.

How much are you worth? I don't know—you tell me! Do you want an annual 5 percent raise? Give it to yourself. Do you want to run the financial show? Run it. You can actually have a more stable income by being self employed than by working for Corporate America.

No More Job-Loss Fear

One of my initial fears, leaving Corporate America behind and pursuing my dreams, was that I would lose contracts—the key to keeping my business alive. But what was more likely? That, due to a failed project or a missed deadline or office politics, a new boss would come in and would be accompanied by inconsistent, seemingly confusing changes that were not communicated to the rest of us, leaving anxiety running rampant? Or that I would be so complacent as to lose contracts and either not get them back or not replace them?

I finally decided to bet on myself, and I am glad that I did. Looking back, I wouldn't change anything, except maybe not waiting so long to take that first step (or leap, as it were). However, the timing does have to be right, and I will help you figure out whether or not it is. Begin by thinking about what an ideal time would be for you. Figure out what is ideal and what isn't—and what is an excuse for procrastination. Ask yourself what your job-loss fears are, and what you can do by being your own boss to mitigate them.

Additional Income

The additional income that comes with being your own boss, in my view, is the icing on the proverbial cake. The maximum amount of income is purely based on your business model, your ability to adapt to change, your effort, your decisions, your relationships and networking, and your business planning. Are you getting the picture? The additional income you can earn is literally entirely up to you. You may just want to earn what you're making now but be your own boss and have some additional freedom, in which case, fine—the goal setting is yours to do. But the possibilities for financial freedom are truly endless.

> It is amazing how quickly you begin a business and then cannot stop thinking of ways to expand it. It seems that from the very same day the concept begins, the planning doesn't stop and you are constantly, sometimes hourly, coming up with ideas on ways to make more money.

Freedom

Ah yes, freedom—that thing we all so cherish, yet seem to freely give up when we happily sign onto new jobs as employees. Many of us have even been guilty of going out and celebrating this relinquishing of our freedom as a great new job with outstanding prospects, only to be disappointed in the feeling of being chained to our desk or BlackBerry. Maybe you have a six-figure job (or more) that you love and you have no reason to want more freedom—but chances are this isn't your position. Freedom, as defined in this book, is the ability to make your own decisions and make changes as you see fit, when you see fit. Freedom comes from being your own boss, and setting your own agenda.

Flexible Hours

Do you want the ultimate in flexibility with regard to your hours? Being an entrepreneur might be exactly what the doctor ordered. Yes, you will need to work a lot to be successful—who doesn't? We rarely hear of stories (aside from in infomercials) where an entrepreneur brags about how little work he or she did to make that half-a-million dollar business streamlined and efficient. But while you may need to put your time in, you will have flexibility in when you do so. One of my primary motivators for having my own business was my insomnia; managers weren't happy about my odd working hours and my decision never to hold a meeting before 9 A.M., despite knowing there was a solid chance I hadn't gotten to sleep until 6 that same morning. So what happened after I started my own gig? I work more hours, but my hours work around me. This is a substantial difference, and in my case a medical necessity. I set my working hours and stick to them. I still don't schedule meetings before a certain hour—only now that time is 10 A.M. This has led to less stress overall and a feeling of control over my own workload and schedule, which was and continues to be vital to me.

The type of flexibility you need will depend on your own situation. Many people are morning enthusiasts and do their most creative work then; others travel so much they forget what time zone they're in or what time it is at all (this is my life these days). Many want the freedom to schedule their meetings, work, and appointments around their children's plays and to work when they are most creative (2 A.M.?). You will indeed get this flexibility as an Accidental Tycoon.

Bringing Your Passions to Work

Every single day when you go to work for yourself, you will be doing what you love and, if you play your cards right, loving what you're doing. This means that your passions don't have to be left at home. Let's say your passion is knitting—albeit probably not common, it is your passion nonetheless—so you decide to build your fortune around knitting (and yes, it can be done!). When you went to your 9 to 5 job, you most likely had to stop knitting unless it was your break time. In your own business, your passion is your business—or should be! Rather than leaving your passions checked at the office door, you're taking them to work with you each day.

Pride of Ownership

Those of you who own your own home after renting for a while know what I am referring to here. Whether it's paying off that car and owning it, paying off that college degree and owning the diploma you worked hard for, or owning your own business, there is a pride that comes with ownership that is hard to describe to those who don't own what is most valuable to them.

If you think homeownership creates pride, imagine knowing that paying for that home does not come from income your boss gave you in exchange for hours, but from your own hard work, your ingenuity, your contributions, your dedication.

The feeling is nearly impossible to describe, but when you reach that destination, no matter the hours you put in, the sense of pride of ownership is overwhelming. I remember my first tax return at the young age of 16 that included my first Schedule C for $10,000 in the computer consulting that I had done in my small business, California Computer Concepts. It was more than I had made doing anything else (like working fast food) and the feeling I got when I fixed company computers and became their hero for the day (by getting their business back up and running) was like nothing else. It was then that I got hooked on self employment.

Earning Potential

Your earning potential is perhaps the greatest reward for many people, particularly if you are underemployed or tired of working for Corporate America and taking whatever they give you—waiting for that December review to see if your pay increase will even keep up with inflation or cost of living.

With your own business, your earning potential is whatever you want it to be. Do you want to make a million a year gross? Net? No problem. Set your own goals. You will find ways to grow your business that allow you to reach these goals and successfully manage your thriving business. You may even find your goals changing as you get into your work, adjusting downward if family time begins to take higher priority, or upward if you find yourself more into your work than you thought—or if the kids go away to college. The key is to set your sights and go for it, and then adjust if you need to. I will never forget the HAM radio club and BBS owner (I am surely dating myself here, as this was the early days of the Internet, accessed by the 300-baud modem into what was known as a Bulletin Board System) telling me one day, "You're very bright, but don't set your sights on a $300,000 per year job. That is tough. $100,000 is more realistic." I'd love to see that guy again now!

Don't let anyone tell you what is or isn't realistic. Whatever limit you are willing to work toward is "realistic." You may not start off with your dream salary—in fact, chances are you won't. But with some creativity and some time, you will find ways to branch your business out to earn something equivalent to what you're willing to put in. Some people will tell you that luck is always involved, and perhaps a little bit is, but I believe in the value of making your own luck.

What about our survey participants? For those who left Corporate America, they were asked what drove them to that decision. They were given the opportunity to select more than one reason, and their responses were ...

- Flexible hours, taking the cake at a whopping 72 percent!
- Higher earning potential, at 46 percent.
- Following personal dreams, at 36 percent.
- Long-term wealth potential, at 30 percent.
- The desire to do something new, at 28 percent.
- The cost of commuting was a factor for 22 percent of respondents.
- Being a "born entrepreneur" was a factor for 22 percent.
- The time of commutes was a factor for 18 percent.
- Wanting to be at home with young children came in at 18 percent.
- Seeing an employer do a bad job in the same industry registered with a full 10 percent.
- Illness was a factor for 4 percent.

What about other responses? Some noted the difficulty in finding a satisfying job in Corporate America, underemployment, not wanting to make others rich, wanting to travel whenever they felt like it, being in control of their own destiny, job loss, and flexibility.

Do any of these sound like you?

Downsides to Working for Yourself

Okay, so we've run through a plethora of upsides to working for yourself, but the reality is that many of you may not have pursued your dreams because of the downsides, or what you perceive as the possible problems as you begin working for yourself.

These downsides shouldn't be downplayed—they are relevant and important and probably quite valid. Chances are they are based on your own life situation and therefore they need to be addressed. Here are some of the most common things I hear, and how to overcome them.

Feeling of Instability

The first day I didn't report to Corporate America, a feeling of sheer panic set over my body—a series of what ifs. What if my clients didn't renew my contracts? What if I couldn't grow my business as fast as I thought, or needed? What if I couldn't pay my mortgage? What if …? These thoughts plagued my mind, and several times I almost thought of taking back my resignation.

The truth is, you will probably feel a sense of instability for a while—this is particularly common in the early growth stages of any new business. You need to have confidence in your idea and in yourself, and this comes from doing the homework necessary to know that your plan is viable. It also helps (although is in no way a necessity, but based on your individual situation) to have six months' worth of liquid capital in the bank so you can pay bills for six months if you need to go back to Corporate America before trying out a new job. Another option is to switch to part time work that will give you time to start the new business and begin generating buzz and income before you quit the rat race for good.

> For some excellent resources on leaving the rat race without starting your own business check out Rat Race Rebellion online—premade, prescreened jobs that might be the boost you need to leave your day job and start something new! Check out www.ratracerebellion.com for more information!

Your own life situation will change how you react to this variable. For instance, if you have children and a hefty mortgage, you might choose the latter option; whereas if you are single, in your twenties, and can rent from a friend if things go sour, you may end up dropping everything and just going for it from day one.

Don't let this worry keep you from your dreams. The more upfront planning you put into your business, the less likely you are to experience financial instabilities. You also need to plan your income, track your revenue and expenditures, and keep expenses low at startup. I'll go into all of this in later chapters.

Potential for Failure

Sure, you could fail at this new business. The business could end up failing you, either due to circumstance, poor planning, lack of interest, or procrastination— or something entirely different. The market could drop out of your perfect new product or service. The world could collapse into a black hole tomorrow. But the upsides are huge, so you need to weigh them against the potential for failure.

I found the best weapon against this fear was a contingency plan; hence starting my business a few months before quitting my day job. You will find a balance that is right for you by exploring your needs versus your desires and striking that just-right equation. Remember: The more you plan, the lower your chance of failure.

Part of the fear you may feel at some point in the process isn't necessarily fear of failure, but fear of success! Yes, you read that right. Many of us, at some point in our lives, are afraid of success. I can almost hear you asking yourself, "Who's afraid of success, and why on Earth would they be?"

George Will once said that "the nice part about being a pessimist is that you are constantly being either proven right or pleasantly surprised." Many people, unbeknownst to themselves, are in some ways pessimistic, especially with regard to their own success, which ultimately becomes their largest hurdle. They believe so little in themselves, and in their own abilities to achieve success, that they never see ideas through to resolution, or perhaps don't even take that pro-verbial first step.

Although the work required to reach your goal may be great, success is nothing to fear and will only be achieved by those who put in the time and energy required. I'm not saying that success is guaranteed, but I can tell you without reservation that failure is guaranteed if you give up on your dreams.

Unforeseen Costs

Probably a new business owners' worst nightmare is the unforeseen startup or other costs that drain your savings account in the first two months while you aren't yet generating revenue. It is absolutely vital that you do your homework to know precisely the type of costs that will be required of you and to plan, at least for the first two years, for every foreseeable cost—no matter how far fetched. Later in the book I'll give you some tools for rating the risk of an unforeseen cost, which will help you determine the probability of it occurring and therefore the probability that you will have to face the issue, and how costly it will be if you do.

Again, planning helps to mitigate this factor. If you can line up one or two contracts before you go live, it might set your mind at ease. Assuming everything will cost at least 20 percent more than you are initially estimating will cover you in case of mistakes.

Potential for Long Hours

Finally, you've left Corporate America—no more 80-hour work weeks! Wrong! The most successful businesses are those that are based on great, feasible ideas and those that also have great effort put into them. Very few people make it on luck and good timing; most of us put in a lot of hours to be successful. The potential for long hours is there, so you will need to ask yourself the fundamental question: "How many hours do I want to work, and if I reach that number, do I want to hire an employee or bring in a contractor to get more work done, or just limit my income potential?" Remember that you don't have to grow your business—if you're happy with its success and would rather work less and just maintain, that is completely your call.

When my own business ran into this issue, I found that bringing in contractors to help was a great solution—it allowed me to grow my business with my core activities while my contractors took care of routine work like faxing, letter writing, mailing, handling packages and packaging for my eBay store, and so on. Since my business was essentially four businesses, there was plenty to keep contractors busy. This also allowed me to focus my energies on my passions and not on busy work.

Lack of Vacations

This one is probably a harsh reality, too. Unless you have an Internet-based business that runs itself or unless your business grows so fast that you can hire employees to run it while you're gone, chances are, for at least the first couple of years, you're going to have limited vacations—or if you take them, you'll be taking your laptop with you. I personally believe this is a fact of being an entrepreneur and one it is best just to accustom yourself to early.

Another option, if your business doesn't require you, is to hire contractors and let them run your business while you're gone—but much like new parents who keep calling home to check in with the sitter, you'll likely be constantly checking in with whoever is babysitting your business.

Still, I have found that no real vacation in over five years is taking its toll on my mental health; in my sixth year I have vowed to make myself let my contractors do my business for a week and leave for seven days that I am sure will fly right by.

Difficulty Building Your Business

Difficulty building your business is definitely something you should be concerned with. It isn't easy to get those first contracts, and then turn the first few into many—and then those many into enough to pay the bills and grow your business.

As you develop your plan, though, you will also develop a strategy for handling this problem; you will find checks and balances to validate your progress and let you make adjustments before things become crucial or life altering. In this book we will work through strategies for building your business and your brand early, and then we will look at how to springboard quickly off that effort.

Work/Life Barriers

Ah, the lovely sound of children crying while you're on a conference call. Work/life barriers, particularly if your office is home-based (which it might be, at least for a while), is not an easy thing to handle.

So what do you do to overcome this? Set clear boundaries. In fact, this is so important that I will cover it in an entire section within the book. Managing work/life balance and making certain your office is nothing more than that—an office—is crucial to your success, and your sanity.

Contrarily, on the home front, you need to find a way to shut out work when it's always waiting for you in the room down the hall, yet not become complacent taking two hours each morning to water the plants and trim the grass before working. I'll offer you many tips throughout this book on how to balance your work and life at home, making sure work gets done—but not too much! Many of us still struggle with this and, after substantial growth, we have had to get offices outside the home to handle this conflict.

Doing the Math

Any new business owner is going to run into financial barriers, questions, concerns, and the like. You will need to do some detailed math to really determine how profitable your business can be, but the following four issues are those you need to consider immediately because they can be incredibly costly and unpredictable. In this chapter, we will walk through many of the things that frighten people—in particular, taxes—in detail.

Insurance Basics

You will need to insure your business. This may be as simple as filing for corporate or limited liability corporate (LLC) status so that your own personal liability is limited. Still, you may need actual insurance for your business. You should talk with an insurance advisor as well as an attorney to know what your potential risks are. They vary greatly based on what type of product or service you are selling, and even based on your location (some states may protect you more than others and some areas may require certain coverage when others may not). For my own business, I have one umbrella policy that lists each of my corporations and my sole proprietorship tacked on to my general homeowner's insurance. It has cost me about $800 per year but it covers all of my assets, including my rental policies. This is often a good and inexpensive route to go, but be sure you are fully protected. Some companies will require more insurance than others and some are higher risk than others.

Tax Basics

Your taxes and the way you file will change when you become an entrepreneur. You will be filing a Schedule C for your business (or another schedule if you run a real estate business with rental property or a farm). You will likely want to talk

> Remember that owning rental property and being a property manager is not a Schedule C business, it is a Schedule E business and therefore an entirely different ballgame!

with a tax planner who can help you understand the ramifications of tax changes. You no longer have a company withholding money from your paycheck, so you have to do this yourself. Your tax rate will vary based on your income, so talking with a planner is your best bet here. You do get some benefits, particularly if you work out of your home, such as in home office deductions including utilities and maintenance, prorated based on the square footage your home office takes as a percentage of total square footage. Again, a tax planner can help and is unconditionally advised.

Let's start with the average corporate worker in California. The numbers may change slightly depending on your state—some states have state income tax and others don't, some offset income tax with higher sales tax while others have no or low sales tax, and still others have higher property tax while some have little or none at all—so your own situation may be different. This is a good example to go from, though.

I'll compare two situations that are nicely laid out on answers.google.com in two scenarios.

Let's look at an employee making $120,000 in an annual salary, with a $20,000 bonus, for a total of $140,000, and a contractor making $140,000 in 1099 income. Sounds great right? The Google Answers column clearly spells out the answer here for the employee:

> You can find the taxable income amount for your tax bracket by going to www.irs.gov/pub/irs-pdf/i1040tt.pdf.

The employee will pay about $29,000 to the IRS, $10,000 to the State of California, $8,400 for the employee's share in FICA/MED, and $600 to State Disability Insurance, or SDI. (The employer is paying medical and dental insurance.) This means the total tax is about $48,500, which is about 34 percent tax in total.

Now let's look at a contractor contracting him or herself out in the city of Los Angeles—someone who is self employed but earning his or her living off contracts from other companies.

The contractor will pay about $33,280 to the IRS, $12,800 to the State of California, $16,570 in FICA/MEDI, $1700 in SDI, and $700 to the City of Los Angeles. This is a total of $70,450.

In this scenario the contractor is paying about 42 percent tax where the employee pays 34 percent.

But—and it is a big but—every single thing that person did as a contractor—advertising, driving, meals, travel, toll roads, paying for his or her own health insurance, and so on—comes off the taxable income, thereby reducing the amount he or she is taxed on by a substantial amount.

This is the real benefit of being self employed. By filing your taxes on a Schedule C of your standard 1040 tax return, you are transferring your business income to yourself and paying income tax on it. But you are first deducting expenses, so you are only paying on the net gain.

> Some states have insanely high tax rates; California, for instance, is almost 10 percent for some tax brackets. One option to discuss with your accountant is how to officially do business in another state or incorporate your business so you can pay corporate tax, which might be lower. In some cases, becoming an S corporation could lower your tax, but an accountant needs to go through the details with you.
>
> For a great article from the IRS on whether you are officially a contractor or employee, visit www.irs.gov/businesses/small/article/0,,id=99921,00.html.

If we take this a step further, as a self-employed business you have an even better situation!

Many things are deductible to a small business owner that are not available to an employee. Here are a few:

- Home office expense
- Car and mileage expenses
- Advertising
- Utilities, on a prorated basis for the area you work out of (if it's your home)
- Contract laborers
- Business parking charges, tolls, etc.
- Home office equipment
- Business travel
- Business meals
- SEPs and IRAs

Many of you won't have businesses where you are a contractor, but instead you will be selling something. You will still set up your business the same way and any large customers (those who spend over $600 with you) may send you a 1099 at the end of the year, which is the same thing contractors get.

So imagine this:

You earn $170,000 in net income. Your cost of goods sold is $25,000. Your contract labor and equipment rental is $20,000. Your professional and legal fees are $5,000. Your home business write off, including utilities, is $3,000. Your meals and transportation costs are $9,000. You bought a Treo, some computers, a new laptop, and gifts for your clients, for a total of $10,000. Your taxable income drops to $98,000, so you're only being taxed on that amount. This means your effective tax rate will drop to below what an employee who makes $140,000 per year is paying! Depending on your state, you will get tax breaks for various small business incentives; but assuming you don't and you pay the same percentage as the contractor, you will still pay $41,000 in taxes. This is less than any other scenario and doesn't include even a fraction of the items you get to write off.

> The following e-how document explains how to file your first Schedule C for your new business: www.ehowcom/how_12326_file-taxes-status.html. It does not, however, replace an accountant!

Healthcare Costs

When you leave your Corporate America job, you will probably be given an option to pay for COBRA (an extension of your health insurance) for a few months. Unfortunately, a few months is inadequate, so you should proceed as though you don't have it and work through your solution.

You will be able to find self-employed insurance policies, and if you belong to a group, you might find even better deals through that group. For instance, the National Association of Realtors offers realtor's insurance through their group plan, even if you don't work for a realtor company. Look into these options, but look first into worst case scenarios for insuring you, and your family, if this applies to you.

If you are already unemployed, lack of insurance is something you have to handle anyway, so it isn't a new risk or a new issue. Just be sure you have some estimates ready to go so you don't get sticker shock. Amazingly, there are some inexpensive plans out there.

Here is a table to show you some costs in California and New York, with one child and one nonsmoking healthy spouse (note that I often choose the two most expensive states so you can see how "not so expensive" it really is):

Company	Deductible	Co-Pay	Premium	State
Anthem PPO	$5000	$0	$165/month	California
Blue Cross PPO	$2500	$30	$349/month	California
Blue Cross	$0	$0	$307/month	New York
Atlantis HMO	$0	$0	$867/month	New York

HMOs offer drawbacks compared to PPOs—for instance, an HMO usually requires a doctor's referral to see a specialist, whereas a PPO plan usually allows you to go to one directly. However, PPOs are usually more expensive because they often have a very high deductible as you can see in the table. You need to decide what you and your family ultimately need, and weigh prescription costs, too, which can quickly add up and eat up many unexpected dollars in co-pays. See also if the company you ultimately go with allows for a self-employed flexible plan, which can allow you to take some of your expenses pretax.

Many people are surprised to learn how inexpensive healthcare can be. Preexisting conditions, obesity, and being a smoker are all things that will impact your quote, so living a healthy lifestyle certainly helps. Check with healthcare providers before leaving your insurance carrier to be sure any pre-existing conditions won't disqualify you from coverage.

Your Personal Break-Even Point

Whether you are unemployed, underemployed, or looking to leave Corporate America behind by quitting the full time job that you joyfully go to each day, you need to find your own personal break-even point. While you may want more freedom, you have to decide what you're willing to pay for it, both in time and money, while you get your business up and running.

It can be hard to quantify feelings; researchers have been trying to do it for years. Writing down the pros and cons, weighting them based on how important they are to you, and then determining how well your new business ranks will help you come up with a proportion of satisfaction. I will supply you later with an example of how to do this, walking you through the quantification process step by step. It isn't as hard as it sounds and it can actually help alleviate worries to get your concerns into numbers and see how the math adds up.

Final Thoughts

You are probably contemplating starting your own business because you are either unemployed, underemployed, or underutilized (your skills and talents just aren't being used to their maximum). Maybe you've always wanted to start your own business but felt there were too many complications. Starting the business is easy—maintaining it is a bit more of a challenge; you'll be able to accomplish both—keep faith, keep focused, and enjoy the ride!

2

Myth Busters!

Small business owners are often put off by lots of myths—the unimaginable consequences of owning your own business. I hear every excuse or reason from "I don't want to pay so much in taxes" to "I can't afford to start a business" to "if I go into business for myself and things don't work out, I'm damaged for life." None of these are true! In this chapter we will explore the common myths, and the real truth behind them.

Common Myths of Self Employment

There are so many myths out there regarding your own business that it is nearly impossible to list them all—it could be a book in and of itself!

Here are some of the most common myths I hear from my students and those I consult with about starting their own businesses, and most importantly, the truths behind the misconceptions. You cannot always believe what you read, particularly online. Usually those with the most unusual stories are the most apt to tell them. They aren't the most common situations in many cases and you shouldn't let them scare you. Arm yourself with good information and then proceed systematically for the best results.

"My Taxes Will Go Up"

They may, if you make very little and suddenly start making a lot—but are you going to complain if that's the case?! Under our current tax policy, being your own boss has incredible benefits because everything you do related to your business is tax deductible. Talk with a tax planner, not just a tax preparer, to understand the ramifications. You might be as pleasantly surprised as I was to learn that my six-figure day job cost me more per year in taxes than my small business does now.

When I say that everything you do for your business is tax deductible, I mean exactly that. Every ream of paper, every pen you purchase, marketing and advertising costs, taking your clients out to dinner—the list goes on. Yes, that's right, taking your clients out for a dinner in which you discuss business or advance your work and relationship with that client is completely deductible.

"My Healthcare Costs Will Skyrocket"

If I could have a dollar for every time I have heard this one! Repeat after me: "Not all employer plans are great and healthcare doesn't have to cost an arm and a leg." If you have a preexisting condition and have trouble getting insurance, you should contact insurance carriers and get coverage before you quit your job. However, most business owners don't have trouble finding health insurance. I was able to get a Blue Cross HMO plan that covered everything I needed, with low co-pays, for under $200 monthly. If you have a spouse who is employed, consider adding yourself to his or her plan during open enrollment, or if you're still a student, consider jumping onto your parents plan if you can, or perhaps even better yet, look into getting health insurance through your school—if it is offered.

I will be bluntly honest about the fact that what your new business is will affect your ability to gain adequate medical and health insurance. A person starting a SCUBA diving search and rescue business will have a considerably more difficult time in securing health insurance compared to a person opening up a flower shop. The same holds true for disability insurance. This is simply due to the level of "danger" to the person(s) within the business, but is no different than securing health insurance through an actual employer if you SCUBA dive five times a week. For some time, insurers didn't want to offer insurance to online professors!

While it doesn't make sense to us, statisticians behind the insurance companies make decisions that don't always favor small businesses.

There are also alternatives to going through traditional channels to find insurance. Keeping with the SCUBA diving example, you can find "SCUBA friendly" insurance carriers through organizations like DAN (Divers Alert Network—www.diversalertnetwork.org). This holds true with other industry-specific organizations, too. If you are a real estate agent, for instance, and are a member of the National Association of Realtors (NAR), you can at least get a group rate, which will lessen your costs. It isn't as good as an employer plan and will generally require health tests and screenings, but it is better than nothing.

> There are many ways to get healthcare that don't involve buying it for full price. For instance, if you are a Sam's Club member, you can get group rates. Lots of organizations have such options; real estate agents have the National Association of Realtors (NAR), AARP offers specific rates; AAA offers alternatives. Look around and see what you can get with existing or new memberships.

"I Won't Have a Fallback Plan"

This one is entirely up to you. You may not have a fallback plan, or you may not want to venture into your new world without one. It all depends on your level of acceptable risk. A fallback plan may be as simple as six months' worth of bills in savings to allow you two months, should your business do nothing in the first four, to find a Corporate America job until the next idea comes along and you can try again. It might be as simple as keeping your day job until you have a few contracts. It might mean cutting costs to nearly nothing while you're in the startup phase, if you have the ability to do that. Really, life circumstance will ultimately dictate how you respond to this.

"If My Business Doesn't Succeed I'll Go Into Bankruptcy"

What did you do before your business? Can you not do it again after a six-month or one-year sabbatical? Enough said.

If you are currently unemployed, you can always get back into whatever industry you are currently looking for employment in or are qualified to be gainfully employed in. If you are underemployed, no doubt you can go back to part time work should you need to. The key is to be comfortable with the risk you are taking and the potential success of your new business. A business failing is not the end of the world, nor should it be. Many of the world's greatest entrepreneurs have started businesses that have failed, before hitting it big with the one that skyrockets them to success. This is of course something that this book is going to help you avoid—by teaching you the lessons that individuals and groups learned through trial and error. Some people are able to learn from others' mistakes but others must make them on their own before the lesson settles in.

"I'm Not Procrastinating; I'm Just Waiting for the Right Time"

Again, I'd be a multimillionaire if I was paid each time a procrastinator told me this. No, you *are* procrastinating! There will never be a perfect time for anything! Start doing your research, get the business started, and when the right time hits you'll know it, because you will know enough about the market, the product or service, and the clientele to know when it's time to launch a full-on assault.

There are many reasons why people fail, but procrastination is a big one. I would hate to think of myself as an 85-year-old person without many good years left, thinking of all the things I woulda, coulda, shoulda done. If you're reading this book, I'm sure you are in the same boat. If you have a few obstacles thrown in your way, figure out what they are, determine the path to overcoming them, write it down, then do it. Go out there and try it! If you believe in it and think it could work, do some homework and then just go for it. You can figure out how to calculate risk factors and protect your family in the process, if that is a concern.

Procrastination is one root of failure. I can unequivocally say that everyone I know who has failed in their own business venture has an excuse—but almost all of them boiled down to procrastination and laziness. What you make of your life and your business world is entirely up to you. Part of your goal here will be to make a solid decision—yes you *are* going to be successful and you *are* going to do this—and then we get to the details. That commitment is vital—no excuses. Once you make the commitment to yourself, try making it to others, too. I have found that this imposes a self-guilt that keeps you on the right track as others ask about how your business venture is coming.

"The Internet Will Kill My Profits—Everything Is About Price!"

In today's Internet age, many people want the best price, and who can blame them? You want the best price, too, right? Any electronics store worker will tell you tales of people coming in to compare products, see what camera they want, then go online to get the best price, save on tax, find free shipping, and delay gratification for a week.

Sure these people are out there, but do you know what many of us hear most often? "Why is there no service in America anymore?" and "Why don't airlines just charge me $15 more and give me a real meal again?" Or "Why did that online company only save me 10 percent and when I had to return an item, charged me a 30 percent restocking fee?" Some segment of the population will only care about price, but this may not be your target market anyway. What you need to do is determine what your target market is, what that demographic cares about and wants, and then hit it—nail it out of the park. If your demographic is primarily concerned about price, I suggest your business be a product-based site that offers, well, you guessed it—the best price. This is all outlined in Chapter 5 on business plans, so for now just get the basic concepts down.

If your business idea is founded on a service or services, then people do still weigh what "bang for the buck" you are offering; so at this point, it is a combination of price, quantity of service, and quality of services. You will also need to be clear about return policies and think about the reasons you will accept returns. This all leads to the general consumer experience. The consumer experience can never be taken back, and word of mouth, whether you are a brick-and-mortar or online store, will kill your business or make it thrive.

"If I Leave Corporate America, I Can Never Go Back"

This is the equivalent of saying that once you leave school, you can never return. There simply is no truth to this myth … none … zero. Some senior leaders do say that they look for consistent work experience on a resume. Is entrepreneurial work not consistent work experience? Did you not learn more, even if your business fails, in the three years trying than from your ten years in Corporate America? Consider that studies have shown that many Generation Xers actually want lateral moves within organizations, not promotions, because they want to learn enough about business that they can leave Corporate America one day.

How will these individuals explain a gap in their employment and do you think it will hurt them if they can answer the question "What did you do the last three years?" with the answer, "Marketing, demographic research, sales, advertising, business planning, getting seed money, and starting a business, which I sold last year?" Perhaps some managers won't accept this answer, but not most. And perhaps those are the managers you would not want to work for anyway. Just a thought!

Since quitting Corporate America, I have had no less than five job offers, about one and a half per year, to go back and do what I was doing before. You have lots of contacts even if it may not feel like it. Everyone from old bosses to new business partners may want to work with you in "Corporate America"; you can always go back to working for someone else should you need or ultimately choose to. This is one reason it is important to maintain your relationships and not burn bridges.

Many bosses see the entrepreneurial spirit as a good thing—a benefit to the organization. Now granted, you may have to convince him or her that you're not going to leave again in six months to pursue another dream/idea/gold vein, but you can certainly talk about the incredible experience you gained during your absence and how you will apply that to the position that you are going to work hard for, back in the corporate world.

Remember, you're not quitting your job to do nothing and sip cocktails by the pool! You are leaving to go to work and apply all you have learned.

"I Need a Lot of Money to Start"

Unless you want to start your own bank, this is not true either (and even in that case, you may get investors to help you). Many (dare I say most?) businesses that I have either helped launch or witnessed the launch of started with less than $10,000. Many Internet businesses start with even less, as the most primary of needs for this type of business is something most of us already have—a computer and storage, which come cheaply these days.

Throughout our time together, we will go through a thorough review of as many potential startup costs as possible, but there will be, of course, some that are only related to your specific model and market. You will need to identify those and then plan for them through careful research and analysis.

"I Can Never Grow This Business"

This one may actually have some validity behind it, but whether or not it is accurate is dependent on you and your own choices, and your upfront research about the environment you are venturing into.

If you've chosen a business model that presents little to no room for growth, than this "myth" is actually a fact. If this is the case, it doesn't mean you cannot earn a living, you just may not enjoy the thrill of a high growth model. Some people like just getting by and not working much, though. You will find ways to grow, particularly as you begin to find new demographics and market segments that are interested in your product or service and that you can sell to. Nearly everything is "growable" with enough creativity and flexibility on your part.

"I Need a Business Degree—Time to Go Back to School!"

This is also just flat-out untrue. Have you ever heard of Bill Gates? Yeah he's an uncommon example, but many entrepreneurs (some experts say most) got the "bug" and either dropped out of college or never went, although many do go back later. Yes, you will learn about profit and loss, financial statements, and investing in B-school (business school). But you won't learn everything, and you won't necessarily learn the real life lessons that you may have gained by being employed in the real world, by being underemployed, or even by being unemployed. This is all valuable life experience you will bring to the table. You will also create a network of business partners who undoubtedly will know what you don't.

Another example taken from real life is Albert Einstein. Although Einstein was always intrigued with math and science, he often grew so bored with school that he just stopped doing his work and consequently failed math in college. So even if you didn't excel in school, this potentially has no bearing on whether you will be successful as an entrepreneur.

As a side note on success, since I just mentioned it: success is subjective. What is "success" to you is not going to be considered success to your neighbor, your

> It is okay to change your definitions of success, just be sure you change your life and business at the same time. I can attest first hand that when these two are out of synch, your life is not a happy one.

friend, your parents, or your significant other. One of my goals is to live in a house in a particular area, in which the average starting price is a whopping $5 million mortgage. Until I can get there and pay cash, I will not be successful. I have known people who would be very happy living in a $400,000 home on a lake where they can fish and have the grandchildren over. In both cases, success is dependent on the person experiencing it.

It's also important to note that the definition of success changes with life circumstances. In our teens and twenties, that definition is often drastically different than in our 30s, 40s, and beyond. Also, our life experiences change the definition of success. Perhaps success before children is working eight hours per day and making $100,000 per year so you can still have time to party. Then you settle down, get married, and have a child—now your definition of success is time with the baby and a college education for Junior.

"Exports Won't Help My Business" or "Exporting is Too Hard"

Have you taken a look at the 2008 U.S. gross domestic product, or GDP? What saved the GDP in the first two quarters of 2008 from going negative? Exports! As the dollar weakens (and this can be for several reasons; other currencies strengthening or the Federal Reserve lowering interest rates, making the value of the dollar weaker compared with currency of other countries), other countries' interest in U.S. products is surging, in part because their relative cost is going down, particularly in emerging markets like Brazil, China, and India. You may find a significant source of your income and product or service interest is actually coming from overseas buyers, especially if you are offering a product at a lower price than what they would be charged if they purchased the same or similar product "at home." Watch out for knockoffs, though, which might damage your business in other parts of the world. In Africa for instance, people knock off items as simple as a toothbrush and its container, or shoe polish to make an extra 30¢ by using a name brand's name. Some areas won't care if your product is authentic, but selling an inauthentic product is bad all the way around.

The 2008 Financial Guide, describes a country's gross domestic product (GDP) as a measure of the total flow of goods and services produced over a specified time period, which is generally one year (calendar).

By definition, gross means that we are not taking any deductions; it is pure sales, not profit. The word domestic means that income arising from investment and possessions owned abroad is not included; and this distinguishes GDP from GNP, or gross national product.

Is it hard to accommodate those customers that require currency exchange? Not really. If you use a credit card company, they will do the currency exchange for you automatically. Just be sure they're translating the currency in such a way that doesn't reduce your earnings. A quick call to the merchant company you are using will help you make this determination. You can ask your merchant account (usually this will be with a major bank) how they do currency translations and then compare and contrast this to others when you select a provider.

With the growing online presence of major carriers such as UPS, FedEx, DHL, and the like, shipping is easier than ever. If you use the United States Postal Service (much improved over the past five years in the area of reliability) and print labels online, you don't even have to stand in line at the post office to ship your packages! Simply put them in any 24-hour drop box. Recently, the USPS made shipping even easier by allowing you to leave items with preprinted labels for your mail carrier—meaning you don't even have to leave home to ship those items. All you need to do is print the labels, affix the labels to the items, and place them by (or in) your mailbox, and your mail delivery person will take them when he or she drops off your mail.

Note: Although this is convenient, you should only do this if your neighborhood would be considered secure, as there is a risk of anyone walking by taking your items before the mail person gets there. Another alternative is to watch for your carrier and hand the items to him or her personally.

Other major carriers, like UPS and FedEx, are also offering free pick up for packages shipped online, particularly with a business account; so as you are printing your labels, you can also schedule them to come pick up your items for free—a time and money saver.

Another fascinating fact on imports and exports: the Small Business Administration (SBA) estimates that small businesses will account for a full 30 percent of exports in 2008, to total over $1 trillion. That's right, one followed by twelve (12) zeros. Now that's a lot of money, all from small businesses—like the one that you are on your way to starting.

"Most Small Businesses Fail"

This is a common myth, that most small businesses fail. Many do, but it isn't quite "most." If we compare them to mid-sized and larger businesses, surely more small businesses, percentage-wise, experience failure. This makes sense due to resources, expertise, availability of credit, and capital.

What are the facts regarding failure statistics? After four years, about half of small businesses are still in business. That number may be better odds than your chances of keeping a day job or finding employment, according to the Research Foundation. The faster that a business grows in the first year or two, the less likely it is to fail. This may be indicative of strong demand, which we know keeps small businesses flourishing. Yet another reason to play well and plan fast! Another quick fact for you: Only about 25 percent of new firms last less than two years—pretty good odds.

"Small Businesses Don't Contribute Much"

Tell this to a small business owner and see what type of reception you get! If you are the type of person who wants to make a great contribution to society and to the country but believe that small businesses don't contribute much, this section is precisely for you!

Companies with less than 500 employees produce about 50 percent of the goods and services in the entire United States economy, according to the Small Business Administration. In some industries, like equipment and machinery repair, or laundry and dry cleaning services, this is even higher—about 80 percent. (As a side note: If you're thinking of starting one of these businesses, this statistic means that competition is more stiff in these areas.) Small businesses also produce anywhere from 60 to 80 percent of all new jobs, also according to the SBA. Which companies are adding most to this growth? Those with fewer than 20 employees! Still think you wouldn't be making your mark?

This country was literally built on small businesses. Look at it this way: even companies like Microsoft, Google, YouTube, or any other conglomerate started at some point, and started at a relatively small size, compared to what they are today. Everyone has to start somewhere. The important thing to remember is that you have to start!

"If My Business Is Small Enough, I Don't Have to 'Legalize' It"

Watch out for this myth, as it can get you into a lot of trouble—legal trouble and financial trouble, that is.

Registration of your company is not based on size. If you are a business of one, as I was for a while, you still have to register and you need to run your business under a legal name.

The same is true if you don't collect much in revenue. If you collected $80, you need to file a return. If you lost money, the government will help compensate you for the loss and the risk. If you had bottom line earnings, then you owe Uncle Sam. You still need to file a Schedule C on your 1040 tax return each year. To be sure you are following all of the applicable rules, consult with your accountant and/or attorney.

"I Can Get a Grant to Start My Business"

Yes and no. There are grants out there, often offered through state (not federal) governments as well as some organizations. These are not readily advertised, but they do exist. The grants that are available are usually offered to those wanting to start or expand a small business and are often in fields like healthcare or housing for the underprivileged.

Furthermore, they are not as easy to obtain as walking up to the state building's door and asking for money. There are many requirements, regulations, criteria, and oversights to adhere to.

Unfortunately, this isn't college and money isn't as easy to get as it was for student loans and grants—and the government rarely intervenes in small business funding. It does, however, help offset failures; if you lose money, you can get tax refunds as compensation for your risk and for the jobs you created. If you need funding, your best bet is a local bank or a Small Business Administration loan.

Some small businesses with really interesting or unique ideas and a killer business plan are fortunate enough to get venture capital funding, but this is another myth—that it is easy to raise funding. I would not count on it (though in this book I will tell you the basics for trying). Note that even SBA loans are just funds guaranteed by the government; the SBA isn't the organization actually lending you the money.

Here is some more information to separate fact from fiction regarding loans. As I said, the SBA doesn't directly lend money, but acts as an agency of the government to guarantee loan programs. There are three primary loan types offered through the SBA: the 7(a) loan program, the 504 loan program, and the microloan, or the 7(m) loan program.

The 7(a) program is the most flexible and allows qualified small businesses to get financing even if they have been turned down by other channels, like your local bank.

The 504 program offers fixed-rate, long-term financing for machinery, real estate, or equipment needed for expansion or modernization. The loan is very specific in what it can be used for; if you don't fit this bucket, you don't qualify.

Finally, the microloan, or 7(m) program, is for small businesses and not-for-profit child care centers and provides only short-term financing and working capital specifically for particular items: inventory, furniture, fixtures, machinery, equipment, and supplies.

Also, remember that not all banks will look at SBA-guaranteed loans the same. This is yet another myth related to SBA loans. SBA loans are based on the prime rate plus some specific margin, and this can change depending on the bank. Each bank may have a different interest rate. Loans can be approved very quickly by the SBA, often within 48 hours. You also don't need to be a market dominator to get an SBA loan. You do not need a lot of collateral, either, and it is often wise to look at these loans before other types of funding because, in many cases, they are the easiest to secure.

The promptness with which you can secure SBA funds depends on the type of business you have, the tax records you can supply, sales data, and how much you need to borrow; so it can take months (but that is unusual).

"I Will Get Rich—QUICK!"

Can you get rich quick? Of course, and there are those who have! Keep in mind, though, that it is a short list, while the list of those who had to put in long days and late nights to reach a high level of success is much longer, and continues to grow. I'm on the latter of the two lists myself, and everyone else I know is as well.

How many people do you know who are super wealthy and made it by making someone else rich—through say … a day job? Probably not many, unless you regularly socialize with CEOs. Unfortunately, the media and infomercials promote this type of unrealistic information and the masses fall for it every time. If they didn't, you wouldn't see the same false information on your television daily.

Many entrepreneurs are savvy enough to know that even if they can take their business "big time," sometimes keeping it small for years is better. The founder of Restoration Hardware knew this, and was able to grow his business slowly and methodically until it reached annual sales of about $100 million.

Chances are better that you will get wealthy with long hours and dedication—and of course, something useful to the general consuming public or businesses.

In closing on this topic, know that I am not telling you that you can't hit it big overnight, as you very well may—it does happen, but also realize that if it doesn't happen like that, you shouldn't throw in the towel and give up. Keep at it, work hard, and your business could be the next Restoration Hardware. Just keep in mind that you need to constantly check your plan against your actuals and make adjustments if needed. The only bad plan is the unrevised, never visited plan.

"Only Born Entrepreneurs Make It"

This is an interesting, common myth because there are so many social and psychological elements tied up here. There has long been a debate in social science over whether leaders are born or made; whether the characteristics that make leaders successful are present inherently from birth and their success rate is dependent on how well this is nurtured and accepted, or whether they are made through education, hard work, and perseverance. Perhaps the answer is in a nice combination of both, tossed in with a bit of risk aversion. This is a question not yet answered by science and may never be, as there are many aspects to the human mind and behavior that may never be able to be tested or explained. What I do know is that the most successful people run with ideas and don't wait around for others who are slowing them down (including potential business partners).

What we do know, in the entrepreneurial world, is that there is no such thing as a "born entrepreneur." Certainly some people are born with more aggressive traits, have more self confidence due to personality or circumstance, and are more or less risk averse, and these types of traits will aid in determining subsequent success and failure. But anyone with an idea, vision, and dedication, coupled with thoughtful decision making and the willingness to act, can be successful.

"I Will Have More Free Time!"

This is a very grey area. You can have more free time. Then again, you may have less—depending on the amount of success you are trying to achieve and based on the amount of effort you put into your new dream.

If you are making the decision to quit your day job or leave the unemployed line for more free time, you are making a grave mistake. If this is the case, chances are your business will be one of those among the 25 percent that fail in the first couple of years in business.

Yes, you will have additional freedom, in the sense that you will select how your days will be planned, who you will hire or fire, what products and services you will offer, and so on. But you will most likely not have more free time if you're giving your business your all.

Every growth strategy, every bit of implementation, every new contract is all about you and how well you sell it, how well you put it into practice, and how well you make it work. This is exceedingly time consuming, probably even more so than you are imagining it to be right now.

You need to go into your new business realizing you will be spending your free time thinking of new ideas—and when they come, you'll want to jump on them immediately. The excitement and enthusiasm is literally so contagious that it's nearly impossible not to. If you find yourself thinking of new ideas at midnight and doing nothing about them, you probably aren't cut out for this.

In starting and running your own business, you will have more freedom—but part of that freedom is the freedom to fail. Is that why you're going into business? Probably not.

"I Won't Have to Work as Hard (or Put in as Much Overtime)"

Unless you have a huge amount of startup money, enough to open with an abundance of employees, this couldn't be further from the truth! In most cases, even if you do start with a full house of employees, you will still be required to work hard, through long days and late nights, to be successful. You will not only be the driver of your business model and plan, but you will be the executioner, final decision maker, planner, and the face of your new business.

As my business grows and gets busier, the busier I get. I cannot just hire out all of my work or I'll lose one of the things that makes my business unique—me. You may be in the same situation depending on what your job is. If you are a consultant, for instance, people are probably paying you for your expertise. While you can outsource or hire people to handle some of the writing, analysis, auditing, and so on, ultimately you are still the face of that consulting service that they hired. Other businesses are more conducive to hiring out—for instance, call centers or customer service people.

As your business grows, it will require more of you and more strategy, more cash, more input, and more responsibility. The more successful you are, the more that will be required of you—it really is as simple as that.

"I Need Small Business Credit to Get Loans"

How many times have you heard young people say "It isn't fair, I have to have credit to get credit!" To some degree this is the case in the private sector with individual credit, but thankfully your business does not need credit to get a small business line. In fact, in my first month of business, Bank of America issued two credit cards, under my businesses tax identification number, totaling $7,000 in credit lines. More came later, after I had proved my ability to make my payments on time.

Now there is a grey area with this myth. In some cases, when a small business loan is really a personal loan gained under the premise of starting a new business, your personal credit will matter, but not nearly as much as it does for, say, a home or automobile purchase. Often your personal credit will guarantee your business credit, which can make it more difficult to get home and auto loans as it will show a higher debt-to-income ratio. Keep this in mind before securing your business debt, and shop around banks to see who will perhaps give you a lending hand without the personal guarantor.

"Being a Franchisee Is Safer and Less Costly Than Starting My Own Business"

So you want to open a McDonald's, a UPS Store, or something similar because you think franchising is an easier road? It isn't! It is often more costly; in many cases you will have limited product offerings based on what the company requires and in most cases you will pay heavy costs to get up and running. If you really want to be a franchise, dig into the details deeply and you might find out that it isn't all it's cracked up to be.

The only benefit that I have ever seen of franchising is the fact that it is very easy and results in a quick startup. Generally, you write the company you are franchising from a check, and they give you all that you need to be successful—sans you, of course, and your new team.

You may have to find the location, or have the location already acquired, but after that, the company usually takes care of the rest: from design and construction of the location to furnishings to equipment and supplies, even extending to training on how they want the business run and what additional local laws you will be required to abide by. Not all franchisors will provide full service; some provide tips, a name, and some software and let you out on your own. Often the level of assistance is tied to the price. For instance, I recently looked at buying into a franchise of a tanning company rather than starting my own. I looked up one in particular, and the $30,000 franchise fee was for the name only. Others provided equipment and a team to train you for two months for less money, but the name was not as reputable or as well known. Sometimes with a franchise, you are merely paying for name recognition.

Another option, of course, is for you to open your own business and then offer franchising yourself. An acquaintance of mine recently did this and in a matter of months had a completely franchised business, charging $20,000 for the advice, the name, and some equipment. You can make money as a franchisor or franchisee—but some people won't feel the same about their business if they buy into someone else's idea and pay money for it. This is something that you need to keep in mind.

In some cases, if you buy into a franchise you may have to pay a percent of profit—you will be continuously paying part of your profits. In other instances, you will be required to pay a fee for the life of your business. When the company upgrades, you must upgrade. When they change logos, you must update your logo. Many of us don't like the idea of giving up that much control.

Another negative aspect, as previously mentioned, is the fact that you are limited as far as the types of products or services you can offer, depending on which products or services are approved to offer through the franchisor. A related issue is the price which you charge for these products or services. You are often bound to the national promotions being run, current "suggested" prices, and so on.

There are upsides and downsides to this pricing situation. On one side, you are limited to the "approved" suppliers that your franchiser has agreements and contracts with. This means that you are forced to go through a certain supplier for your products, who may actually be charging you more than what you would pay if you purchased the exact same product through a different supplier. Let's say you franchise a McDonald's, and they only approve Supplier A. Supplier A charges one cent per hamburger patty. If you had started your own fast-food restaurant, and were able to "shop the competition," you would have found Supplier B, who for the same (or similar) product, charges one cent for three hamburger patties. There are upsides and downsides to everything.

The downside of this pricing deal is the fact that you are limited to what you can charge your customers for a certain product; oftentimes you will have to follow nationwide or regional marketing campaigns. However, the product or service may be worth more or less in some regions than in others. Smart franchises know this and allow you to make adjustments; others are more rigid. If you want to buy into a franchise, pay careful attention to those types of details.

Final Thoughts

So now that we've covered some of the basic ideas of entrepreneurship, what you need to consider before moving forward, and even debunked some common myths, what do you think? Do you have what it takes? I believe that we all do, with the right motivation and the right tools for success. Throughout the remainder of this book, I will unload a plethora of research, personal knowledge and insights (and plenty of stories), tools, and more motivation than you may be able to handle. So what are we waiting for? Let's get started and get you one step closer to becoming the next Accidental Tycoon!

What did our survey respondents have to say about flexibility compared to Corporate America? A whopping 89 percent, nearly 9 out of 10 respondents, said that owning their own business provided more flexibility than Corporate America—6 percent noted it was about the same, and only 4 percent said less flexibility. One enthusiastic responded by saying that "more flexibility is an understatement!"

3

Dreams to Dollars

This chapter may be perhaps the most critical one in the entire book—without a dream, you have no passion to follow through on! Without any passion you have no business and without any business, you have no dollars. Many of you may have ideas or are searching for one; this chapter will tell you how to turn those ideas into a business, a profitable real life entrepreneurial piece of art!

You Have an Idea, Now What?

Chances are, you are picking up this book because either you had an idea and weren't sure how to implement it, or you are intrigued by the idea of becoming your own boss and want to learn how to realize "the American dream." In either case, you will need an idea to run with, to analyze, and then, potentially, to market.

If you already have an idea in mind, then you're in a good position to begin analysis—determining the sources of your revenue streams, setting realistic start times, identifying your initial strategy, determining who to talk with and how to evaluate your goals and strategy, deciding who your target demographic will be, and figuring out how to analyze your startup costs. If you fall into this category, proceeding through the rest of this chapter will be easier for you.

If you don't already have an idea, or you aren't sure what you want your new business idea to be, now is the time to start brainstorming. I always recommend thinking about what gets you excited. What are you passionate about? What do you do now that you'd gladly do for free if you didn't have to worry about finances (e.g., paying bills)? What do you enjoy doing with your time when you have a moment of it to spare? Analyzing your passions and brainstorming what they are is the first step in beginning to find your new business.

You can turn your passions into profits, but first you have to know what those passions are. This goes for those of you who already have your business idea, as well. Make certain it is something you are passionate for and about, and if it isn't, then perhaps you should reconsider a new idea.

To facilitate this search, I recommend taking some time for yourself—to really connect with what brings you joy in life. Try sitting, alone, and think about what makes you happy. Try going for a walk in the park or along the beach—what do you want out of life and what makes life enjoyable? Whatever helps you think clearly and undistracted, do this, and jot down everything that comes to mind.

Now at this point, use a branch-out method that will help you see how you could potentially turn your idea into something profitable. I'll walk you through a scenario. Say you enjoy shopping—immensely. When you have an hour of free time it is best spent at the mall finding bargains. Now what if you routinely know how to shop to get designer goods for 90 percent off? What if you created a discount boutique and resold these items at half off? Perhaps you even had an eBay store to accompany the brick and mortar or on ground store? The potential for large profits here is astounding, albeit with a relatively easy startup. This is a small example of the way to begin turning the things you love to do into ways to make money.

One way to try to conceptualize your business is to draw a picture of your work, and to "branch out" your next steps from there. To create this map, place shopping at the center of the bubble. Draw lines from the bubble, and write words or short phrases that come to mind when you think of shopping—perhaps eBay, "hard to find items," "antiques," and so on. Use this as the basis for your brainstorming. Often this is the most effective and fastest way to brainstorm and still be able to maintain a sense of your original ideas. Also, in the process you may find other ideas you hadn't thought of—perhaps even another new business!

The following is a pictorial reference of what I am referring to, although it is a very simplified version.

An example of the branch method of brainstorming.

If there is anything I have seen "kill" a new business in record time, it is lack of interest in what you are doing. Unless you are driven by sheer dollars and cents and are making a happy living doing a job that makes you less than such, you need to love what you do. Don't take this introductory section lightly; in my view, flushing out what you enjoy most and then analyzing each item based on the fundamentals in this chapter is your best shot at success. It is much easier to remain dedicated to something you have your heart and soul already invested and interested in.

First Steps

With any new business venture there are crucial first steps that you will need to take to determine if the idea is feasible, if it will generate revenue, if it has a market, if it has established competition, and whether or not there are any barriers to entry (meaning obstacles to entering a particular market).

Identifying Potential Revenue

If you quit your day job to live underneath a bridge, what is the point? The idea is, after all, to make a good living—a very good living in fact—being your own boss. Right? Of course it is, so it makes sense that you need to analyze what your potential revenue sources are, and then how much realistic revenue you can earn as a result. Later we will expand into other markets that can grow your earning potential, but think worst case scenario and then document it.

What are the markets and demographics that will buy your product? In other words, who are your customers? What will they buy and how will they buy it? What will they pay for it? Are your potential customers "customers for life," or will you need to be constantly marketing to a new group. For example, if your business caters to "the party crowd," then your customer base will constantly be changing, as today's partier is tomorrow's professional.

What did our survey respondents say about the price they charge compared to what they feel their product is worth? Forty-five percent felt that they charge what their product is worth. Thirty-two percent said that most of the time they get a fair price; twelve percent said some of the time, and 10 percent said they do not get a fair price. One very astute respondent said that this is not a get rich quick scheme, and it takes hard work and dedication! Indeed it does.

In our survey, 51 percent felt they were making about what they expected, 32 percent said they make less than expected, and 16 percent said they make more than expected. Most noted that the harder and longer the work, the more income they make—definitely a solid correlation there!

Feasibility

Feasibility has a number of factors to consider. Some of the questions that you need to begin to ask yourself include:

- Are others doing the same thing?
- Is there a very high cost to get started?
- Do you really know the product or service well?

- Are you highly (I cannot underestimate the value of this) passionate about the product or service?

- Do you know who will buy it and—perhaps most importantly—can this group afford your product or service?

- Do you have the means to get started?

- Do you have the support of those who can affect your profitability? Specifically, do you have the support of significant others, family members you are caring for, and so on?

- Are you willing to give up free time to grow your business? (If you are passionate about your idea, this should be a quick "yes.")

- Do you have your goals well defined?

- Do you know your own definition of success? If not, you should begin to think about this. Success to you might be freedom and working fewer hours, or it might mean a fabulous paycheck that lets you buy your dream home and pay your kids' college education and the retirement home in cash, no matter how many hours you need to work to achieve it.

What are some other factors to consider with regard to feasibility? Think about your own personality characteristics. Do you start things well but don't finish them? Then this may not be a good decision for you. Do you like making decisions on your own? Do you plan well? Do you take advice from others with ease?

Of course there are additional factors, too, such as your willingness to take risks (financial risks, personal risks, and risks with your feeling of security). Do you understand the labor required to get the job done? Are you competing with major players that are well established? This is a red flag. Do you have a strong, suitable list of suppliers to help you accomplish your goals? Will you be able to meet your income requirements, initially and as you expand? Are there areas to expand into? Are there market conditions—like the cost of fuel—that you have no control over and that will have a direct impact on earnings or profits? If the answers to any of these are "yes," list them all out and have a plan of action ready in case you find yourself in one of these situations. Also make sure you have a solid idea of what your overhead is going to be, and calculate this into your costs because not doing so can kill a great idea and a great project really fast.

Market Analysis and Target Demographic

One of the very first things you will need to do is begin to analyze the market you will compete in. This includes the demographics of the individuals who are most likely to go for your product or service (their age, generation, gender, spending patterns, average income, geographic location—everything you can imagine that defines who your target customer is would fall into "demographic information"). Do you know where these particular individuals hang out? Do you know how to reach them? Does your product or service have a complementary product or service that would serve as a solid means for advertising and promotion and, later on down the road, cross promotion and partnerships?

Competition

Knowing your competition is crucial. Would you want to compete with Best Buy? Do you want to open a store that directly competes with Wal-Mart? Chances are this wouldn't be the best strategy for you, and it would likely be setting your business up to fail, at least initially.

Once you know your passions, you can figure out what your niche is within that passion. Is your knowledge of the subject so substantial that others would be willing to pay for your advice? That consultation ability alone may be sufficient to begin your business. You need to thoroughly analyze who is out there and who is doing what. You can't do this on the Internet alone. You need to ask people who would potentially be buying your product or service what they think, and where they currently go for it. Polling or surveying is an excellent and highly recommended means of accomplishing this. (You can even do it using tools like SurveyMonkey.com.)

After this, you may need to do some sleuthing; even perhaps visiting the competition if you have a competitor with an on-the-ground or online presence. Sun Tzu (the author of *The Art of War*) warned, "If you know yourself but not the enemy, for every victory gained you will also suffer a defeat." Business, in many ways, is a fight—a fight to come out on top—and in essence, your competition is "the enemy." Many of the most successful businessmen throughout time have been quoted as saying that *The Art of War* was among their most useful and educational books with regard to their own businesses and success.

It is important to note, the competition in the Internet era can be your friend. Competitors often buy ad space on each others' websites for example, and can be a source of revenue. We will discuss this in Chapters 4 and 5.

I don't suggest being dishonest or calling others for bogus consultations, but I do recommend that you flush out your competition thoroughly, and begin to understand what they do—and don't—bring to the market. What they don't bring to the market is your niche! You can do this yourself, and use market research firms as an alternative if you have more money than you do time.

Determining Need

To determine the need for your product or service, you need to know first who will be buying it and what need they expect it to fill. You can do this by conducting surveys yourself or by buying marketing data on your particular product or service, widely available using a search engine and "market data"—if your product is knitwear, you can type in "knitwear market data" to get some good results (nearly 30,000 hits on Google alone). Just be sure to verify the source of the data to be sure it is as unbiased as possible.

If the data supports the idea that there is a strong need, that is a good thing and can be a starting point for your work. I've had colleagues come up with ingenious ideas, only to find out that the people they thought they'd sell products to didn't see it as a need, and economic conditions at the time meant that people were, in general, only buying things they needed, not things they wanted. Economic conditions play a role here, so don't underestimate them. Generally, in an economic downturn or in times of uncertainty only the super-wealthy consistently buy things they want—so unless you are selling private jets to recession-proof individuals, think about your demographic and how the economy may hurt or hinder their ability or desire to buy. Remember that consumer sentiment plays a role in how they spend money, too.

Growth

I am referring here to the ability to grow the business and sustain that growth, once achieved—are there natural segments of the population that will be interested with minor modifications to your product or service? Does your idea have the potential for expansion? Is it limited, does it have a presumable natural path for progression? After you answer these questions, you need to determine how much of the product or service you want to offer up front, as opposed to growing the business gradually. This information comes from market analysis and knowing whether or not offering a "second tier" of products and services will be a turnoff to first-time buyers.

Growth can be both local as well as global, with the latter being laden with its own extensive list of benefits, potential pitfalls, and requirements. An entire book could be written (and many have been) on expanding a business to operate on the global stage, so for the sake of our discussions, we will address expansion in more general terms.

Deciding on an Initial Strategy

To begin any project, you need to decide on an initial strategy for developing your business. This involves many things, from deciding when to quit your day job (or stop looking for a job if you are unemployed), to when to commit full time to your business, to how to get your first customers.

Your initial strategy also needs to have an analysis of your costs, your risks, your personality—everything bulleted in the feasibility section of this chapter. Your initial strategy also needs to include the method you will use to "roll out" your new business, and you need to add information about methods of advertisings, and don't forget the initial "blitz" campaigns that really get the word out early and fast.

Initial Strategy

Your initial strategy needs to be well developed and needs some thought. I have literally started businesses in one day—all in 12 hours; business plan, vision statement, mission statement, filing a fictitious business name statement, setting up a bank account, and template-based website. These weren't my most successful endeavors, though. My most successful endeavors were those that required time to start: time to think, strategize, research, launch, and market.

So what do you think about? For starters, what do you really want to do?—What will captivate you enough that you can do it full time and be content, even happy—happy enough to stick with it when times get tough?

After you know what you want to do, it's time to begin setting up the stages of your business—setting a plan of short-term goals. For example, in one year I want my business to be generating $20,000 in revenue. (You will determine your profit margins later.) *Another short-term goal might be: "I want to spend one hour per day—my lunch hour—marketing my business until I have five clients, then I will quit my day job because this will net me $50,000 a year."*

Realistic Time to Start

A realistic time to start goes beyond when you would like to begin business and moves into when you feasibly *can* do business. There are many things that might impact your ability to begin, such as …

- Familial obligations.
- Startup costs—if they seem out of control, see what you can do to get control.
- Difficulty finding initial clients—you may need to get super creative here!
- Limited time to devote early on, due to job or family constraints—not devoting time early on can kill a great idea very quickly.
- Caring for sick parents or family members—for most individuals, this will obviously take priority over a new business, so if you are facing this, it might not be the best time to start. But it certainly doesn't mean you can't brainstorm.
- Financial constraints that go beyond startup costs, like a rising mortgage payment, and so on.
- Difficulty leaving your day job.
- Religious days—Do you not work on a specific day of the week? Is this going to hinder your success? Theoretically it should not, but what if you take Sundays off and, as it turns out, your clients want most of their business conducted or service performed on Sunday?

- Recreational obligations (softball practice, etc.). Sound silly? Low priority? An individual I used to know actually let his small business fail to not let his softball team down for those three months while spending it on the softball field!

First, you'll need to identify what your short-term goals are, then work backward to determine how long it will take you to get there. If your one-year goal is $100,000 in revenue, and you are planning to charge $10,000 per client for your new solar panel, you will need to sell 10 of these per year. If your profit margin is 50 percent, you will net $50,000.

If your day job pays you $75,000, then you can plan on being able to quit your day job in about 18 months, since that is when your business would, all things staying equal, be able to sell about 15 per year, netting the same pay.

You may have available time that you didn't even think of. One technique I like to use is to create calendar items (what I call calendaring) every single thing that I have to do in a day with the time it takes me to do it. When I was working a day job and planning to leave Corporate America, I calendared my day job. I tried my best to keep my working hours to 10 per day at my day job, and I took my full hour lunch, often sitting at Starbucks, working on my laptop on my side jobs. Then after work was over I'd use time I scheduled in to do additional work on the business. Soon, in about a year, I found I was needing to schedule about seven hours per day for my side job. Calculating my pay and realizing it just barely exceeded my Corporate America job, I knew I could quit, as I had eliminated my quitting as a potential financial burden.

Now there is a not-so-obvious issue here—and that was that I was used to getting paid double! I had my salary from my day job, and my contract wages from my side job (which my employer knew about and supported—another thing to consider). As I increased my "moonlighting workload," I had become accustomed to making double my income and I hadn't even realized it! Once I had officially moved on, I now had to live on "half" of what I was used to making, even though it was the same as it was just a few months earlier at my day job alone.

This sounds like a good problem to have, but it is tough to go from making X dollars to X divided by two, regardless of how you got there! So the key is to plan early: save all the money you make from your business to reinvest in your business. Try to avoid getting caught up in the excitement of the paychecks, and save that cash so you can use it as first-year startup money, or to pay the bills if you have a bad month.

> If you are underemployed or unemployed, you will have more time to devote to your business. Keep in mind that some states, once you earn a 1099, will ask for unemployment money back. So talk to an accountant about this, or at least do the legwork yourself if you don't have the funds available for professional advice. Contact the department that handles your unemployment (or other subsidies that you may be receiving).

Identifying Basics

There are lots of basics you will need to identify before you start your business. First, you'll need to know what genre of work you want to be in. At some point you'll need to narrow down to the specifics. You will need to determine what you are an expert in. You will need to determine how much time you can devote early on, as we just discussed. You will also need to determine who your customers are, and how much of a product or service they buy. You also need to do one very important thing—come up with a budget. What is the minimum you need to live and pay the bills, and what will your business easily earn? Not so easily? With some effort?

Your Go-Live Day—Making the Decision

The day I quit my job was the best day of my life. I've been laid off before due to budget cuts (information technology management is notorious for it), but quitting my job? Not going back on purpose? I never thought that would happen! I dreamed of the day, but I was always too nervous; I always thought I wouldn't be able to make it on my own and the income would be too variable. The income *is* variable, but it is terrific to be in charge of my own destiny.

You will need to determine your own go-live date—and it needs to be data driven—based on when you can afford to go live, and when you think you have enough excitement about your business generated—enough buzz, in marketing speak—to take it into full swing. If you just opened up a boutique for gifts (for instance, a very successful one around the corner from my house had the most unique gifts and charged a pretty penny for high quality items, then wrapped them—and catered to a high-end clientele), you will want to get the storefront ready—for months even before you open—and let everyone possible know about your new business. This is all about creating buzz and anticipation; building up the momentum and the "I can't wait until that store opens" feeling. The more excitement you can create before you even open, the more loyal a customer base you will create.

> Be careful with deep discounts. In some markets and with some products or services, like dry cleaning, it is acceptable and normal to see lots of coupons, especially for first-time customers. But for some products you will cheapen your brand, so do some market research before you even make your decision to go live.

The day you decide to say "I quit!" and hand in that resignation that day will feel like no other. While you can celebrate, the standard two weeks that ensue need to be carefully planned and impeccably executed so that you are earning what you planned for on day one, week one, and month one.

Service or Product

One of the decisions you will be making as you work through your business planning is whether you want to offer a product or service. These need not be mutually exclusive; many successful business owners offer both. For instance, when I was running my first computer consulting business, I fixed computers for small businesses onsite with a guaranteed four-hour response time, day or night. But they often needed parts, so I sold them equipment, too. They needed it fast, so they were willing to pay a substantial markup.

In the days when computer parts were a commodity and a standard markup was 5 percent, I was paying retail and still marking them up 50 percent. I wasn't being dishonest with customers—that is a quick way to lose them. I would tell them that they could go to Best Buy, buy XYZ parts, and save some money, or I could go get them and here was the bid. Over 95 percent of the time, they wanted my expertise in selecting the product and I got the service sale—and the product sale. This was one of the few businesses where my product profit margin exceeded my service profit margin, which is opposite of how it usually works!

Whether you decide to go with a product, service, or both is highly dependent on what you want to do with your time (and on what your passion is). In the beginning, *you* may be the only service provider. If you are going to be a land-scaper, do you want to be out there digging up concrete? Do you need a crew? If so build this into your cost plan. If you are going to repair computers, it might just be you—you better love repairing computers or you will be one unhappy camper. Services usually generate higher profit margins, and you can decide how much you are worth per hour, provided what you're offering is something people are willing to pay that price for.

Products are good because they're usually low maintenance (except for dealing with warranties and so on), but the profit margin—unless you are selling a prod-uct with a generally higher profit margin that is not a commodity—is generally lower.

If the product can be quickly and easily found on the Internet, you might want to bundle it with service or find something else—unless you can sell a lot of these widgets. Anything sold en masse means your margins will be lower. For instance, if I want to buy a cell phone, I can go to many online providers, even eBay or Craigslist, and have many options. The profit margin is low because of the competition. If I had a unique product—wine rated by the feedback of other users, for instance—people might be willing to pay for my atmosphere (if I was an onsite location) or my knowledge as an online club member (for a web version of the same sort of company), and loyalty can be generated. People often pay a bit more because they are loyal to one place or another. But there is a fine line. You don't want to be so overpriced that people go elsewhere.

Many successful entrepreneurs bundle products and services. I was once strictly in the service business, but I found myself answering the same questions over and over. One common one was "What are some schools' human resources addresses I can use to get jobs?" Realizing that sending custom e-mails to people for limited money was time consuming and not worth it, I created an online product for sale and a document that is sent out to individuals. This is one way you can tie product and service together, but if you want to maintain a brand they need to be complementary.

Deciding If Your Plan Will Work

After you've decided that you want to make the jump, you need to figure out if your plan—the one you have by now fully documented, including short-term goals—will work. To do that you need to talk to people—lots of people—and you need to get the advice of experts—lots of experts! You also need to do your homework. Again, check the feasibility section of this chapter—read and re-read it—because it is important that you're able to answer those questions, and that the answers favor your business.

Who To Talk To

One way to find out what people are buying and how much they are paying for it is to talk to others in the business. For instance, if you are a wine expert and want to sell wine (and your expertise) on a website or even at a wine-tasting bar, you can visit wine-tasting bars, see what is on the menu, what the traffic (how many people are entering the place) looks like on various days and times of the week, and who is frequenting the place. Lots of people visit the competition to see what they're doing to replicate it. This is one good place to start.

You also need to talk to a tax advisor who can help you plan. A financial planner isn't a bad idea either if you have excessive obligations or if you are going to take a significant cut in pay early on. You might also want to talk to the Small Business Administration (SBA) and see what kind of financial assistance is available for individuals like yourself—entrepreneurs looking to make a living for themselves.

Evaluating Whether Your Idea Is Marketable

Another thing you'll need to do is determine how marketable your idea is. Here are some questions to get answers to:

How easy will it be to reach my target market? Will it be as easy as placing an ad in your local newspaper or journal, or will it require an ad campaign? Will it be beneficial to join social networking websites to advertise, or will it require a simple flyer posted at the local coffee shops?

How will my idea be received by my target group? This is a question that is a mix of both intuition and research. Even if the research that is conducted points to an acceptance of and strong demand for your products, services, or both, this doesn't automatically mean that you are guaranteed success. Similarly, just because the research indicates that you are "doomed" if you proceed with your original idea doesn't automatically mean that you will fail. This question is highly subjective, and will require both adequate research as well as a "sense" of the wants and needs of your target market.

Who is already doing what I will be doing? This is where research and investigation into your soon-to-be competition comes in. Who's already selling the same products? Who's already providing the same services? What are they charging, where are they lacking, where can you improve their models, etc.? Do they have an online presence? If so, evaluate their website. What are the pros and cons?

> Your own level of willingness to assume risk and how strongly you feel about the future of your product or service plays a role here. You may get a cool reception to the idea simply because it hasn't been thought of before.

What can I bundle with my products or my services to make them more appealing? Bundling is similar in marketing nature to "upselling" any product or service, but with some distinct differences. Upselling is selling a secondary or complimentary product, based on the sale of one product or service. We see this in its simplistic form in the now well-known phrase, "Do you want fries with that?" In more high end forms we see things like necklaces with the purchase of a watch; even recently a free compact car with the purchase of an SUV! You can figure out profit margins and make accommodations based on them.

Bundling is different than upselling in the sense that you are combining two or more products, services, or both that will increase the potential of the initial sale. For example, many cable television companies are now bundling their cable TV service with cable Internet service and telephone services. Often the goal of bundling is to make something simpler for the user—a single bill, for instance, for three utilities. By advertising the "package," you may be more likely to attract a wider customer base, instead of waiting for a customer to sign up for cable TV service and then trying to sell the additional services through direct marketing.

This concept can cross the product-or-service divide. For example, if you were offering window washing services, you could advertise the inclusion of a supply of window washing liquid (your own cleaner, for instance) for those smudges in between window washing visits. Carpet cleaning companies often do this. You could also offer a package of window washing and plant watering and maintenance.

Perhaps the most important question is, "What is it that people want that they aren't getting?" Wal-Mart answered this question with "low prices," and then figured out how to offer them; among other ways, by buying in such large bulk that they were able to put price pressure on suppliers and beat their competition. Apple answered it by offering products that were "cooler" than the others and by selling products to kids in schools so they would be used to their gadgets and computers at a young age. Samsung answered this question by maintaining tight family control over its operations and creating high-quality goods with great distribution. Toyota answered this question by offering a quality product at a great price. eTrade answered it by creating the guaranteed two-second trade and excellent online service. eBay answered it by disintermediating the market—removing the middle man and letting buyers and sellers work together in a huge global marketplace—and offering a platform for feedback and payments.

Have you noticed that "generics" tend to not do so well? What does Sears offer besides tools you can get elsewhere? What does Kmart offer? Do you want to be a company that has to fight and face bankruptcy each quarter? What does Ralph's offer over Stater Bros? What does CVS do to lure prescriptions from Wal-Mart? What does Maxtor do to make their hard drives the choice over others? You may have an answer if you're brand loyal to one of these companies, but in general, you won't see high profit margins or incredible growth out of these businesses. The key is that you don't want to be a generic anything unless you are running a low profit margin high volume business.

Figure out first what your customers want, then figure out how to offer it. It is kind of like writing a dissertation—you need to figure out what isn't out there before you can figure out what you need to offer.

Determining If Your Idea Will Supplement Your Income

One major decision you will need to make for the long term is whether this business is going to supplement your income or be your only source of income. If it is supplementing your income, figure out how many hours you want to spend on the business, and how much it will supplement your income by. Also determine for yourself if you will want to take this full time as the primary or sole source of income in the future, or if you want this to be a part time business forever.

If this business will be a supplement for the long term, you don't need to be as strict with regard to planning. You might find yourself launching the business and only breaking even for a year or two (if you are lucky), knowing that in time it will be profitable. This goes back to personal needs and decisions.

Determining If Your Idea Will Be Your Only Source of Income

If this business will be your only source of income, you need to be very serious in your planning. You need to know precisely what your bills are and what your business has to cover. The main difference between the business being your only source of income and a supplementary source, of course, is that the business needs to pay you a salary, so you need to cover not only your business's expenses but your own, too.

Try to limit your own personal expenses by getting rid of unnecessary debts before you take the plunge. Convert debt to lower-interest credit cards, for instance, remove as much revolving debt or as many variable rate loans that could change unexpectedly as possible, and then figure out what you need to make yearly. Remember that you need money to reinvest, and even if you have a well run business, you'll still have costs you don't realize but which creep up and get expensive, such as bringing on help when you need it, postage, ads, and so on.

Time Constraints—Do the Underemployed Have Time?

You need to figure out what your time constraints are for your business before you start it. We discussed some things earlier in this chapter that might affect your free time, like family and work.

If you are underemployed, you might have enough free time to still work eight hours a day on your business, but you'll need to be willing to commit to a very long work day for awhile. Beginning a new business is no picnic. If you want this business to fill an employment gap and then eventually take over as your only job, you'll need to work harder. This is why I am a big fan of scheduling your day, and making certain to schedule in time to think of new ideas, too.

I've found that every time I fill my day with 18 or more hours of work, I lose my creativity and the new business ideas that help my business generate more income. Be sure you schedule time, even if it's just for a walk, to brainstorm ideas. Try to have a life while you are at it! (Easier said than done!)

Getting Startup Money When You Are Unemployed

Although your being unemployed could be a warning sign to some lenders, investors, or both, if you are unemployed or even underemployed, you may still be able to find sources of startup money.

Banks do loan money to new startup businesses that have a business plan that is well laid out, pending you have adequate credit to minimize the risk that the bank will be evaluating. We dive into this in depth in Chapters 8 and 10.

Other sources are investors that are interested in high returns. It will cost you in high interest, but if you are confident in your numbers and know you can pay it back, it might be worth the risk.

Another option is small business loans, grants, or both through the Small Business Administration (SBA). Contrary to popular belief, the federal government does not loan money to startup businesses or entrepreneurs, nor do they give out grants. Any government funding that you may have heard of, or hear about, is coming from the state and local levels, and the criteria for these programs is very strict and can be difficult to navigate. Even these sources of funding, however, are not directly allotted and dispersed through the SBA.

The SBA deals with private and public lenders to assist small business owners acquire financing, usually through guaranteeing the loan itself. Obviously there are numerous requirements and chains of command that need to be negotiated, depending on the loan program you are applying for, but if you fit within the criteria set, this is usually one of the most attractive financing choices. SBA-guaranteed loans are often easier to secure, compared to soliciting your local financial institution on your own, and will often fund you with much lower interest rates. To learn more about the SBA's loan programs, visit sba.gov/services/financialassistance/sbaloantopics/index.html.

The SBA also deals with grants, although not necessarily as the grantor. The SBA's website specifically states: "Please note that the U.S. Small Business Administration does not offer grants to start or expand small businesses, though it does offer a wide variety of loan programs. While the SBA does offer some grant programs, these are generally designed to expand and enhance organizations that provide small business management, technical, or financial assistance. These grants generally support nonprofit organizations, intermediary lending institutions, and state and local governments." In other words, unless you fit a very specific group, with very specific needs, you will not qualify for a SBA-brokered grant. For more information on the SBA's grants, visit sba.gov/services/financialassistance/grants/index.html. (Small Business Administration, 2008)

> The SBA is a fantastic resource for more than just financial backing. In addition to their many financial aid resources, they offer free training, help in acquiring government contracts, help in understanding laws and regulations, and much more. Visit sba.gov/services/index.html for a breakdown of all that the U.S. SBA can do for you!

Startup Costs

Every business has startup costs; how much and what type will depend greatly on what you're going to do for a living. If you are going to be office-based or you're going to have a storefront, your costs will differ than someone who is going to run an Internet operation. Here are some basics for you to consider:

Office

Whether or not to have an office is a difficult choice. I was chatting with a multi-billionaire gentleman who is quite famous, and he was remarking how he used to have a highly impressive office, but then realized (paraphrasing here), "Heck, I just want to wear my shorts all day, why do I need this office?" and converted his living room into his office. Even his employees, when he has them, work from there—or from their own homes. I've had both—a home office and an outside office. I'll describe each and give you some of my personal pros and cons.

When I was running my computer consulting business, I was a "kid." I say this because I was in my very early 20s, and I had started it in my teens. I decided one day that I wanted a place to store equipment and I wanted my contractors to have a home base—I wanted a desk, and I wanted legitimacy. I think legitimacy was the biggest reason I wanted to move my office out of my laptop!

One of my clients happened to own the office building where his practice was and he offered me a suite, five rooms for $300 a month. In today's money this would be about $550—still a really good deal. It would come complete with a sign on the door—and a sign on the street in the business complex. I was a legit business! I moved in, they paid for new carpet (talk about lucky), and I bought IKEA furniture, a few file cabinets, some whiteboards, some entryway furniture (that I never used, because not one client came into my business), and I was happy. I left work at lunchtime and then again after work and I'd go to my office, do my work, pay my contractors, answer calls that had come in, schedule appointments and work for the next day or week, run quotes, and pick up equipment. I staged new systems there, had my "ghosting equipment," hardware that copies computer hard drive data running with a very strong up-time, and my contractors worked from there. I paid nearly nothing in rent.

This was a bad move! Why was this bad? Because I didn't need it! Not one person ever came to my office but my team, and my team could stage their computers from anywhere. My work was onsite—I went to my clients. That was the entire idea behind my service—so I didn't need the not-so-fancy office with new carpet. I moved out about two years later and moved back into my laptop. While it wasn't nearly as fancy or nearly as "legit" feeling, I got to keep an extra $300 per month for myself and pump it back into my business. (The constant barrage of solicitors stopped, too—they couldn't knock on my laptop!)

Years later, I began another business—online education and real estate consulting. While they sound highly dissimilar, they have more in common than one might think. I taught online—one class or so here and there—for about ten years. One day toward the end of my doctorate, my dissertation chairperson said, "Hey I do this full time." I was shocked. He really taught online and made a living at it? I thought to myself, "Wait, he lives in a lower-cost area than I do; I pay nearly double the tax he does. I'd have to do double the work." Turns out, I have double the energy and half the family commitments (and I can type really fast!).

So began the quest for a few additional schools to add to my income and fill up my free time, eight years after my first online teaching job. After less than a year and a Ph.D. almost finished, I had equal pay from schools as I did from my day job. To my astonishment, I was winning quality awards—in both of my careers! Obviously the quality of my work wasn't suffering. What if I added to my workload? So I did, and so I left—my day job, that is. I eventually decided to market my additional expertise—my advanced concepts of statistical models and my expertise in technology, management, real estate, entrepreneurship, and so on—and decided to design courses, further expanding my offerings. I began writing books about what I was seeing in the market—again an expansion. Then the television appearances started, the expertise began to flow, and the research I embarked on more than doubled. Products were added to my list, and the product/service mix was working very well. But guess what? This was all done from my home office—the loft in my 2400-square-foot home.

The lesson here? I was too focused in my early days on what it meant to have an office and not what it meant to have a business. I was looking at what would make me feel good, not what I needed. In the right career, working from anywhere would make me feel good. I toy now and again with the idea of renting space in a gorgeous tower off the 405 freeway, but then I remind myself that it would all be for show.

I did find a nice compromise, one you might find useful yourself. I moved into a new home last year, a bit larger, with a casita—a guest house. The guest house is … yes, you guessed it, my new office. It's a building apart from home, giving me home/work separation, but a low cost one—and a tax write off to boot!

Technology

As with anything in life or business, what you need depends on what you're doing. The same goes for technology. I am an online professor primarily, an author and a speaker, and an analyst. What am I using as my home PC? A machine I built seven years ago. I've upgraded parts as they've died off (that old IT business expertise comes in handy once in a while, like when I try to figure out just where the smoke is coming from in the grey box under my desk), but I have a (very) fast Internet connection, a large monitor, a comfortable chair, and an old—a *very* old—PC. My websites are stored on some virtual server somewhere in who-knows-what-country, and they are reliable and cheap.

If you're going to host a site like eBay or Amazon, you obviously can't do this. You need to analyze what you do need. How many calls will you make? Do you need a fax? Will a free electronic fax do? Can you use a cell for all your calls? What sort of backups do you need? Do you really need QuickBooks, or will your bank offer you a small business service that lets you invoice clients and handle payroll online?

Once you get a good list, figure out what it will cost and then set a budget and stick to it. Try not to get sucked in with all the bells and whistles. You probably don't need Blu-ray on that work computer!

SURVEY SAYS

What do our survey respondents say is most vital to their success? Respondents could pick up to five.

- 82 percent indicated that a laptop is most vital
- 62 percent said a cell phone is most important
- 48 percent said a calendaring system
- 44 percent said a scanner
- 40 percent said a desktop
- 40 percent said a fax machine
- 38 percent said automated backups
- 32 percent said dual monitors
- 32 percent said a PDA
- 28 percent said manual backups
- 28 percent said VoIP

What about some other miscellaneous items? Client management software, digital cameras, digital voice recorders, K7.net, voice-mail services, accounting software, and point-of-sale systems were all mentioned.

Staffing

To staff or not to staff—the age old question. You may want to begin your business with just you—for a while, you may well *be* your business. If you're going to hire staff, though, you will need to consider all costs involved. In each state, this will vary greatly. The U.S. Department of Labor has some great resources that will help you determine the cost for employees. Here is how they break it down (keep in mind that this is for workers of all categories; these are averages including highly skilled workers with doctorates all the way down to the lowest skilled, most uneducated workers)—the key to take from this section is how much more it will cost you to employ someone than just their wage.

Overall in the United States, a worker earning a salary of $18.67 per hour (average for December 2007 in private industry) cost the employer an additional $7.75 in fees, resulting in a cost of about $26.42 per hour.

In the Northeast, the average salary is $20.99 per hour, with an additional $9.20 in costs, for a total average of $30.18. In the West, this is $20.05, with an additional $8.22 in costs, for a total of $28.27. In the Midwest, it is $17.93 with an additional $7.71 in benefits, for a total of $25.63. Finally, in the South, it is $16.99 in wages and $6.65 in benefits, for a total of $23.64.

In nearly all cases, benefits are running about 30 percent or more for employees! Some benefits are legally required, some are not. In some states, for instance, you must provide healthcare and in others you don't. Legally required benefits are Social Security, workers' compensation, and unemployment insurance. These average around $2.50 per hour per worker. Note that these figures assume straight time, and no overtime or bonuses. (U.S. Department of Labor, Bureau of Labor Statistics, 2008)

What is the take-away lesson here? Having employees isn't cheap. You may only need moderately skilled workers who you can pay less than the average; remember that these numbers include the highly educated and senior professionals.

There is another option, and that is contractors. There are rules, though, about contractors that you need to strictly abide by!

Initially it is up to you whether you want to bring someone on as a contractor or as an employee. But this is subject to potential review by the IRS and state workers' compensation and unemployment compensation agencies. The IRS is most likely to classify a person as an independent contractor if she …

- Is capable of earning a profit or loss from an activity.
- Provides her own materials and tools needed to do the job.
- Is paid by the job.
- Works for more than one company at a time.
- Pays her own business and travel expenses—you don't reimburse her for mileage, and so on.
- Pays and hires assistants.
- Has flexible working hours.

There are common law rules according to the IRS, too. Does the company control or have the right to control what the worker does and how the worker does his job? If so, he may be considered an employee. Does the business provide tools and reimburse for travel and mileage and expenses? If so, he may be an employee. Are there written contracts or benefits like vacations, pension plans, and insurance? If so, he may be an employee. There is no magic bullet that makes a person an employee or a contractor. The entire relationship is taken into consideration, including flexibility and control. The IRS does offer form SS-8, Determination of Worker Status for Purpose of Federal Employment Taxes and Income Tax Withholding, available in the References section of this book. (Internal Revenue Service)

If you are going to hire contractors, you must require a W9 form from your contractors, which is a taxpayer identification number and certification. You can get the W9 form online at www.irs.gov/pub/irs-pdf/fw9.pdf?portlet=3. Then you file a simple 1099 MISC form at the end of each year. The money you pay them comes off your taxable income and you don't withhold taxes from them.

Life is a bit more complicated with employees. You must withhold federal income tax using form W4. Publication 15, "The Employers' Tax Guide," available on the IRS website, will walk you through this. Grab Publication 15A, "The Employers' Supplemental Tax Guide," while you're there.

Social Security and Medicare taxes pay for benefits that workers and families receive under the Federal Insurance Contributions Act, or FICA. You must pay a portion of these as well. Social Security tax pays for benefits under the old age, survivors, and disability insurance part of FICA. Medicare pays for benefits under the hospital insurance part of FICA. These also need to be withheld and you pay a matching amount yourself, which adds costs.

You will have to file quarterly Form 941, the Employers' Quarterly Federal Tax Return.

You will have to file Form 944, the Employers' Annual Federal Tax Return.

There is yet another tax you must pay on your own: the Federal Unemployment Tax, or FUTA. This pays unemployment compensation to workers that lose their jobs. Employees don't pay this at all! *You*, the owner of the company, pay this entirely. You report it on Form 940.

You must deposit withheld income taxes and employer and employee Social Security and Medicare taxes, minus any Earned Income Credit payments, by depositing electronically or delivering a check, money order, or cash to a banking institution that is an authorized depository for federal taxes, or by using the electronic federal tax payment system available on the Internet at the IRS's website. It is discussed in great detail in Publication 15, under the How to Deposit section. This is one thing the IRS makes it easy to do—pay them!

You also must prepare a Form W2 each year, on the last day of February for paper forms and March 31 for electronic forms. You can do this online using the Social Security Administration's online W2 filing system (www.socialsecurity.gov/employer).

If you can fit individuals into contractor status, this can save you a lot of money. Think about this decision carefully! Also ask yourself if you need anyone at all, and if you don't, then ask how you will know when you need additional help. A general rule of thumb I live by is, "If I have to turn down jobs because I need more hands, I bring on more hands."

Vehicles

This consideration is more pertinent if your new venture is service based, but even product-based businesses could be affected.

Rehashing an earlier example, if your idea is for a landscaping business, even if you are planning on being a sole proprietor, you will likely need a truck, and perhaps a trailer. If you are going to employ a crew (or more than one), you may even be considering a "fleet" of trucks. There are many aspects to this that need to be considered.

First, if you already own a truck, and you are planning on only using your personal vehicle, you will be allowed certain tax advantages. Similarly, if you don't own a truck (or opt not to use your own vehicle), and you want to buy or lease a "work truck," you will be eligible for some different and/or additional tax benefits. For example, if you lease a truck, your lease payment now becomes a business expense, as do your insurance payments and the costs of fuel and maintenance. You will not necessarily be eligible for the same tax advantages if you are using your own personal vehicle. You will need to consult with an accountant, not merely a tax preparer, for an interpretation of the full letter of the law. It is advisable to consult with a tax professional before making this decision.

Insurance

I don't mean only healthcare insurance (as I discuss this in the next section), but the other types that are often not considered, and which generally fall under the main category of "business insurance." These include professional liability, business liability, general liability, umbrella liability, workers' compensation, etc.

Here's a quick breakdown, based on an injured party and insurance plans that cover the injured party:

Injured party:	Property
Insurance:	Property insurance
Injured party:	Employees
Insurance:	Unemployment insurance
	Workers' compensation insurance
	Health insurance

	Disability insurance
	Key employee insurance
Injured party:	Customers/Others
Insurance:	Liability insurance
Business Operations:	Business interruption insurance
	Key employee insurance
	Surety bonds
	Employee practices insurance

If you're feeling a bit overwhelmed, you're not alone. Insurance is often overlooked for this simple reason. Here is a bit of a further breakdown from Microsoft's website, which you can read for yourself at www.microsoft.com/smallbusiness/resources/finance/business-insurance/protect-your-business-7-types-of-insurance-coverage.aspx:

Business owner coverage. Otherwise known as "catch-all" coverage, business owner insurance provides damage protection from fire and other mishaps. Owner coverage also offers a degree of liability protection.

Property insurance. This can augment the property coverage offered by business owner insurance. Property insurance covers damage to the building that houses your business, as well as to items inside, such as furniture and inventory.

Liability insurance. In our litigation-looped society, this may be as important a form of coverage as you can get. It covers damage to property or injuries suffered by someone else for which you are held responsible. This can take in a range of disasters, from the postal worker who sues you for a dog bite incurred during a delivery to your home business to the clumsy customer who scorches himself after you make your complimentary coffee just too darn hot.

Product liability insurance. You might want this form of coverage if you make a product that could conceivably harm someone else. For instance, catering businesses worried about some dicey-looking truffles or Brie would do well to tack on this coverage.

Errors and omissions insurance. This coverage is particularly important for service-based businesses, offering protection should you make a mistake or neglect to do something that causes a customer or client some harm. A good example is doctor's medical malpractice insurance, which practicing physicians are required to carry.

Business income insurance. This is disability coverage for your business. It ensures you get paid if you lose income as a result of damage that temporarily shuts down or limits your business.

Automobile insurance. This last item should come as no great surprise. If your business uses cars or trucks in some manner, you have to have this type of insurance for collision and liability coverage. (Wuorio, Microsoft, 2008, retrieved from www.microsoft.com/smallbusiness/resources/finance/business-insurance/protect-your-business-7-types-of-insurance-coverage.aspx)

Other types of insurance may be necessary or unique to your particular business. For instance, a book author or consultant may want to carry a policy that will protect them from libel, plagiarism, or negligence lawsuits. For professionals in the medical field or legal field, professional liability or malpractice insurance is important. The cost of insurance can have a significant impact on your bottom line, so find out what you really need to be protected and what your umbrella policy covers.

One thing that should be clear from this section is that you should never, ever settle for insurance you know to be inadequate, such as $300,000 in property insurance for a shop worth well over half a million dollars. You need to find a good insurance agent who you can trust, and make sure that he or she helps you get the right type of insurance plan(s) for your particular needs. Spend some time in choosing your agent. You need someone you can be comfortable with on a long-term basis—someone who will advise you well so that you can spend your time on your business, not worrying about the fine print of the coverage.

Healthcare

Ah, healthcare. Although mentioned in the previous section, it can get so confusing and is so often misunderstood, I'm devoting a section to it all on its own.

We hear companies complain all the time about how expensive it is to provide healthcare. We already ran through the costs for individuals and to insure your own family, but what about employees?

The price will depend on which state you live in, how healthy your employees are, and how many people you are employing, among other things. Allied Quotes at www.alliedquotes.com provides small business health insurance quotes, so you can check them out. Shop around—you will be amazed at how drastically different prices are.

You should know that health insurance, in general, is the most expensive employer-paid benefit. Many companies are cutting back by either providing lower quality service or increasing co-pays or both. The cost of healthcare is rising at a rate nearly twice that of inflation. Most small businesses in America don't provide healthcare. For instance, in California, full time workers at small businesses account for over 20 percent of the uninsured. As of April 2008, more than half (56 percent) of all small businesses don't offer healthcare because of the costs (SurePayroll Survey at www.surepayroll.com/spsite/press/releases/2008/release041608.asp). It is also important to note that you do not provide healthcare to contractors. One way many employers are handling the healthcare issue is to give a self-insured healthcare credit to employees, requiring them to buy a plan and helping them offset the cost with a check each month.

Final Thoughts

Once you have an idea and you have made the decision to "go for it," there are so many things to do that it can feel and become overwhelming. I recommend that you write them all down, in order, with specific details as to when you will do each one. Be as aggressive as you can so you don't lose motivation or momentum, but also watch for potential "gotcha's" as you move through each of the requirements and each phase of business planning. Catching them now is better than catching them a year into your work!

4

Your Path to Entrepreneurship

By this point, we have established that you have an idea (or you are well on your way to discovering an idea) for a business and that you have what it takes to be an entrepreneur—you are committed, prepared to plan, prepared to sacrifice, and you realize that sometimes it takes many flings of mud for one to stick.

Now begins your personal path to entrepreneurship—to owning your own business!

Types of Businesses

There are four primary types of business models and many subtypes. Your accountant can help you determine which one is best for you; even if you use this book and do your own research, you should run the ramifications of your choice by a tax accountant or legal advisor (I recommend both), because individual circumstances, like personal write-offs and other legal implications, can drastically change the outcome of your selection from a tax perspective.

Additionally, each method of structuring your business offers various types of protection for you and/or your family, should your business be sued or be negligent in some way.

Sole Proprietorship

The first and perhaps easiest of the four structures is a sole proprietorship. A sole proprietorship is the method many of us use to begin with, until we get big enough to form some kind of formal corporation, or unless our liability from the start is substantial. There are many examples of substantial liability, but some are: businesses teaching people how to fly small planes and get their pilot's license; day care facilities, restaurants, and so on. Anything involving more risk than you care to assume on your own should possibly be put into a corporate format. Also, if your company manages property or owns a building or premises in which someone could be hurt and sue for damages, consider other options than a sole proprietorship. Another case in which you would want to consider a structure other than sole proprietorship is any time that an individual must drive for you and they are your employee, like a pizza driver.

A sole proprietorship is easily established. You will need a name and a business checking account, and you will report income on a Schedule C with your Form 1040 for your personal taxes.

First things first! Find the name that best suits your business. Go to your local government, which will usually be your county—most counties have the information on their website about "how to start a small business." They will usually require a small business license, which can range from $10 to $500 per county. After this, you need to establish that the business is, in essence, you. Entrepreneurs do this through a DBA, or "doing business as" request. To do this, you file a DBA form through your county, which will usually require that you publish the name in some media form (usually small town newspapers qualify, and the government will most often give you a list of papers and prices) for a certain number of weeks, which again varies by county or city. In my experience, it could be as little as one week or as long as two months. (Be prepared—many companies scour these parts of newspapers to start sending bulk junk mail, usually arriving within three to five days of when you first publish!)

After the DBA is established, you bring the business name certificate and business license, along with identification, to a bank. Show them your documents, and establish a business checking account. Essentially this method will work for all types of corporations, too. Remember, it is essential to keep personal and business funds separate, regardless of what business model you choose. If you need cash to cover business expenses, you need to write yourself a check and document it as owner's equity (or document it based on the advice of your financial planner or accountant). Most accountants are well versed in the common bookkeeping software most of us use, so if you run into any concerns, most will assist you with how to make the entries into your own system.

After you have your business checking account and business license, you're free to do business—just be sure to keep your business and personal expenses separate. I like to use NeatReceipts Professional to scan all of my business receipts and automatically categorize them into IRS buckets—the lines the IRS uses in Schedule C. Using this method saves both time and money come tax time, as not only am I having to take up less time during my annual session with my accountant, but I am also saving personal time when preparing for that appointment, which in turn allows me more time to work and lets me focus less on administrative stuff.

If you are in a riskier business or want to start off as a separate corporation, look into other options, which are discussed later in this section of the book on corporations.

A sole proprietorship is easy to manage and fast to set up, but offers you no protection. You and your business are one and the same—that is why you are "doing business as." As you and your business are inseparable, if at any point the potential for a lawsuit were to present itself, the lawsuit would be filed against you directly, placing your personal assets at risk.

Partnership

A partnership is essentially set up the same as a sole proprietorship with one exception—you have a partner. Each of you owns a named percentage of the business, which is also reported on a Schedule C with your Form 1040. This is very similar to a sole proprietorship, in that it offers little to no protection from risk, but it is very simple and straightforward to set up.

When you fill out the business registration forms with your county, one of the check boxes will be for a partnership. Generally the same rules and procedures are followed regardless of the county, city, or state, and both names go on the business checking as "DBA." Keep in mind that you cannot take a person off a checking account once it is opened, so if your business partner leaves, you have to reopen your checking and refile both the business license (some counties and cities will let you do a business modification) and a new DBA form, since your partner is no longer doing business under that name.

There are obvious risks here, like your partner leaving or having a medical crisis, and not having full control over your business. Everyone has her own rules, but (after hearing too many horror stories) I personally believe—no partnerships. Save them for marriage, and perhaps private lending. There cannot be two kings (or two queens)—someone needs to have the final decision. That is only my opinion, however, and many former business school peers or friends have successfully started partnerships with no issues.

> Think about the not so obvious before starting a partnership—Does one of you have an ego? Does one of you need to be in control? Are you *both* control freaks? If only one of you needs to feel the power or control over the business, or has a stronger personality, it might work out okay. If you both do, you should reconsider—unless lines of responsibility (and profit) are clearly delineated up front and adhered to by all involved parties.

In this scenario, since risk is passed off to both parties, you are assuming the same percentage of risk as you own in the business. If you have a 60/40 split, the partner with 60 percent assumes 60 percent of the risk, unless otherwise documented.

Also remember that your accountants will need to work together, or if you are preparing taxes yourself, be sure to read the IRS's rules about how to file for partnerships.

Note that partnerships are not limited to two persons. In most cases, you are allowed one or more additional parties, which will lessen the risk potential of each involved party, pending a fair split of responsibility and ownership.

Corporation

There are two primary types of the basic corporation—S corp and C corp—each with its own pros and cons.

A corporation in general has one big advantage, and that is limited liability due to you and your business being two separate entities. In essence, your business is now its own living and tax-paying being. Upon structuring as a corporation you will receive a tax identification number or Employer Identification Number (known as an EIN), which is similar to your own Social Security number. The corporation will be required to pay taxes to the IRS just as you are. Another advantage, speaking of taxes, is the corporate tax liability (which is often less than personal tax liability) and a true separation between business and personal taxes (although this can be a grey area with an S corp, as it is considered a pass-through structure).

Generally, corporations file quarterly taxes, making life a bit more difficult for the entrepreneur, especially if you're just starting and don't have much to report. You will usually make estimated tax payments as a corporation. For more information, see IRS Publication 505, consult with your tax professional, or both.

Structuring your business as a corporation as a way to separate taxes is a tricky situation, however, as the IRS considers an S corp to be a "pass-through" entity, meaning that all of the tax liability will pass through to your personal bottom line. I cannot stress enough that you should consult with a tax professional, accountant, and legal counsel prior to making the decision to structure your company. At the very least, consult your state tax laws, the federal IRS tax laws, research thoroughly, and consult with your local SBA office.

Double taxation, according to Investopedia, is "A taxation principle referring to income taxes that are paid twice on the same source of earned income." Investopedia continues with the following explanation:

> "Double taxation occurs because corporations are considered separate legal entities from their shareholders. As such, corporations pay taxes on their annual earnings, just as individuals do. When corporations pay out dividends to shareholders, those dividend payments incur income tax liabilities for the shareholders who receive them, even though the earnings that provided the cash to pay the dividends had already been taxed at the corporate level." (Investopedia, 2008)

Note that you probably won't have shareholders beyond yourself and/or your business partners in the beginning. Also remember, though, that you don't have to be a public company to offer shares of stock. Plenty of private companies have stock available for sale.

Remember that you can always become a corporation later on down the road and start off the easier way by becoming a sole proprietor (it is far less paperwork and less difficult to file taxes), unless you will have a significant level of risk immediately upon starting your business, or you are looking to turn a substantial profit and you will have substantial startup costs.

Limited Liability Corporation

A limited liability corporation, commonly referred to as an "LLC," is one way to limit your liability without creating a big headache come tax time. I have an LLC that is easily managed and is easy to file taxes for.

A limited liability corporation is set up to do precisely what it implies: limit the owner's liability. It is reported like a regular sole proprietorship on a Schedule C with your 1040, and can provide the same benefits—like a home office write-off—that sole proprietors enjoy, yet will limit your liability because it protects you as an individual from your business. Two exceptions to this are farms and real estate rental properties, which require a Schedule F and E, respectively.

As an example of an LLC used to own and manage a real estate business, I use my own LLC to deed my rental properties into the business, rather than having them owned by me personally. Since real estate transactions are a bit different and my LLC has relatively little credit or positive net assets (and most banks won't lend to LLCs to buy properties anyway), I buy the properties myself, then using a quit claim deed form, I "give them" to my LLC. My LLC files its own Schedule E, for real estate businesses and income-generating properties, and has its own Employer Identification Number. My LLC is free to hire employees as any corporation is, but if an individual is hurt in my property beyond what my insurance covers, my primary home cannot be touched nor can my personal property.

Are you protected individually with an LLC? Yes. But remember, all assets that your LLC owns are at risk. If you own assets that have to have insurance, be sure you add your LLC as a named insured. In the case of real estate investment properties, the mortgagee, the second lien holder, myself as an individual, and my LLC all must be specifically named insured on the policies. If you have an umbrella policy, talk with your insurance broker or representative about adding your LLC to the policy, too.

Overall, the pros and cons of an LLC are as follows:

One advantage to the LLC structure is that it allows for an unlimited number of members. If the LLC has just one owner, however, it will be taxed as a sole proprietorship. Also, the LLC model provides for limited liability for all members, which means that they are personally protected from any liability of the LLC and successful lawsuits, as well as from the LLC itself.

Some of the disadvantages include the fact that, as a member of an LLC, you are not allowed to pay yourself a salary, and the managing member's share of the bottom line profit of the LLC is considered earned income, meaning it is subject to self-employment taxation, which can be higher than corporate taxes.

No Such Thing as a Bad Idea

Now that you know what your options are and will be consulting with experts about your own situation, we will move onto ideas and inspiration, the next step on your path toward entrepreneurship.

We've all heard our teachers tell us that there is no such thing as a stupid question or a bad idea! Perhaps our teachers were right all along. Some of the wackiest ideas have certainly made people a lot of money. Do you think this isn't true?

Read on! The most unique or creative (some would say stupid) ideas have really made it big!

The Worst Business Ideas That Made It

We've all laughed at the Pet Rock right? How much money did that inventor make, exactly? We know it was well into the multimillions. Unimaginable now, but many people scoffed at the notion of eBay or Amazon, too. Look who's laughing now!

Crazy business ideas can catch on. If they didn't, why would people pay for expensive nighttime infomercials that make people millionaires in a matter of months? I had two really bad business ideas that, embarrassingly enough, I will share here. They didn't take off, but it goes back to the "throwing mud at the wall until some of it sticks" theory. What were my two ideas? The headband holder, which was really a paper towel holder, fixed so that it couldn't roll. And? The small pet food dispenser: a coffee dispenser made for pet food. Yes, brilliant. It is amazing how excited we can get about these crazy ideas! I got the products up on eBay within hours, showcasing how well the headbands really were held and the pet food organizer really stored food. Oh well—two down, two thousand to go!

This is the stuff entrepreneurs are made of. Do you find yourself sitting there saying, "Hey—I thought of that already!" or "Why not use this device to do this? And then remarket it?" Yep, entrepreneur material. If this doesn't sound like you now, don't worry, ideas will come to mind. Of course, I cannot take all the credit for my two wacko ideas—a good friend and I nearly simultaneously found these "solutions" at the Container Store and got them for sale available online to the public almost immediately.

The point is, you will have some great ideas that go nowhere—and that idea you think really stinks just might be the one that sticks. Just run with it! See where it takes you and what happens. One day, something will stick.

So what are some other worst business ideas that actually did make it? In no particular order, here are a few:

1. Rescue Critters (www.rescuecritters.com). Want to practice K9 CPR? Rescue Critters sells animal rescue (CPR and First Aid) mannequins.

2. FlexPetz (www.flexpetz.com). Want a few days with a well-trained dog, but don't want to actually own one? FlexPetz offers animal rentals.

3. Beach'n Billboard (www.beachnbillboard.com). If you want to advertise your business or event to the beach crowd, but don't want a traditional billboard or plane-towed banner, contact Beach'n Billboard. They will sculpt your advertisement directly into the sand at the beach(s) of your choice. Talk about going green!

4. Santa Mail (www.santamail.co.uk). Even if you don't believe in Santa Claus, your child probably still does. Keep the tradition alive with a customized letter from Santa. Contact Santa Mail today!

5. The Million Dollar Homepage (milliondollarhomepage.com). The genius Alex Tew came up with the idea for his million-dollar home page, which he allowed others to use for advertising, charging one dollar per pixel. He had one million pixels available … a million-dollar idea one buck at a time!

6. Antenna Balls (www.antennaballs.com). Offering everything from basic shapes and designs to custom decorations for your vehicle's antenna, AntennaBalls.com was grossing over $1.15 million after only two years of operation.

7. Diapees and Wipees (www.diapeesandwipees.com). Tired of having to lug around diapers and baby wipes in a diaper bag that clashes with your outfit? Have no fear—Christina Leigh has the solution for you. Check out Diapees and Wipees for fashionable diaper bags created for fashion conscious moms-on-the-go!

8. Doggles (www.doggles.com). That's right, even your canine friend "needs protection from the sun's UV rays. Contact Doggles for sunglasses (and other pet supplies) for your beloved K9 friend.

9. Jewels et Jim (www.jewelsetjim.com). No more plain and unsightly medical alert tags and bracelets. Now you can alert medical personnel of your medical history and issues without having to disregard the latest fashion trends.

10. I Want NY Pizza (www.iwantnypizza.com). The idea behind this business is just as the title states: if you want a traditional NY pizza, no matter where you may be, contact I Want NY Pizza and they will arrange the delivery!

Testing the Waters

Before going full-board with your idea, you might want to test the waters a bit. How do you do this? Run the idea by family and friends. Try selling a few of your inventions on eBay, Craigslist, or other free or nearly free sites. Set up a simple website that allows basic PayPal or Google Checkout. If, with some advertising and word of mouth, your idea is resulting in zero sales (as my pet food holder did), it is time to put your energies into something else. I prefer to put my energies into numerous projects at one time, so if one fails I am already onto the next, but many people very successfully take the opposite approach and stick with one idea for a year or two and then make a decision whether to take it big or start again.

If you have the resources, you can of course hire focus groups, but this will cost you some money. You can also collect research using online surveys with tools like www.surveymonkey.com and post the link to online forums where people who would buy your product "hang out online." However, this isn't quite the same as an in-person focus group. If you are trying to decide whether your new perfume smells good, for instance, you may need to go this route no matter what.

So let's assume you do need a focus group. What are some firms you should check out? A great website that I have found is www.GreenBook.org. GreenBook is a company that provides comprehensive information "to buyers of market research services" (their slogan, in fact). Offering online research, quantitative research, qualitative research, interviewing, and even international research, GreenBook provides a great starting point for your research needs. Note that GreenBook is a directory of research providers, not the provider of the research itself. Through GreenBook you can search for marketing research groups by category. Additionally, you can also search your local yellow pages or contact your local SBA for marketing research companies in your area.

Doing Business with Family and Friends

Many times the best ideas come to mind over a family dinner—and they belong to the family member or two or three who decide to run with it. Sometimes you need inexpensive labor, so you bring on the 17-year-old cousin you rarely saw to help with the business. Or sometimes you just want to keep profits in the family.

Lots of people go into business with family and friends. Restaurants are often family owned and run, as are dry cleaners, manicure and pedicure shops, and so on. This often works best with "communal" property, where the individuals all share expenses and the income "… goes into the household kettle of funds, which everyone involved can draw from."

If you are an independent person with your own family—and your partner is, too—you might give this a second look before going for it. Many people have reported family tensions or even complete disconnects. Money is a very powerful thing—sometimes it's best not to mix money with people you care about. I have a couple of personal stories to share here—while for the sake of keeping boundaries, I refuse to go into business with my family or even discuss finances with them, there have been occasions where I've made mistakes, and friendships and even my marriage has suffered as a result.

The first mistake wasn't so much my decision, but my husband's. Just after we married, I was going through files (to throw them away—not much excites me more than cleaning out cabinets! Hmm … business idea—note to Palm Treo!) and found some documents about an investment in a movie company for what I consider a substantial amount of money, but my new husband did not consider it "a big deal." He had invested in a family member's C-list (at best) movie—neither of them having any movie experience. The family member involved was a mortgage broker on top of it, so my skepticism about his ethics are questionable to say the least.

When I asked my husband if he had been paid back, he said that the deal had "gone south" and he wouldn't be paid back. I was furious! This seemed like such an obvious waste to me. That was money we could have used toward the purchase of our new home, our wedding, our retirement. I am still shocked that this particular family member would even ask my husband to invest in something with such a high level of risk, with no documentation whatsoever about what their recourse would be if they didn't get their money back. To this day, I have never thought the same of that individual—because I'd never ask for an investment in something so ludicrous, I have had a hard time understanding this other individual's thought process—or lack thereof. Did it create marital tensions? Definitely—particularly when I informed my accountant and subsequently wrote it off as bad investment debt, as per my accountant's instructions. (Too bad we can't screen for this stuff before marriage! Hmm … another business idea ….)

As you may already know I am also a coauthor, and I tend to be very candid and open in my writing. I think that sharing personal, human experiences with readers makes your work more usable, more informative, more real—and creates a human connection through writing.

I have had three coauthors in my life. While all three wrote their halves of the books technically, my involvement was significantly greater than the 50 percent I will earn one day in royalties. I tend to go all-out with marketing, hiring publicists that are more than most mortgages and cars combined, updating the website daily, and so on—and my partners frankly don't.

I realize this is a matter of personality and drive and perhaps a bit of internal motivation that leads me to never stop trying—and all three of course had families that came first (I am the only childless one, so I am certain that played a role). In fact, I'm not sure (beyond one who traveled a bit and tried to get on television regularly) what they did when it came to trying to sell our books. About a year later, one other coauthor stepped up and held seminars and forums that took some time to try to sell books and stepped up to help financially with some television media, but it was rough for awhile. I had to officially "let it go," realizing that no one will care or be as involved as I am because of my personality type.

This type of situation can lead to personal tension between friends, family, and so on. I've been able to separate work from business now, knowing that it "isn't their thing," to work 80 or more hours per week to accomplish a goal. These were partnerships by agreement, not by business creation, but they resulted in the same downside nonetheless. One of my dearest friends and I got into a heated discussion with a lot of hurt feelings midway through one book. He is such a good friend that I decided not to ever write with him again, because I care about him too much to do that to our friendship. From this point forward, I will never write with a coauthor. It isn't due to writing issues or their not supplying content and not being experts, but to the all-important promotion up to and after the release of the book.

This brings up a very essential point: find out, if you do intend to have business partners, how they see their involvement. Do they see it as a "full time part time" job like you perhaps do—part time officially, but one that will take 30 to 40 hours per week of your time? Will they sacrifice personal time like you do? Think of all these things before engaging with a partner. It may be hard to tell a friend or family member "no," but sometimes it's best for the relationship.

Consider these risks before you take the plunge with family and friends. It sounds terrific to work with people you already inherently trust, but trust me—there are downsides. Be prepared for them. Even the people you think are least likely to leave you hanging with a majority of the work may do so, as everyone works differently. If you are like me, and tend to work very fast and dedicate 18-plus hours per day to your work, partnering isn't always the best idea because you may *never* feel like someone is pulling his own weight, even if he is just behaving like a normal person.

Understand your personality and assess others' personalities, and if you still want to go for it, be very thorough in documentation, noting who will do what and when and how. Keep it in writing and have repercussions for an individual who doesn't live up to expectations.

Pros of Family and Friends

There are advantages to family or friend businesses. One is keeping the profits with people you care about, which is a big one particularly if you become highly successful. The idea of working day-in and day-out with someone you really like or care about or love is another great benefit—laughing while you work is great! Sometimes the inherent trust that comes with knowing someone you go into business with makes it all worth it, too.

Another benefit is that of "backup." Working with family and friends, you will never feel "alone" in your endeavors. Those who you work with are familiar to you and you are familiar to them, which means you will likely be able to step into each other's roles more easily (particularly if you share information about your day jobs, should the need arise). You will also be there for each other in business as you are in your personal affairs.

Easily accessible resources is yet another huge benefit to starting a business with friends or family or both. Oftentimes when friends or family get together to start a business, they will pool resources, financially and otherwise. This is obviously much easier than having to hit the pavement with lenders on your own.

Cons of Family and Friends

I gave some personal examples of the disadvantages, but here are some more general ones. Resentment if the business doesn't go so well, and it was primarily one person's idea, is a big one. This can happen in any business partnership, but when the one that you begin to resent is your family or friend the tension and emotional burden is far greater. You may find yourself trying to figure out how to get out of the relationship on the business end, while maintaining it on the family/friend end. This flat out may not be possible.

Another is a 50/50 split of revenues without a 50/50 split of workload. This can happen with any business partner, but this again leads to resentment; and resentment at work is one thing—resentment that carries over into Thanksgiving dinner is another.

Another big downside is if or when one person wants to leave the business, if the other cannot afford to continue or buy out the partner. While this can happen anyway, it is particularly difficult when family is involved. What if your brother whom you are in business with needs out to send his kids (your nephews) to college? How do you say no without feeling terribly guilty later? How do you say no at all? What will this do to your relationship if your business was just booming?

Another downside is, particularly with spouses or family members you live with, never getting away from them. Everyone needs their adult time, their alone time, their time to get away from their loved ones or friends. Sometimes too much of a good thing isn't so good. There can also be issues later, with regard to who owes who what, and how revenues (if there are any) should be split or reinvested into the business.

Remember, although it is counterintuitive, it is sometimes easier to share your thoughts and feelings on your new venture with a random business partner than with a loved one.

Home Based or Office Based?

Another major decision you will need to make fairly quickly on your path to entrepreneurship is whether you will be home based or office based. You can have both if you have a separate building on your property, such as a casita or guest house, but you may still feel like you never leave home.

I have had both a home-based and an office-based business. I can speak first hand about some pros and cons, and I'll include some additional expert knowledge, too.

In our survey, a whopping 89.4 percent of respondents worked from home, and 8.5 percent worked from a totally separate office building. What did the survey respondents say about the difficulty in working from home? Fifty-two percent said it was not very difficult and 34 percent said it was not at all difficult, but 13 percent said it was very difficult. No doubt the type of business is driving these statistics.

Pros of Home or Office

The pros to working in a home-based office include a very (very) short commute and the ability to get to work quickly should the need arise. (This whole issue of no commuting could be by far one of the best advantages right now, considering the recent rise in fuel and other transportation costs.) If you have small children and need to be close to them or you are caring for another individual, a home office can be a great option for you. It also gives you a nice tax write-off for home office deductions.

The upsides to an office-based business is the feeling of getting away from work—when you leave the office and go home, you're home—not at work. You can still write off your expenses associated with your business rent, utilities, and so on. It is easier to expand in an office-based solution, because usually you will have room to extend the suite, or add desks at the very least. You also get the feeling of ownership in a different way than a home-based business provides. There is something about walking up to a building with your company name on it that gives you a sense of pride and empowerment that, in my view, a home-based business doesn't give you. Also, if you need to meet clients and customers, you automatically get additional credibility.

Another great benefit to working from home, which I take full advantage of, is no dress code. If you have the ability to conduct your business either primarily or entirely out of your home, you can wear whatever you want. I often spend a great majority of my day in my gym clothes—they are simply more comfortable to work in. If I need to do a web- or camera-based interview, most of the time the only things that change are the hair, makeup, and top part of my outfit. Sometimes my television hits that are remote (not in studio but from a remote facility) are done wearing a jacket and nice shirt with gym shorts.

The downside to this is that I don't often get to see myself fully dressed in any of my many business suits, which makes me feel empowered and capable. Having to get dressed up in my fancy threads does provide me with a sense of accomplishment and success that I don't get when I forego them for gym clothes. Of course, going out to events, speaking engagements, residencies, and in-studio interviews takes care of that problem right away.

Now that I work from home, I am generally much healthier as well. Even though I live part time on one side of the country and part time on the other side of the country, I have a gym in both places and it is up to me when I go. It is up to me what time I eat and what I eat. Rather than having to cram all of my personal errands and lunch into a one-hour block of time, I am not restricted to the local fast food stop. I can actually cook a healthy meal or take the time to go to a real restaurant, which in turn has provided me with an overall healthier lifestyle. Keeping with this same benefit, I can be much more flexible about when I visit the gym, and can go at a time of day when I feel strongest, rather than at a specific time my employer deems is okay. Any time I have a block of time free, I can take the five-minute drive to my local gym and work out.

Are you a night owl? I am, which is why working from home is a great option for me. I can work until 2 A.M. and then sleep until 10 A.M., should I choose to. I typically do my best thinking late at night. In fact, it's quite late as I am writing this section. Not having to report to an in-office boss at a particular time allows me the option of working as late as I need or want, still being able to sleep in, as long as I don't have any meetings, travel, or media spots lined up for the next day.

Cons of Home or Office

There are also downsides to both a home-based and an office-based business. For starters, home-based businesses don't often allow you to disconnect from work. For years I was working in my loft; day-in and day-out, the loft in my home was all I saw for 10 or more hours on end. Yes it was convenient, but it was also convenient to go upstairs and check e-mail at 11 P.M., when I should be trying to unwind and head to bed because I had an early morning television interview the next day. A nice middle-ground solution for me was to find a home with a casita—I leave work and walk into the house, and it isn't quite as easy to go into the office right before bedtime or at any point during the night.

Another downside to a home office is lack of expansion. Even in my new casita-turned-business-office, I only have room for two desks. Should I hire a third person, one of my file cabinets has to go—and it will definitely be a cramped space. I may be able to add on to the building, but that is expensive.

You may not also get the same feeling of really running and owning your own growing business at home that you would in an office building. Running your latest venture from home means that your client meetings may need to occur at Starbucks. I certainly don't have room for a conference table and I don't know many home businesses that do. I once recently went to a meeting at someone's home where she had converted at least three of her bedrooms into offices for her employees and the conference room was the kitchen table. It didn't feel the same discussing business on placemats with the kitchen appliances sitting next to us. You'd be surprised how much the setting of an environment actually impacts the actions taken—a meeting over a dining room or coffee table will often prove less productive than one in a boardroom, unless you exude great discipline and focus!

When you are working from home, it can also be hard to get into "work mode" if you don't set a routine and stick to it. The first two years of doing my online teaching business full time, I worked in my loungewear or gym clothes, which often didn't come off until I went to the gym around 6 P.M.—then back to loungewear. The only time I put on real human clothes was for conferences or for television segments.

It is also, of course, much easier to feel isolated at home, particularly if you are a business of one. As I stated earlier, the walls of my loft and my computer screen were all I saw for hours and days and months on end, with my only interaction with others being that of the random front-desk staff at my local gym, and my husband when he got home from work. Now that I have consistent contractors, I actually have someone to talk to during the day, bounce ideas off, laugh with, strategize with, even have lunch with when time permits. Life is a little less lonely this way. They always say life is lonely at the top—if that is the case, I must have been on top! Since I wasn't, suffice to say it can be lonely by yourself in your home office!

Office-based businesses also have their downsides—commutes, for one thing. Hopefully, if you do select an office, you select one close to home; but you may have to select one close to your clients, and the two may not be the same thing. Office-based businesses, particularly small rented suites, may also give you luxuries like a shared administrative assistant, cubicles if needed, conference rooms, mailing services, access to technology (fax machines, copiers, etc.), and so on.

An office is often more expensive, however, and is another added cost to your startup, which you may not be able to afford immediately. Sometimes entrepreneurs start at home, and when they get too big they move into an office. This is a great alternative, particularly if accommodating your growing office needs would mean moving to a much more expensive home. However, you won't have your work at your fingertips should you need it, and rolling into work in your pajamas isn't quite as easy!

Tax Implications of Your Business Location

There are tax implications for both choices. Home-based business write-offs are determined, in general, by the percentage of your home that is used for business. Take the square footage of the business portion, and divide it by the total square footage of your home. This gives you a percent of the home used for business. Then figure out what percent of that is used purely for business and not for family sharing (like e-mailing). Here is an example:

2000-square-foot home

200 square feet used for office space

10 percent of the home is used for business purposes

Of that, you spend 60 percent of your time doing work things in that space and 40 percent of your time doing personal things in that space. Sixty percent of 10 percent is 6 percent—so you can write off 6 percent of your home expenses.

What are home expenses? Mortgage interest. Association fees. Insurance. Utilities that are commonly shared with the house. And so on. If you use a separate phone, that is fully deductible, too.

Again, talk with a tax accountant on this because home offices are one of the biggest reasons returns get audited.

If you are an office-based business, then all costs associated with rent, utilities, and so on will go on various lines on your Schedule C of your 1040 tax return.

Legal Advice

As you proceed with your business, you will want and need to get legal advice. When exactly to do that is up to you, but I recommend planning with at least a tax accountant. Remember, tax accountants aren't bound by client confidentiality. If you have potentially sensitive tax questions, a tax attorney is your best bet.

D.I.Y. Legal Work

There is a lot of legal work you can do on your own. A great resource that I have found to be paramount to the others I will list is www.business.gov. Business.gov provides information and resources that help small businesses comply with federal, state, and local business laws and government regulations.

Some other great resources are:

Nolo.com: Nolo provides law forms and do-it-yourself legal kits and books for consumers and small businesses, including information on estate planning, business law, debt and credit, etc.

SmallBusiness.FindLaw.com: FindLaw's Small Business Center provides information and resources for small businesses, including employment law, human resources, an overview of legal issues faced by small businesses, and more.

LegalZoom.com: LegalZoom was founded by renowned attorney Robert Shapiro, whom you may remember from the O. J. Simpson trial. LegalZoom provides all sorts of valuable legal forms and services for both personal and business use.

How to Get Sound Legal Advice

As you proceed you will undoubtedly run into questions that an attorney is best suited to answer. When (not if) this occurs, be sure you have already found an attorney to rely on. Make sure your attorney specializes in business and tax law for businesses. You don't want someone inexperienced handling matters that could send you into financial ruin and incredible stress if not handled properly. I often ask colleagues and friends for referrals—if they have worked with someone successfully for a while, that makes me feel more comfortable.

> By far the most important aspects of your choice of legal counsel are whether he or she is bar certified, experienced, and recommended by others in your line of work. You can check this status by contacting your state bar association and validate there are no complaints against the attorney. The attorney will most likely have his state bar ID number listed on his business card, which will make checking his status easier. You can find your local bar association's contact information by searching online or contacting your local court system.

What to Ask to Find a Good Attorney

So what do you ask to find a good attorney? Well, first, as I mentioned above, you want to be sure he is board certified. You also want to make sure that he practices the type of law that you need advice on and/or representation in. For example, if you are involved in a real estate deal, you will need a real estate attorney, not a family law and probate attorney, and vice versa.

Next, you will want to know what type of record he has. How long has he been in business? Has he ever had any actions taken against him by previous clients during the course of his career? What is his win/lose ratio—if the need should arise that a court case is presented? Don't be afraid to ask for references; the selection of an attorney is a big deal. Remember, you often get what you pay for, too. If you live in a big city, consider driving an hour to the suburbs for lower costs but still quality practices.

Locating an attorney can be a daunting task, like finding health or life insurance, but there are some ways to make it easier on yourself. First, ask your friends, family, and colleagues who handles their legal work. Personal referrals can often prove to be the strongest methods for finding a good lawyer, and some lawyers may even offer a referral discount to both you and the referrer. If this doesn't pan out, you can contact a lawyer referral service. Although there are hundreds (dare I say thousands?) of these services out there, in my view the most reputable ones are those that others recommend to you without bias—without getting paid for a click-thru or a link on their website. You can also call the courts and ask for recommendations. A simple call to the court clerk or county bar association will provide you with contact information for any local lawyer referral services, organized by type of law. Another benefit of this is the ability to receive information on reduced-cost legal services that may be available to you, depending on the situation.

Just like asking your friends and family, you can ask other business owners. If you don't know any other local business owners, again, contact your local SBA office. They will be able to put you in touch with valuable resources, whether those are other business owners who you can inquire with or a listing of recommended legal counsel.

What You Need to Know to Move Forward

So what else do you need to know to move forward? You have an idea, an initial marketing plan; you've registered your business and have done your preplanning with an accountant and/or attorney. From here, you need to make some additional decisions: How many resources (capital, human, technological, and financial) do I need? Am I going to start slow or go all-out from day one? Am I going to quit my day job now, or wait for business to pick up? How much working capital do I have? And so on. Go through the checklists throughout this book. Once you've done so and can answer the questions, it's time to begin!

Paying Yourself

As you begin your business, one of the first things you're going to have to do is make sure you can continue to eat and pay the bills. If you quit a day job to start your own business, you will need to figure out how much you're going to pay yourself. Chances are you aren't going to be making the big bucks from day one, so you will need to preplan your needs and the minimum you can pay yourself now, and cover your expenses. Remember that you need to reinvest as much as you can in your business to help it grow. If you pay yourself a salary, you can reinvest the rest of the earned money back in the business. If you pay yourself all the earnings, then you will need to use your own money to build the business.

Determining Your Own Worth

This is a bit of a trick question, because you are your business! Your worth is invaluable, immeasurable. If all of your contractors and employees disappeared, your business would still run. Nonetheless, you'll have to figure out what you are worth. In the early stages of your business, you will pay yourself the most you can afford while maximizing reinvestment and paying the bills. As you move forward and become more successful, you will need to assess your worth, allowing yourself a higher wage while still maintaining business needs. Again, it is very dependent on whether you still have your day job and what revenue and profit your business is making. This is a decision to make as you go. Most likely what you are worth isn't what you'll pay yourself—it will be considerably less until the profits of your business support what you deserve.

Deciding How Much You Should Pay Yourself

Deciding what to pay yourself and what to pay others is tough. You cannot promise wealth to these individuals because you don't know the outcome of your business. If they work hard, you can promise you will do your best to match their earnings to their contributions.

Often the business owner ultimately profits less than lower-paid employees after bills are paid. Little discretionary income is common among small business owners, particularly in the first five years. Chances are you won't be able to pay yourself what you're worth, but be sure your clients do. This will ensure your continued success. Pay yourself as much as you can, and need (so you can pay the bills), but as little as possible so you can reinvest.

> Find out what your employees or contractors are motivated by. It may not be money—find out and give it to them. Examples are titles, nonmonetary gifts, "atta boy"s, additional responsibility, and bonuses.

Making Enough Money to Not Only Survive But Thrive!

Remember that your business goal isn't to make enough money just to survive, but to thrive! Keep close tabs on your expenses and income and you can readjust your own pay monthly or even biweekly—paying yourself more in "good months" and less in "bad" or slow months. Be sure you compensate those who contribute greatly to your success, because money is a common motivator.

Final Thoughts

Keeping a close watch on your business will ensure your success going forward! Don't be afraid to make adjustments along the way. The most well run, successful companies have had to embrace change—particularly if it's driven by the customer.

5

Business Plans

Business plans aren't the most exciting part of starting a business, and many business owners start a business and become quite successful without them. Planning isn't a requirement, but it sure does help with your success rate and the chances of meeting your goals! Some estimates indicate that businesses that don't have business planning fail as much as seven times more often than those that do.

So what do you need to prepare to write a business plan, and when should you do it? I generally recommend writing before you launch and revising as you go—your business plan is a living document that you will modify continually and check against your actual progress. You will find most of your revisions occur in the first year, and the first few months may even include daily revisions. Your business plan should be reviewed often, not only to keep you on track, but to allow you the opportunity to make revisions if your goals change or if anything in the external environment affects your business.

My first few months included daily spreadsheet updates on cost, profits, revenues, and task lists, and a check of whether I had met those monthly goals. To this day, I reread and revise the entire business plan for each of my businesses about every two months or so, no matter how well my businesses may be doing.

It is important to review your business plan often to ensure that you are still creating and growing your business in the manner that you originally wanted. If you've come up with better ideas or different methods, update your plan. Your business plan is quite literally your map—where you are now, where you want to go, and how you are going to get there.

In some cases, it might be best to put the plan into what is known as a GANTT chart. It is a tool that project managers use to map a critical path so that they are successful in their endeavors. Particularly in the early stages of a business, this is important. A GANTT chart can be created in Microsoft Project with an easy in-application tutorial. A GANTT chart will show you which processes in a particular project are dependent on others, will show you what the critical path is (what cannot be late to avoid a project that comes in late overall), and what must be done before another task.

The Basics of Business Planning

Details matter! You should be as detailed and as thorough as you can be when drafting your business plan. Although you can simply lay out a two-page plan on where you are, where you want to be, and bullet steps you need to take to get there, it is in your best interest to be as thorough as possible, even to the point of writing out weekly activities and then keeping track of your success in accomplishing them. I generally choose the latter, even though it is time consuming initially. Once you get the basics documented, it is easier to maintain. If you are going to use your plan for any sort of funding—securing venture capital, hard-money loans, or even SBA-backed loans—you need to have a solid plan to present. You also need to be able to answer questions that will arise.

> I always recommend showing a business plan to at least three trusted colleagues (and have them sign it). This way, you can be certain that you can answer the common questions that someone who doesn't understand your business might ask, should they come up in a presentation.

Basics

So what are the basics? Well, first you need to clearly state where you're starting from—where are you now. This includes money, time, goals, direction, and who will be helping you, if anyone. You will want to document anything financial, especially anything you need to look out for that could be a red flag for your business failing. Some examples of these red flags are income streams falling below a particular threshold or inventories not moving as you had expected.

Be sure you include a contingency plan, too—if A, B, and C occurs, then X, Y, and Z are my potential reactions. Sometimes we think less clearly when we are stressed, so your business plan can quickly be referenced to keep you focused and progressing forward.

Laying Out a Five-Year Plan—And Why Five Years?

We all hear of the five-year plan and the five-year business plan. In some industries, like information technology, which experience rapid change, it's tough to plan beyond two or three years. So why five? Five years is looked at as the standard for planning. Banks will want to know your five-year projections and investors will want to know their five-year returns. Five years is the point at which your business is considered relatively safe, so your initial plan should cover through that length of time.

There are many fantastic online tools, but the best one I have found is www.score.org/template_gallery.html. Score is a resource partner with the SBA, which, as we have already discussed, is a fantastic resource in and of itself. Score calls themselves the "Counselors to America's Small Business" They are a nonprofit organization, their mission being to educate entrepreneurs and to positively impact the formation, growth, and success of small businesses nationwide.

Another great online tool is BusinessPlans.org, because of all of the samples of completed plans that you can view to get an idea of what you are shooting for within your own plan. BusinessPlans.org offers much more than business plan templates and examples. They also offer additional resources that you may be interested in, such as free business software, investor directories, marketing strategies, and even a newsletter to help keep you up to date with the rapidly changing entrepreneur environment. Their library has over 600 resources—all within a mouse click!

Yet another great online resource is MyOwnBusiness.org, because they literally walk you step-by-step through the creation process of your business plan, and other aspects of starting your first business. Visit www.myownbusiness.org/s2 for their section on business plans.

Please also refer to the Resources list, found at the back of this book, for some excellent tools and ideas. I recommend using a template to get you started. Even Microsoft Word Online has some good templates to begin with. You can download them directly into Microsoft Word and begin working on your business plan immediately.

Identifying Needs

Your plan will need to identify starting needs as well as needs to sustain your business through the first five years. Some business owners plan for three; this is okay, but five is recommended to maximize the potential for bank loans and investors. Why five years? We want to have a roadmap to fall back on. For example, when you are trying to decide whether or not to do something or to take action on a particular new venture within your business, you can quickly and easily decide yes or no by whether or not it's in the five year plan. While plans change with markets, they don't change without reason and can serve as a good guide.

What kind of needs will you need to identify? Here are some examples, although there are many more:

- Capital equipment. This is any major purchase, like computers, furniture, servers, copy machines, and so on—generally considered anything that will depreciate over time.
- Monthly expenditures until the business is self-sustaining.
- Office supplies (paper, pens, and so on).
- Office space rental costs, until the business is self-sustaining. If this is your home, it may be zero.
- Utilities, especially if you are renting an office building or office space (e.g., electricity, water, gas, cell phones, Internet).
- Services, such as legal services, accounting and payroll services, etc.
- Advertising and marketing, including your website! This is your monthly budget for advertising and marketing until your company is self-sustaining.
- Any professional and/or legal counsel you will need to start up and sustain your business until you are profitable.

- Uniforms. If your business provides a service, this is especially important to consider.
- Cleaning. Some office building or space rentals include nightly or weekly cleaning services. If yours does not, contracting an outside company for this needs to be considered, unless you will have time to clean house yourself. (Note that these costs also could extend to window washing and plant maintenance services.)
- Cost of capital (e.g., if you take money from a home equity line of credit [HELOC], the interest payments to the loan).

Note that although these suggestions are excellent starting points, there will be many that are specific to your business idea. Researching your own demographic, competition, and so on is highly advised to help in your business plan creation.

Calculating Revenue, Costs, and Returns

In your plan, you will need to estimate revenue, costs, and returns or profit. This can be the most difficult part of the plan. How, after all, are you going to know how many widgets you will sell? This is where your upfront planning and market testing comes into play. You can also get an idea, as noted in Chapter 4, by posting a few on existing sites like eBay and Craigslist and seeing how well they sell. If you're a service business, you should have some idea how many clients you will have because you are already beginning to let others know about your new business and are tracking the response of interest you are getting.

After you calculate your estimated revenue (plan for a worst case scenario—better to have a pleasant surprise) you will need to calculate your monthly costs of operation. I don't recommend calculating this on a yearly basis because some things will be due monthly or even more often, like utilities and employee paychecks. You need to be sure you have working capital every month, not just at the end of the year. Try telling Sprint that you will pay next year and see what they say!

So you've estimated your yearly revenue and then divided it by 12 to get your estimated monthly revenue; assume that you will sell more of your products or services toward the end of that year than in the beginning, because people won't be aware of your business right away. Then estimate yearly costs and divide by 12. Revenue minus costs is your projected return or profit—the bottom line.

Your bottom line may well be "in the red," or negative, for the first few months—this is somewhat normal, depending on the type of business and how quickly your company grows. Even retailers often run in the red the entire year until Black Friday, or the day after Thanksgiving, which officially kicks off the holiday shopping season. Many retailers wait all year for Black Friday, so named because it is when they go "into the black" and turn a profit for the rest of the year, making up for the losses over the previous 11 months.

> If you don't see yourself coming out of a hole in three years or don't have the financial means to sustain yourself during the time you're in the red, you need to either find financing or revise your plan, and perhaps even your idea. See why it's important to do this up front?

You may have a black "year" and not a Black Friday—in other words, you may run in the red for quite some time, especially early on in your business. Just know what to expect and how long to plan running deficits for, so you can keep an eye on cash flows and know when you expect to turn a profit.

Getting Started

To get started collecting data for more than just the basics, you'll need to think through everything you anticipate encountering over five years. As daunting as this sounds, it actually is rather simple, as long as you do your homework. This includes employee growth, unexpected demand for your product or service, unexpected lack of demand for your product or service, a recession, an economic boom, high interest rates, low interest rates—your plan needs to be contingent on everything you can feasibly put into one document. Remember, this won't just serve you for investments but will also be your personal guide to success.

> A wise manager once told me that if I didn't know what decision to make, I simply needed to check the company mission and vision. If the idea wasn't aligned with one or both, don't do it. If it was, "go all out" and don't let anything stand in my way or in the way of the idea.

As said by Gertrude Stein, "It is awfully important to know what is and what is not your business," meaning you should start by having a mission and vision statement in your plan.

Your mission is what you will accomplish in your business, and your vision is what you see it doing, attaining, the goals you see it fulfilling. Your mission and vision are closely tied together because your mission should fulfill the vision you see for your company.

If you don't know where or how to start drafting your mission or vision statement, or both, check out the article "Developing Effective Vision and Mission Statements," written by Jay Ebben. In his article, Jay details what makes a strong mission and vision statement and what to avoid. You can find his column published on Inc.com's website at www.inc.com/resources/startup/articles/20050201/missionstatement.html.

Collecting Data for Your Plan

As you get deeper into your plan, beyond first year or year one-through-three financials, you will need to collect more data. This includes what your potential market base is, how much of that market you can reach with your plan for advertising and marketing, what it will take to achieve your goals, how high you want to aim, and so on. Remember the old adage about reaching for the stars—it is engraved on a plaque I earned in elementary school—"Reach for the Stars—If You Don't Reach Them, You'll Land Pretty High Up Anyway"—or something to that effect. It's premise has held true for me throughout life and throughout businesses and change.

I am not suggesting by any means that you rely on luck for your business growth, but I am suggesting that you can make your own luck by taking every opportunity, meeting every possible person who can benefit from you (not the other way around!), and offering value to everyone you work with. If you help enough people, you will more often than not be paid back with endless help from others.

So what else is in your plan? Most business plans follow the following organization and include the following sections:

> I read somewhere that Venus Williams's sister, Serena, once told her something to the affect of "Everything is an opportunity, and the more opportunities you take, the more will open." That is a powerful message that we all need to remember. Build opportunities into your plan for future growth.

Executive Summary

This section should be detailed, yet succinct. Your executive summary will usually be one to two pages in length, highlighting the important aspects of the business, the founders, and the plan. In essence, your executive summary should read like an overview of your plan as a whole. Just as you may read a movie review when determining which movie to see this weekend, those who receive your business plan (usually investors, bankers, loan officers, etc.) will read your executive summary to determine if the rest of your plan is worth reading through—does it peak their interest?

Description of Business

-Name

-Organization structure—this is where you will explain the legal structuring of your business (LLC, Inc., 401[c]3, etc.)

-Introduction of founders, owners, stakeholders, etc.—traditionally this section will include a brief but detailed biography of each founding member, including education, relevant experience, key connections, etc.

-Length of time business has existed (or what starting date the business will exist from)

-Accomplishments to date (if business already exists, as applicable)

Description of Product/Services

This is where you get to really boast about your new business. What are you offering? Why is what your offering different than everyone else's? How much are you going to charge? What types of products/services will you offer in the future?

Note that this section can be included as a part of your "description of business" or can be a stand-alone section.

Marketing Plan/Strategies

-Industry

-Customer/target demographic

-Competition (competitive analysis)

-Advertising and PR

-Location of your storefront (when applicable)

Suppliers, Contractors, Vendors, Etc.

Operations and Management

Who will lead your business, who will handle the day-to-day operations, who will work on forming strategic partnerships, who will work on expanding your client/customer base? These, and more, are all questions that will need to be answered within this section. You may want to state that resumés/CVs are available for key managers—your investors/lenders will want to see what makes them "right for the job"!

Financial Plan

-Current standing and position: profits and losses

-Projections: profits and losses

-Need

If you are seeking funding, state here how much, with verifiable data that supports your request.

Technological Plan (as applicable—recently becoming a popular section)

-Computer requirements

-Peripheral requirements (printers, fax machines, scanners, etc.)

-Backups

-E-mail

-Company-wide calendaring

-Remote access capability

-Disaster recovery plan

-3 to 5 year growth strategy for technology

-Web hosting

How to Get Information That Is Reliable

One of many things even managers of big firms grapple with is determining what information is reliable. I heard on a major news network this past year that even information from the Associated Press has to be fact-checked before going to a story with it—and it never used to be that way. We are not short on data these days, with everyone posting everything and anything on the Internet, so you need to know how to spot reliable and unreliable information. As a professor of statistics, I can shed some light on this, although I'll spare you the scholarly verbiage and confusing analytical mumbo-jumbo.

First, look for bias within the analysis of the information. Does the researcher or the author have a reason to publish or print a specific finding or "fact"? If so, toss it out unless she was honest enough to list biases with regard to her research and what assumptions were made for the study. For instance, if you are reading a document on marketing and it is written by a company that provides small business marketing, it may simply be promotional material disguised as research.

If the information you are looking at is actual research, are assumptions and limitations listed? Assumptions and limitations are the basics of all types of research. Assumptions are the things the researcher assumed in doing the study and limitations are the things the study didn't touch or reach. An assumption is something assumed for the research that may lead to bias. For instance, I may assume that the sample that I studied is representative of the population at large.

In my survey for this book, I assumed that people answered honestly and had no reason to lie. Limitations are things that limit the scope or results of the study. My study was web based, so that is a limitation. If a small business owner did not have web access, he or she did not get an opportunity to respond to my survey. If you read research material, look for these elements because they need to be well documented in any research you read.

The next thing to look for: What is the sampling rate? If you are looking at a survey that interviewed 20 people, you may not have a reliable survey. For social sciences and business, we generally look at obtaining 1016 or so participants when conducting a survey, which gives us a 95 percent confidence in the data the results produce. I won't bore you with the mathematical equation behind this, but you should know that polling many more people than this doesn't change the confidence level much, but polling fewer definitely does. A confidence level is how sure the researcher is that the results are accurate. Common confidence levels are 95 percent, 98 percent, and so on. These are also known as Z scores, but that is much more than you need to know for the scope of this book.

That said, you can have a valid and reliable survey with a small sample size if the sample that is tested is representative of the population. Look for studies with small samples to mention this in the limitations. While small samples don't make the data necessarily bad or unrepresentative, they do mean that the researcher had to take special precautions and use specific tests to keep validity intact. If she didn't, toss it out.

I used two words here that are key—reliability and validity. Validity is how accurate the information is with regard to its representation of the population at large. If airlines survey 30 passengers on one flight and try to apply the findings to flying in general, they are using a highly skewed, invalid sample.

In the airline example, they are also using an unreliable sample, because reliability refers to repeatability—if a new researcher ran the exact same study on that same population, would she get similar results? If so, it is reliable. If the survey is representative and repeatable, you have a reliable and valid study—the stuff that good things are made of!

Note: When it comes time to present your idea to lending institutions, venture capital firms, and investors (whether they are strangers or family and friends), being able to produce statistically valid and reliable data will greatly increase your chances of a successful meeting, as it shows a great deal of attention to your planning and an understanding of "the numbers."

Creating a Plan That Works for You and Achieves Your Goals

Ultimately, the plan you create may be viewed by quite a few people, and you should get feedback on it. But remember that the goals should fit your goals—your lifestyle requirements and how fast you want the business to grow—which may not be the same as how capable the business is of growing. You may want it to grow faster than it can, or you may not want to invest the time it takes to make it grow as fast as possible. Bottom line—keep your goals in mind when you create your plan and pay particular attention to ensuring that they are aligned. If you have data that doesn't make sense, you can be darn sure the money lenders will notice and ask.

What to Do When the Plan Comes Together

At some point during your writing, you will have time to reflect on where you're at. You should have a flow chart or map that indicates what you need to do, including tasks as detail-oriented as you can handle or want to plan for. (This often depends greatly on personality type—as my husband will tell you, I would gladly make a list of items to be done and even write out the specific steps to get there, but that would drive him insane!)

Run your plan by others—other businesspeople or friends who you trust. If you show it to someone you don't know and don't completely trust, make sure that he or she signs a nondisclosure agreement. You can download many of these forms online, free of charge or for a very minimal fee. LegalZoom.com has some great agreements for a small price.

Once you think the plan is solid, it is time to begin marketing your plan for startup revenue, if you don't already have it yourself.

Marketing Your Plan for Startup Revenue

If you do need startup revenue, a good place to start is your local bank or SBA office. In any event, no matter who you approach, they will most likely want to see a copy of your business plan, which is why you will want to have this done before starting your search for financial backing.

Regardless of who or where you ultimately get revenue from, you need to offer a return—even if it's to family—and it needs to be in writing (remember my personal story in Chapter 4?!). Even if the return doesn't begin for three years, note it and document it and then follow through by ensuring that in three years you indeed get that return you assumed by pushing the limits of your business within your comfort zone.

Family and Friend Investors

Family are often where startup businesses get their money initially. Family members certainly are a good source of investment income, as are close friends. However, there are risks with both options. If your business goes bad, how much worse will you feel about losing your mother's money than a bank's? Also, if the deal goes sour, it could strain family relations, no matter how strong your ties were when the loan was made. Last but certainly not least, do you want your family bringing up at family dinners that they haven't gotten paid, or asking, "So how is business?" when you are trying to enjoy Thanksgiving dinner—knowing what they are really asking is "When am I getting my money back?!"

A good source? Yes, absolutely. But weigh the pros and cons carefully before jumping into the business bed with your friends or family, or both.

Angel Investors

Angel investors are a certain type of investor that is greatly growing in popularity within the world of entrepreneurs. Unlike venture capitalists, who lend pooled money from others, angel investors, or "angels," invest their own funds. Some angels invest on their own, while others may team up with other angels to create "angel groups," which are exactly what they sound like—groups of angels that get together to invest in small businesses.

One of the largest pros to going through an angel is the fact that, since it is his or her own money that he or she is investing, you only have to convince that person (or that group of angels—depending on the situation) that your idea/business is worth the risk. When you approach a bank or venture capital firm, on the other hand, your presentation must not only convince the person you present to, but do so in such a way that he or she will turn around and convince those above him or her, who actually have control over making the final decision on whether or not to lend you the money.

One of the largest cons to angels, in probably about half of the situations, is that you are limited to the amount of money that the angel has allocated to lend. If you need $100,000, but your angel only has $75,000 to lend, you now need to search for someone else to lend you the remaining $25,000. One fact that you can take comfort in is that angel investors often know other angel investors, even if they don't belong to a group. Keeping this in mind, if you can convince one angel to back you, and he or she knows another angel, chances are high that you will be able to convince their "angel friend" to jump on the bandwagon as well.

Angels and angel groups are now going online or virtual. You can actually search for angel investors online, no longer limiting you to the angels in your neck of the woods. Sites such as FundingUniverse.com are popping up all of the time, connecting angel investors and entrepreneurs across the globe.

Saving Up Your Own Money

You could, of course, start your business with your own capital, as many of us do—myself included! You can take a 401(k) withdrawal, for instance (be careful and talk to your tax planner on the ramifications of this), or a home equity line of credit (HELOC). Don't forget to include repayments to your 401(k) or HELOC and interest as well as opportunity costs in the startup costs section of your business plan.

You could save up for a business you intend to start sometime in the future, too. Any long-term, high-return account would be great for this, such as a high-yield CD.

Starting Your Business with $10,000 or Less

It is possible to start a business with $10,000 or less. Many people do—I did, and I continue to start my new ventures with less than 10 grand! How? I use the 10 grand as borrowed money and then repay a small amount at a time. If you are really a risk taker, you can even take a cash advance on a credit card and pay the high interest to that credit card. Where there is a will there is a way. I've done it five times and regretted it once. Not a bad ratio for me, but it may be more than you are comfortable with, or you may have other financial goals and ideas. Figure out what works for *you*. You can start your business out of your home with a simple website, relatively inexpensive marketing, and lots of word-of-mouth advertising, while keeping your day job going at the same time until the business is running full speed ahead.

Making Sure Your Plan Fits Your Goal

I want to go back to this a bit again, because so many people I have worked with have downsized after years of success. This section has a lot of personal anecdotes and things I have learned along the way because many of these lessons have had a great impact on my life, including quality of life, happiness, and marital satisfaction.

As a personal example, a good friend of mine was on the same path with his business plan that I've taken for years. We were comparing our successes and both of us were moving along quickly, referring new clients to one another. I thought life was good, but he got fed up. At some point it got to be too much for him and he said NO MORE! He dropped most of his clients, kept two, downsized dramatically, and went on vacation. I dream of doing that, but my personality doesn't allow for it—*I* won't allow for it. I guess one could say that ultimately it isn't what I want. For me, that was failure. For him, quitting those jobs and taking back his freedom was success. For me, buying a bigger house in the hills was one of many markers of success. For him, it was adding onto his existing home and having his own quiet home office where he could be with his child. What do you want? I can't stress enough the importance of your business goals being aligned with your personal ones. If they aren't, both your business and you, including those close to you, could suffer greatly.

I am reminded by little things every day that one woman's definition of success is not another's: my family who have corporate jobs with no potential to expand earnings beyond a specific corporate salary (yes!), my friend's 18-year-old sister who has "low aspirations" (but high for her) to earn an associate's degree and be a mom, the family members who don't understand or appreciate my lack of desire to replicate my DNA and have children at this stage in my life due to the interruption it would bring to my business, and so on. Everyone has their own personal priorities and you shouldn't sacrifice yours. You may find however that they change over time.

Whatever decisions you make, you will constantly be tested and reminded that what is good for you isn't so for everyone else. Also be prepared to take criticism. I hear the snickers and feel the lack of warmth from my extended family who aren't happy about the fact that we don't have a bunch of little babies running around and all the cousins aren't growing up together. Being the sarcastic one in the family, I played an April Fool's joke on my family, saying that my husband and I were combining names to create one family name. We would become Babbica—a combination of both of our names. My husband's family did not find this funny (although they play it off as though they did). While I justified the joke idea as being easier than hyphenating for those future babies they so badly wanted, they didn't find it funny at all.

> Think carefully about your definition of success. It might not be what you thought it was once you achieve it. Success is personal. I have to remind myself of this every day. Also, don't be afraid to alter your definition of success. What was success for you yesterday isn't necessarily what you might consider success today.

While this is a bit of an aside, remember that all the decisions you make in your personal life, once you're tied with family in business, will take on a whole new meaning. If you join the two together, you have to watch your boundaries a bit more (and, in my case, your choice of practical jokes, too).

To be blunt, the point is—whatever makes *you* feel successful is what your plan needs to assume. Unless of course you get very big very quick and become a large-scale corporation—then what your shareholders want will matter more. But that is another book for another day!

Keeping the Plan Updated and Relevant

If you don't know where you want to go, you certainly won't get there—unless you are darn lucky. You need to keep your plan relevant, current, and updated. Did market conditions change? A new competitor come on the horizon? Did your target demographic change their purchasing habits? Is the economy in your market sector not doing so hot? Update your plan and figure out what you're going to do about it! A relevant and current plan is a useful plan. An outdated plan is useless to you, and to your team, should you bring one on.

Also keep in mind that if you have investors, whether friend or foe, they could request to review your plan at any time, so it also benefits you to be able to produce a current plan. Keep your investors happy and stay in charge and on top of your business—running it rather than letting its last minute changes run you.

Don't Be Afraid to Change Course!

This is an important lesson that I had to learn time and time again before it really sank in. Sometimes your career and business takes you places you hadn't imagined or didn't originally want to go. Your ultimate goals may even change entirely—don't be afraid to change course. If you are enjoying what you are doing, if there is a market for what you're doing (and it pays the bills), and if it falls in line with your personal vision and mission as well as your business mission and vision, go for it!

This brings up another important point—we talked earlier in this chapter about your company mission and vision. But you need to have a personal one, too. Make sure the two align, or you will be miserable.

Revisit the Plan—Be Sure of Its Accuracy

Revisit every element of your plan from start to finish at least once per quarter; more often if you're having unpredictable revenue fluctuations—either positive or negative. Be sure your contingency plan is updated, too, and be certain you are taking into consideration market changes that you have no control over, like exports, the value of the dollar, consumer discretionary spending (if that affects you), and so on.

Initial Phase Importance

It is extremely important that you plan out your initial phase—those first few months—with extreme precision. Know what you're going to do then roll with the changes. Not doing so could throw you off kilter for a very long time.

Transition Time—Decisions, Decisions!

You have a plan, you have some startup capital, and you're ready to transition to your new job. You may have been unemployed or underemployed throughout this process and you're ready to tackle this new challenge. Whether you are underemployed or unemployed or just wanting to change jobs, it's decision time! (Again!)

Move Slowly or Make the Switch All at Once?

First, are you going to move slowly into the new business or make the switch all at once? Obviously, moving slowly means you'll have time (if you are employed) to continue earning a paycheck, but you'll have less time to spend on your new business. Moving at once has the opposite affect: less money but more time for your business. Take into consideration personal bills, finances, and your family's worries and concerns when making this very important decision.

Transitioning Into Your Business Plan

It is tough to not just begin one day typing e-mails to people to talk about your new business. Make sure you do your homework first, and put your business plan into action. Follow your first-few-months plan, marketing according to what you thought best. Update that if you need to—but remember that your business plan was written when you weren't in the heat of the moment, which means you were probably of sounder mind then.

Putting Your Plan Into Action

Sometimes your enthusiasm becomes contagious and your plan has to be modified to make that work for you. If it does, go for it. The most crucial step here is putting your plan into action. If that means leaving your day job, time to write the resignation letter. If that means launching the website, do it. You should be doing everything in your plan listed as prelaunch. If you are unemployed, you should be doing that and more now! You should be bouncing your ideas off of family members, focus groups, really grasping the concept of your target demographic, and working to immediately build a business—even if it's only a web presence for now.

Quitting Time—Leaving Your Day Job

If you are underemployed and quitting your part time job or fully employed and also leaving it behind, you will already have planned your quitting time. If now is the time, don't burn any bridges. Write a great letter of resignation, and even perhaps get your bosses on board (if you think they will be) ahead of time and ask them to allow you to even promote your new business. Imagine an e-mail blast to 10,000 workers telling them about your new adventures! Sometimes the best contacts are those you already have through other people and the networks you've built.

Send an e-mail to your officemates informing them of your decision—and your new business. A simple but effective template that I have used many times myself is:

Dear <enter name>,

Let me start by saying how much I have enjoyed working <with, for, alongside, etc.> you. I have learned a great deal from you and I hope I have been able to offer the same.

Recently I made the decision to <insert decision>.

This has been a decision that I have spent many hours analyzing and feel that it is in my <my family's, etc.> best interest to pursue. My final day with <enter company name> will be <enter date>. During my future endeavors, I plan to start a business doing <enter the business>. I hope you will join me in celebrating this moment that I have dreamed of.

I sincerely hope that we can remain in contact in the future. My contact information is:

<enter contact information>

Please do not hesitate to contact me anytime. If you wouldn't mind taking a moment to reply to this <e-mail, letter> with your latest contact information, I would surely appreciate it. Also, don't hesitate to ask any questions you may have about this latest chapter of my life; I would love to answer any you may have. :-)

Sincerely,

<your name>

Coping with Anxiety and Stress

This is going to be a high-anxiety, very stressful time for you. You will need coping mechanisms that preferably don't involve things that will limit your ability to do your job or the time you can spend on it. Hitting the gym, eating well, meditation, and so on are all listed as common and healthy ways to combat stress and anxiety. Sometimes it helps me to revisit my plan and to document my income sources so that I know, in fact, that bills will be paid. I often even hold onto money for three months of mortgage payments to make myself feel better in case I lose a good contract.

As one of my dear friends writes in my newsletter column: don't forget to laugh, don't forget to spend at least a few hours a month with friends, and don't forget to share your burdens and your success with others. It makes hard times that much less difficult, and happy times that much more sweet. If you're like me, you rarely celebrate an accomplishment, feeling like it is a beginning rather than an end. I remember earning my Ph.D., hanging up from my dissertation defense call, and thinking, "Okay, delete 'get Ph.D.' from my PDA." Guess what? That is exactly what I did, and moved on. I don't even recall having a dinner to celebrate until I met a man that I would later marry—we celebrated about two months after my degree was officially conferred. If you are a go-getter, every success feels like one more step to the "ultimate," whatever that is. Try to remember the accomplishments along the way, though, because it makes it easier to fight burn-out and to feel successful. That is important for your own mental health.

Setting Limits and Boundaries

Now is the time when you will be so excited that setting boundaries and limitations—especially with a home-based business—will be critical. Set them and stick to them. I don't encourage type-A personalities to avoid their business after certain hours—some of us work best at 10 P.M. Just be sure you keep a balanced life or you'll burn out, like my aforementioned friend who drastically changed his job after not having enough time with his family and friends.

Final Thoughts

When you begin to get your arms around your business, you're going to run into many obstacles; from naysayers to doomsdayers to those who get in your way out of jealousy or trying to cause disruption. Choose your business partners carefully; choose to bring in family members knowing all it may bring, and remember to stay true to what you want out of your business. This is your life and your baby and ultimately it needs to bring you satisfaction; not the rest of the world!

6

Raising Capital

Many entrepreneurs feel the task of raising capital is daunting, overwhelming, and in many cases even keeps the entrepreneur from pursuing his or her dreams and goals. Raising capital is definitely a unique skill to learn, but it is incredibly valuable and imperative for both the budding and the experienced entrepreneur.

This chapter, devoted to the many aspects of raising capital, will identify numerous sources, ways of tapping into them, the pros and cons of each, and the nuances within them all.

Types of Capital-Raising Endeavors

There are many ways to raise capital, whether you have a new business or you have a business that you want to grow and expand. It isn't easier or more difficult to raise capital in either case, but the methods can be somewhat different.

Hard Money Loans

Hard money loans are often not so easy, and not so cheap in terms of interest rates and payments—but they are sometimes the fastest way to raise the money that you need.

A hard money loan can come at a high price—some say your dignity—as you ask what many call "loan sharks" to help you raise immediate capital while they ask interrogationlike questions and scrutinize your taxes and credit.

Contrary to what some believe, "loan sharks" are legal, as long as no laws are broken during the course of the transaction. One example of a highly accepted version of hard money lending would be all of those payday-advance businesses popping up across the country—which are actually regulated by state and federal laws. Hard money lenders, though, generally require additional collateral.

These loans also come at a high interest rate; it is not uncommon to see 15 to 25 percent (or higher) for a relatively short-term loan! But there is an upside, and that is fast money, which could ultimately make or break your business, depending on the situation. For example, if you start a cleaning service and win the bid for a large retail complex, and they want you to start in one week, it will often take much longer than a week to secure the funds through a bank loan for all of the new equipment you need. A "hard money lender" may be willing to lend you the money within 48 hours; provided you pass the tests (like collateral) and have reasonable credit scores.

If you have strong reason to believe you will be able to pay the loan back fast, this might be an immediate good option.

So how do you find a hard money lender? You can talk with investment bankers who typically know of many. A good source I have found, believe it or not, are mortgage brokers. Their business often relies on them for down payment money, and so they may have a good supply of people to talk to.

Loans from Friends and Family

In the "old days" (one year ago) borrowing from friends and family wasn't so practical and secure because your family member had no recourse—the loan wasn't reported on credit (which if you are on time with payments, helps you build credit, too) and there were little assurances besides a promissory note and your word that the individual would get his or her money back. Talk about risky business.

In Chapter 4, I talked about a personal experience with my husband's family member who ripped him off with a business venture. Due to keeping everything so informal, my husband had little recourse—then and still to this day.

> No matter how small or large the loan may be, if you are receiving it through a friend or family member, seriously consider paying the minimal fee to validate the loan through Virgin Money's process. As the lender (your friend/family member) will be able to ask that the loan be reported to your (or your business's) credit report, you will be able to grow your business's credit quickly, which will help you as your business grows and you find yourself needing larger lines of credit.

Today, though, there is one particular online system that makes this transition easy, and that is Virgin Money. Virgin Money, created by Richard Branson—the same brilliant individual who founded Virgin Records, Virgin Atlantic airlines, and Virgin America airlines—came up with this novel approach to officially loaning money to your friends and family, and receiving money from your friends and family.

With Virgin Money, you can have the payments automatically made from a checking or savings account, and your family member can report the loan to your credit and even hold collateral.

Although Virgin Money will handle everything from student loans to retirement loans, the short and simple version of how Virgin Money handles business loans is this:

> You find a friend or family member willing to lend you the amount of money you need to launch or grow your small business. You contact Virgin Money and they literally handle the rest.

Below is an excerpt from Virgin Money U.S. that helps to define what they do to help small businesses and consumers and to help with business loans. It costs between $100 and $300 depending on what you want them to handle, including credit reporting:

"Whether you're looking to finance your friend's startup, or expand your own business, use Virgin Money to manage your loan. We'll provide the documents and support you need. So read up on our products, give us a buzz, or have us send you a guide. Now let's get down to business, shall we?

Virgin Money manages business loans between relatives and friends. Using us means that the business of your loan—legal documents, transfer of payments, year-end reporting—will be taken care of. (Which we think will come in handy, because, really, you've got enough on your plate.)

Virgin Money business loans are flexible, fast, and fit your financial needs. When you use us, grace periods and deferred payments are easy. It's up to you and your partner. You pick the terms; we create the documents and manage repayment. Not sure about lending? Need advice on how to ask for a loan? We can help. Request a guide. Call one of our specialists. We try to please.

Our goal is pretty simple. We want to make friend and family financing a real alternative for startup and growing businesses. We offer a top-notch small business financing option, protecting both money and personal relationships. Hey, we didn't say it was a small goal. But we like to aim high."—Business Loans (Virgin Money, 2008)

Sound easy? That's because it is. Not only is going through Virgin Money easy, but it will provide both you and your investor(s) a sense of protection, and lessen the potential for any awkward moments, which can arise when combining friends or family and business matters involving money!

Venture Capitalists

Venture capitalists are groups of investors who come together with a common cause—their own business that invests in others' business ideas. Many dot-com organizations were created and founded on venture capital (VC) money. VCs will require many things from you, but all of it is doable and VCs are a good source. VCs usually lend others' money or pooled money, and not their own. If they lend their own money, they are referred to as angel investors and not venture capitalists. VCs are usually much more strict and will have more significant guidelines and requirements than angel investors will.

First, you need a well prepared business plan with a one-page executive summary. Generally each VC group will have their own submission guidelines, which you can typically find on their website or have mailed to you by contacting them directly, should they not have a website. They will initially read the executive summary—and then the rest of the business plan if the summary is solid and piques their interest. To quickly expand on "piquing their interest"—I say this because even if your business plan is solid, if it is not a field of business that they typically want to invest in, they could turn you down on the basis of that fact alone. VC firms, like angel investors, will often only invest in a business that they "know" or know enough about to make an informed decision as to whether or not your plan and projections are viable.

What kills a VC deal? Many VC investors say that many business owners come in not even being able to answer simple questions like "How much money do you need?" or "Who is your target market?" You need to know your business! Like I mentioned a moment ago, the VC firms you present to most likely invest only in particular types of businesses, which means that you are dealing with an educated bunch of people. If you don't know your stuff, their confidence in you will drop tremendously, as will their willingness to back you financially.

So how do you find VCs in your area? A simple Google search to see who has funded similar types of business is a good place to start. My recommended search criteria are precisely this:

"venture capitalist AND <insert business genre>"

What do you need to do to prepare? First, you shouldn't even think about approaching a VC firm without an extremely thorough business plan, chock full of market research, unless you have the cure for diabetes or something similar. Next, as already noted, you will need an executive summary—in some cases the venture capitalist will want to see only the executive summary before meeting with you about the rest of the plan. Each will have their own rules to live by.

If your business plan makes it past the initial review, you will likely be called in for an interview, allowing you to present your business idea as well. Make sure you walk into this meeting well prepared. Call it cramming, call it rehearsal, call it what you want—practice, practice, and practice some more. You don't want to find yourself at a loss for words or without an answer to a question. Remember, there is a very high likelihood that they already know the answer to all of the questions they ask you. They are asking you to see if *you* know the answer.

Lastly, dress for success, even if this means you have to go out and purchase a new designer suit for the "big day." Although it would be nice if the world operated under the theory of "never judge a book by its cover," it simply isn't so. Imagine if someone came to you asking for money wearing a tie-dyed shirt and gold pants, versus a nice three-piece suit.

There are some upsides and downsides to VC money that I feel obligated to mention, in the interest of full disclosure.

The advantages are as follows:

- The VC firm has a fairly constant influx of financial resources
- The VC firm will be able to provide highly trained and educated management and personnel resources
- You will have access to market expertise that you may not otherwise have available

The disadvantages are as follows:

- You will likely have to forfeit some managerial control, even to the point of not being a part of the management team at all
- You may have limitations, with regard to operations or growth, or both, placed upon you by the VC firm
- Your preferred exit strategy may not align with the VC's idea of the best exit strategy

A note on VC firms—people talk. Just like doctors fraternize with other doctors and lawyers with other lawyers, venture capitalists socialize with other venture capitalists. This means that if you "blow it" with one VC, the chances are high that within a short amount of time other VCs will know about you and that you are looking for money for XYZ. This stacks the deck, so to speak, against you, so do your homework and make the first presentation count!

There are many other nuances to venture capital, and there are terrific web resources in the Resources section of this book on the topic. A great place to start your search for additional knowledge is www.AskTheVC.com. Another resource is the National Venture Capital Association, which can be found at www.NVCA.org. You can start your search for VC firms at www.VFinance.com, which is a directory of active venture capitalists.

Small Business Administration

The Small Business Administration, or SBA, doesn't actually lend money, as we have discussed. But they are an invaluable resource to you, as they will connect you with lenders that specialize in small- to medium-sized business loans. The SBA acts as a guarantor to the lenders that they work with.

The SBA specializes in helping small businesses secure funding when traditional funding outlets are not viable or have been exhausted without success. The lenders that the SBA works with have considerably more lenient lending practices than your traditional bank, but this does come with the potential downside of not being able to secure the amount of funding that you may need. In this case, you may need to secure more than one loan.

Let me stress the fact that the SBA themselves do not have funds to loan. They match you with private-sector lenders, which are in turn guaranteed by the SBA.

Most lending institutions are familiar with the various SBA loan programs, so you can contact your local bank or credit union to inquire as to whether or not they offer SBA-backed loans. A more direct route to take is to contact your local SBA district office and request information on local lenders offering SBA loan programs. They will usually be able to provide you with a list of qualifying institutions in your area. To find your local SBA office, visit sba.gov/localresources/index.html.

You need to be prepared for your SBA loan application, too. You need to bring, at a minimum, your financial statements, business plan, personal identification, your business identification and documentation, as well as your business license. Various banks will require different documentation.

So what banks work with the SBA? Most major banks and even smaller ones that have business checking. Some of the larger participating banks include Bank of America, Citibank FSB, Wells Fargo Bank, Washington Mutual Bank, and many more. To find out what other programs and resources the SBA has to offer, you can start by checking out their website, at www.SBA.gov.

Bank Loans

Once you open up a business checking account with a particular bank, your chances of getting a line of credit or a bank loan for your business is much greater. Often this comes in the form of a business credit card, particularly one with a high limit and low interest for a period of six months to one year. For instance, I earned a line of credit on an LLC about one year after opening my business checking with a $30,000 line and 0 percent interest for 12 months. This is a great way to get seed money to grow your business. Some use this money to expand into another business venture; be sure you record this carefully for your accountant if you decide to do so, because that transfer of funds must be recorded in your accounting and tax files.

To get a bank loan, you will need an official business with your business documents filed, and you will need to bring profit and loss statements. You may need to secure the loan with personal credit depending on how established your business is.

Keeping an Eye on Economics

We already know that economic conditions—from home sale prices to the cost of money (the worth of the U.S. dollar)—affect us as individuals. But they also affect our businesses and in many cases, more so. In particular, taxes have a great impact, particularly on small businesses. Small businesses provide an incredible amount of jobs in America; while we would think preserving their viability would be paramount, it isn't to all politicians. We often see politicians try to raise taxes on businesses, which directly impacts your bottom line. The smaller the business, the more impact raising taxes will have.

You need to watch conditions of the market; what is the consumer sentiment? Are people spending? How is the gross domestic product (GDP) doing? Is it growing? If people are spending and have discretionary income and feel wealthy, they are more likely to spend money eating out, on clothing, and on more expensive or designer goods. You may have to adjust your business—from your prices to your marketing strategy—based on consumer sentiment.

The Impact of Market Conditions

Many people don't realize how much impact the Federal Reserve has on the wealth of the nation. When the Federal Open Market Committee (FOMC, or Fed) adjusts the reserve requirements or the interest rates, they either contract or expand the economy. When they raise interest rates, banks are more likely to want to lend because they will earn more, but fewer people will want loans because they cost too much. Also, the higher interest rates are, the more people will invest money instead of spending it because the incentive to do so is higher. This is a contractionary climate, where we pull back spending and make the cost of money more expensive.

What impact does this have on your business? Plenty! First, if people want to put their money into a certificate of deposit (CD) this month because they can earn 8 percent, they're less likely to buy your designer handbags or eat at your restaurant. Also, if there is a higher opportunity cost to spending money (e.g., there will be less money to invest in a high-return environment), they're less likely to spend money on goods and services. We know that even gratuities (tips to your waiter or waitress, valet, etc.) go down when we have a contractionary climate.

On the contrary, when the economy is in expansion mode (as it was in the early 2000s), money is cheap and people borrow like crazy and build like crazy. They expand their businesses with inexpensive loans, and people feel more wealthy. The downside to this, as we saw in the mid-2000s, is that the build-up can be a house of cards that crumbles, as the mortgage implosion showcases so well.

When the economy is expanding, people feel the wealth effect and they spend money more freely. In these years, GDP tends to climb and spending climbs. People build houses, build shopping centers, and invest a lot in their businesses, the cost of money being inexpensive. Banks protect themselves by offering variable rates—the rate plus a margin—but when the Fed changes its policy to be more contractionary, business owners often aren't prepared and get hit with higher finance charges. This startles businesses back into contracting and not expanding as much.

Be careful and watchful of the economic environment in general. Watch what the Fed does with rates, the state of banks, and the health of the stock market. All are indicators of not only consumer sentiment, but also the health of our economy in general. Watch unemployment rates; anything above 5 percent is considered above the natural rate and may be cause for concern. People without jobs are people not buying. This is also a time many people start businesses, as they are feeling overlooked by Corporate America.

The Impact of Taxes and the Political Climate

All politicians like to take our money and spend it. Individuals in surveys are less sympathetic to taxing a business than they are to taxing an individual, although most don't realize how closely tied the two are. Even if you don't enjoy watching politics for instance, I suggest you find a half-hour or one-hour business show and watch it diligently each day; read a business newspaper or a business magazine and keep current on what is happening in the political and tax climate. Politics, economics, and government regulation affect businesses and you should be aware of what is happening.

You also may need to make forward-thinking adjustments to the type of corporate structure you have if you see taxes increasing in the relatively near future (say one year out). If you are working with a CPA, ask to be on his or her business e-mail list. Most will send out quarterly e-mails with tax changes and credits. Sometimes you will see random credits people aren't aware of, like a credit to buy a vehicle or the ability to write off a capital asset in one year, for only that year. This is all information you want to know.

As of 2008, the corporate tax rate ranges from 15 percent to 39.6 percent, depending on structure and amount of revenue. (Small Business Taxes and Management, 2008) You will want to work with your tax accountant or advisor to see how to best structure your business to keep taxes low.

Dollars and Sense

Every dollar you spend is a dollar you cannot reinvest in your business, its infrastructure, its employees, or its growth. It's also a dollar you don't have to give yourself a raise! It's easy to go to the local office supply store or shop online and order 100 pens and pads of paper although there are plenty in the supply closet. Watch even small expenses very closely because that end-of-the-month credit card bill can sneak up on you, particularly if you give your employees their own cards and allow them to make purchases up to a certain limit without your approval. Authorized users in some cases account for 50 percent or more of spending in a business.

Watching Your Pennies and Tracking Your Expenditures

The amount of accounting required to truly watch every penny and categorical expense can feel daunting, and for good reason. There are tools, though, to help you. Two that I personally have used since their inception are QuickBooks, by Intuit, and NeatReceipts.

QuickBooks (quickbooks.intuit.com) helps you track your income by category, client, and type; expenses by category, client, and even employee; outstanding invoices, accounts payable, accounts receivable—you name it. Many medium-sized businesses don't even feel the need to "scale up" when they grow because the software is very powerful and can handle quite a bit of growth. It has particular add-ins if you run a certain type of business that requires additional tools, like property management. Reports are run quickly and easily, and can be used to present to your team—to document or explain, for instance, why costs must be cut for the next period. You can also look at profit margins and profitability by client, by service, or by product, and so on. You can also run reports to show you which clients are delinquent and need to pay up.

NeatReceipts (www.neatreceipts.com) is a fairly new technology and business, but a great way to make tax time less of a nightmare. By scanning each receipt that comes in, you make audits less scary and daunting, and you can easily classify your expenditures and know what you're spending on a daily, monthly, or yearly basis. After scanning the receipt, it keeps and stores a PDF copy of the receipt so that you can simply transfer the information to your accountant or onto your tax return at the end of the year.

Making Investments

If you want your business to grow, you will have to invest in it. From websites to new computers, everything you spend on your business should be a "value add"— that is, it should add to the overall well-being of the business. This includes money spent on consultants, legal or professional help, software, hardware, equipment, and even major expenditures like manufacturing equipment, if that is your business type.

Although you are keeping a digital copy of all of your business receipts, you are still required by the IRS to keep hard copies of all tax-related documents. The use of NeatReceipts makes organization very easy, especially when gathering all of your documents in preparation for filing your taxes (both personal and business), but it does not waive you from retaining the physical copies of your receipts.

After I scan my receipts, I simply toss them all into a plastic bin and at the end of the year I seal the bin and store it. Each container is one year's worth of receipts, should I ever be audited.

Like everything else you do in business, you must know what type of expense your purchase falls under. There are general expenses, and then there are capital expenditures and then assets that must be depreciated over time. The IRS's rules are best to follow. You have buckets like office supplies, cost of goods sold, insurance, office expenses, utilities, and so on. You can also write off business use of automobiles using one of two methods: a flat rate amount or a per-mile rate. Be sure to keep track of your mileage at the beginning and end of the year, and keep a driving log indicating where and how you used your car for business. If you keep a log or hang onto receipts and label them, you can have an accountant sort through it or you can get a copy of a Schedule C from the IRS and see how they categorize items into specifics. This often helps with planning.

Calculating Returns on Everything from Staples to Furniture

It seems silly to figure out what the net benefit is to buying staples, right? One rule of thumb is to agree to spend X dollars on office supplies—no more. The truth is that everything has to have a return. Some are harder to quantify—like pens and paper—but are necessities. These fall under office supplies on your tax return. You might not stress so much about the little things, but do watch your expenses.

Bigger items are another deal altogether. A personal example—when I moved into my new casita-based office, I had to buy all new furniture. I wanted to feel like I stepped into a professional office; I also wanted to spend a little bit of money. I had to find a nice balance between the two. If your business is more image-driven, consider that when making purchases. If image is irrelevant and you do all your work on the back end, consider how you feel about your business space and if you want to be there. Sometimes that affects the bottom line, too.

Will your office help retain top talent? As frustrating as it might be to always pay for the office snacks, it is okay to set a monthly limit and spend that much money if it helps morale. On the other hand, you could offer a place for people to store their own goodies and reinvest in your business.

To calculate a return on investment, use a simple formula like this:

A = cost of the item

B = value of the item to your business

If you divide A by B and you get a low number, consider whether it's worth the purchase.

Some purchases are not quantifiable, like those that improve morale or make people want to be at the office and—hopefully—be working while they are there. Be careful of employees who "hang out," eating and drinking your office-supplied snacks and Red Bull while not doing productive work. This is purely a cost to you. I had a boss once who would let us hang in the office late if we could show that productivity resulted. Often he'd treat us to lunch if we were far ahead of deadlines. Those small gestures went a long way for the team members who realized that he had to pay for those things out of his own pocket; therefore, they meant a lot to the team.

> What many of your team members or contractors may not realize is that everything the "business" spends is really your money because it is your business! Be sure to educate people about this without beating them over the head and making them feel uncomfortable. If you feel a team member is taking advantage, be sure to speak up. They may be used to feeling like "the businesses should be paying" when really all you owe them is a paycheck in exchange for work.

What to Do When the Signs Look Bleak

You are already analyzing your numbers on a regular basis—running cost-benefit analyses regularly and analyzing your expenditures on a return-on-investment (ROI) basis.

But what do you do when the signs aren't looking so hot? When your expenditures are greater than your income? You need to immediately look for ways to cut back if you don't believe the situation will turn around fast. Bring your team together if you have one, and ask for new ideas to bring in new revenue (and reward them if they pan out and are followed through on). If you have an open line of credit or can get one before even one bill is late (you do not want to damage your business or personal credit), and you know your business will be okay in the next 30 to 60 days, consider using the line and riding out the low tide.

But if you believe the short rainfall could be a drought, it is time to take action immediately. Cut all expenditures that aren't necessary. Hopefully you have already been calling companies you do business with regularly (including utility companies) to be sure you are on the best rate plans, but if you haven't, do so right away. Call all clients with balances beyond their due date, and cut back on staff hours if you need to. You may need to take on more of the burden yourself for a while, until the business is doing better again.

This is really time to reassess whether your projections are accurate and if so, by just how much. If they aren't, you need to adjust them, and fast. Figure out if you're on a path to destruction or if this is a temporary glitch by examining why business isn't doing as great. The key is to act quickly, but don't overreact if it's a temporary problem. You may also wish to spend money, as counterintuitive as that is, on advertising, marketing, and public relations to draw in more business. Spend money where it makes the most sense and draws in the greatest number of potential customers.

Warning Signs of Financial Insecurity

What are some warning signs of impending doom and the need for quick change? Running a monthly deficit is a big one. Barely meeting payroll each month is another one. Paying employees a day or two late is a red flag. Not being able to pay yourself your full salary that month is another big one. Rapidly declining sales or other competitors and new entrants into the marketplace may threaten your business's security and stability. Not being able to fund a great opportunity when it comes along, or consistently paying bills barely within the grace period, are other bad signs. Needing to put your personal money into your business account to keep your accounts in check is another, as is the cost of your services not keeping up with inflation, or people being unwilling to pay the same as they were in the past for your services. Lack of response to a good marketing campaign may also require attention, as it may mean you need to find another niche.

Raising Capital Quickly

Venture capitalists and even banks aren't necessarily going to be fast in getting money pumped into your business. Often the fastest way to do this is to raise your price (if it won't affect your client base negatively), downsize or rightsize (which is similar, but it is designed with a specific approach to be sure the company needs exactly the staff they have), and raise capital through quick-to-get high interest credit cards. While these can be dangerous in the long term, they can get you through a hard time fast.

Another method which could be a fairly quick means of raising funds is to set up an initial public offering or IPO. With an IPO, you are selling shares, or interest, of your company. This won't happen until you have enough cash flow that you can show value for stock holders.

If your business is growing quickly and you have a lot of interest in your company, you could sell and issue stock to those wishing to "get in on the deal." For instance, some of the most common purchasers of stock through an IPO are employees and initial investors. Creating and selling stock is fairly simple and straightforward if you have already structured your business as a corporation, because in doing so, you established a certain number of shares when you incorporated with the state.

> Be sure that you don't sell off more than 49 percent of the shares you have available. As long as you retain 51 percent of the shares available or more, you still have the controlling decision with regard to the operation of your business. If you sell 50 percent to a single person and retail 50 percent for yourself, you have officially taken on a partner, who will have equal control of your business. If you sell off more than 50 percent of your available shares and have retained 49 percent or less, you are officially no longer able to control your company. You may continue to run your business, but those who own the majority of the company can take over at any time, whether in regard to a single decision or to the total operation of your business.

Keep in mind, however, that in going about raising capital this way, you now have shareholders, meaning that you will have to take their votes and opinions into account when operating your business. Your board will have say over the direction of your business. As soon as you sell a single share of your company, you are obligated to turn a profit. This is referred to as fiduciary responsibility.

It is your responsibility to ensure that you operate your business in a manner that turns a profit, increasing the value of the shares that you have sold and issued.

There are many other obligations tied to issuing stock. I suggest you research this method deeply and consult with both legal and financial counsel before moving forward with this option.

Lastly, you can always form a strategic partnership with another business, whether a competitor or a complementary business. If you are the one who will benefit most from the partnership, you will most likely end up receiving the short end of the stick with regard to overall benefits of the partnership, but if it keeps your business alive or growing, it may be your only choice. An example of a strategic partnership would be if See's Candies partnered with FTD. The joint marketing potential would be that if you purchased a box of candy, you would get a discount on a dozen roses, or vice versa.

Throwing Good Money After Bad

I have personally seen so many business owners throw good money after bad that it is nauseating. If you know something isn't working, don't continue to do it! Taking that phone book ad resulting in one call every quarter with someone just checking on price (and more calls soliciting business than buying anything) and then renewing the contract is an example of throwing good money after bad. Keeping that super-fast Internet connection when the fast one sufficed just fine (or you couldn't even tell the difference) is another.

> Continuing to pay an unproductive employee is another example of throwing good money after bad (a good reason not to hire family or friends—they are more difficult to fire).

Knowing When to Change Direction

One of the most difficult things for any business owner to do is to change course, and to do it quickly before the situation becomes critical or results in late payments to anyone, including yourself. When you need to change direction, it may be time for you to step away from your business for a few days, and even take a few trusted colleagues with you to strategize. Be candid with employees about what is going on and that you're figuring out what the cause is. Ask them, too.

Many times, they're working with the customer and you aren't—they may know something they are too afraid to tell you. This is another reason why you need to keep the lines of communication open. Don't wait until a crisis to communicate.

Your course shift may be dramatic and drastic, like an entirely new line of business, or it may be more subtle, like a small website change that will, for instance, accept Discover in addition to MasterCard and Visa. It may be as simple as advertising more, or as serious as a lack of demand for your product or service that will continue into the foreseeable future. I highly recommend you write down expansion ideas and new business ideas as you come up with them throughout your years as a business owner, and now is the time to crack open that book.

Should you need to downsize or rightsize, chances are whatever you choose will be difficult because your team may feel like family. This is often the case with small businesses or individuals you have mentored, especially if you have done so on a personal level. I can say that in all my years as a senior leader in Corporate America and a business owner, the hardest decisions I have had to make were along these lines. The key is to be candid, open, and honest. The following is an example of what not to do, a real story that occurred within an organization I worked for, IPC Communications in California (headquartered in Michigan).

Our plant focused primarily on fulfillment and CD/DVD replication, while the headquarters in Michigan was mostly a print house. The print consumers wanted DVDs and CDs, which created the need for our division. Many of these were customers like Apple and Microsoft and were located in California, which I understand is the reason our division was located on the left coast. From my first day, I could feel the tensions between the two locations and between the staff members. Rather than bringing the teams together, senior leaders in Michigan stuck up for only their people in Michigan. As our division's profits tanked due to corporate's pricing strategy and lack of leadership, rather than bringing in support from Michigan, they had a plan to shut down our facility. We all felt it; it was "in the air," so to speak. But no one discussed it except those in our own plant.

We had very tight security; we replicated CDs for big companies that had a high degree of theft for product serial codes, and so on. We had a huge warehouse with stored product that we "kitted" and assembled for big companies like Toshiba.

Every day we went through airportlike security—including going to lunch. One day, while walking into the building (note we had no prior warning at all), we noticed there were seven guards instead of the usual one or two. Next to the guards and lining the hallways were boxes! You do the math—if you worked there, what would you do? As senior leaders, we were all instructed by the president, who visited a couple of times a year at most, to organize our teams into conference rooms at specific times—those who would keep their jobs for 30 days in one room, 60 days in another, those asked to help shut down the plant and incentivized with bonuses in yet another. Everyone knew what was going on, and the management from Michigan still waited until the end of the day. People sat in rooms waiting for the axe to fall, trying to figure out why they were separated, realizing it was by time left with the company—just not knowing how much time.

The job market wasn't so great for IT workers, which was the group I led. I did my best to persuade the president to keep my staff on as long as possible, but they fired the people who ran the customer-facing software first (and subsequently had to rehire them back with contracts at five to six times their salary when systems didn't work and they had no choice but to pay up or be nonoperational). As leaders, we were required to help people pack their things and make sure nothing disappeared out of the warehouse on their way out. Some people were walking around hallways crying and hugging; even HR was devastated. Others were just ticked. We all went our separate ways; many went to my next organization when I was able to hire back a lot of my previous staff. My direct boss at the time hired most of the rest of the team at his company, so most fared okay. But morale? And trust in Corporate America? They suffered forever. In fact, most of us became entrepreneurs within 10 years, and we will never fire ourselves in the manner we were treated—without dignity or trust.

Final Thoughts

There are so many sources of raising capital; yet at the same time it feels often like there is none. During the credit crunch of 2007 and 2008, many small businesses and medium-sized businesses faced great difficulty getting loans. It is important to have a variety of places and people you can turn to should you need cash flow to keep going. But remember, you need a long-term plan. If sales are on a continual decline, you may have to make some tough decisions while you restructure. Business owners face many difficulties, and we touched on quite a few—remember, there are answers to everything. I personally enjoy and find solace in online networking groups (I like Entrepreneur.com's groups) that help one another in particular industries, particularly when it comes to raising capital. University organizations that offer think tanks or product development teams can also be helpful!

The First Year

7

Your first year can be the most exciting: the startup, experiencing changes galore, bringing in the right team, expanding into new products or services, launching your marketing campaign, and watching the growth! Who wouldn't find this a thrill? There is something inside of an entrepreneur that doesn't die off very easily, regardless of difficulties, costs, or obstacles thrown at you. The entrepreneurial spirit is alive and kicking in America.

Your first year needs a roadmap, though, as do the others. This chapter is devoted to some advice to keep you on track, and out of trouble so you can have an exciting year two, three, and so on, too!

Making Your Business Legal

In Chapter 4, on starting your business, we discussed a bit about creating a DBA and getting your name filed. We will expand a bit in this section on what to do if the name you want is taken, how to check to be sure you are following all the rules, and where to go for help.

Naming

Hopefully by now you have selected a business name. The only requirement for a sole proprietorship is that the name not be taken in your county. However, if you have the exact name as another business in another part of the country, you could still run into legal trouble; particularly if you start to expand into other parts of the nation.

So how do you figure out which names are legally taken and which names are legally open? Turn again to the Internet for the start of your search, but also realize that if you are ever going to go national, you will likely have to pay for a name and trademark search, as the amount of hours it takes to search the country is astronomical. There are services that will take care of this for you, for a fee.

To search within your county, simply look up your county online. Once you have your county's official website pulled up, type into the search bar "business name" to quickly find the section of their site that allows for the searching of current DBAs that have been issued.

Another method you could use is, using your preferred search engine, search for "<name of county> AND <the business name you want>" and/or "<name of county> AND 'doing business as'," which should bring up, within the top search results, the page associated with your county's listing of current and past DBAs. If you want to see if the company is listed nationally, you can do a general Google search with the name in quotation marks.

Note that even if the business name you were hoping for shows up on a list of DBAs, that does not immediately mean it isn't available. The person who originally owned the rights to that particular name through the DBA could have let the DBA lapse, meaning that you may now take that name. Also, some counties will allow for similar or even exact same names, or same names with different spellings, etc. However, note that your name may infringe on copyright if it is too similar or detracts from the other business and you go national, so I always recommend checking to see if the name is available nationwide. Contact your county clerk's office for more information and to inquire about the rules and regulations of your jurisdiction.

Ok, so you want to go national, or the possibility is there for you to go national (or international?) in the future. You will need to search the entire United States to see if anyone already has the name you have in mind. As I stated earlier, it is a daunting and near impossible task for you to undertake on your own. This is where business name/identity search and verification services come in. A quick Google search just revealed 72 million results for "business name search." That's right—72 million! Searching for "business name search service" comes back with 68 million results.

A website I mentioned earlier, LegalZoom.com, is one of the best known sites that I can recommend. It provides both a nationwide search as well as the registration of your chosen name, should it be available. They will also offer recommendations of similar business names that are available for registration if your original choice is already taken.

If the name you want is taken, try to think of a modification that would still suit the business but not break copyright laws. For instance, changing from Inc. to Corp. may be sufficient. Note, however, that some jurisdictions, such as the State of California, do not count words like "A," "The," "Corp.," "Incorporated," etc., as part of the business name, so the addition or removal of these will not change the result if the name you had your heart set on is already taken. Due to many governing bodies following this same method, some entrepreneurs choose to add words to the name to really distinguish it from others.

Copyrights

Before you sell anything, apply a graphic to your website, add a company motto—you name it—you need to be sure that someone else doesn't own it! If they do, you could be liable for any damages done to that company and its reputation or business, and you will have to handle numerous attorneys' fees and the costs of changing your business name—not to mention the detriment to your own business when you have to make changes down the line. Protect your name completely. How do you do that?

According to LegalZoom.com, "Copyright does not protect names, titles, slogans, or short phrases. In some cases, these things may be protected as trademarks." Under these circumstances, a trademark is what you (and your business) will need. LegalZoom.com continues, "However, copyright protection may be appropriate for logo art work that contains sufficient authorship. In some circumstances, an artistic logo may also be protected as a trademark." (LegalZoom, 2008)

Business Structure

You already know the official structure—corporation, sole proprietorship, partnership, and so on. But what about the business model? Will you be an online or on-the-ground company? Will you be a hybrid? Will you have a store along Main Street, U.S.A., but also sell on eBay or Craigslist?

What about your management model? Will you have all people reporting to you? Will you hire managers as time goes on, or in the beginning? Will you hire professionals for advertising and marketing, or anything you aren't particularly good at, or will you do it all yourself? Will you have a matrix style management style? A top-down management style? Let's review these two, to get you started.

Matrix management style: The matrix management style is where an individual (the employee) has two supervisors or bosses to report to, one being a functional boss and the other being an operational boss. This can sometimes lead to staff confusion, as employees aren't sure who to report to or have a different boss for different projects. This management style works best with those who can operate well under ambiguous rules but not so well for people who like structure.

Top-down management style: The easiest explanation of the top-down management system that I have found to date was written by Jyothi M. John in his article "Top-Down Management Versus Bottom-Up Management." In it, he simply defines the top-down management style as "a management structure in which the managers are appointed directly, with or without relevant experience but with the necessary qualification." In top-down management styles, direction and strategy is pushed from the highest level of the organization down to the lowest. In bottom-up organizations, management tries to get input from all levels of the organization before making any decisions. You will find most companies to be top-down. As an entrepreneur, particularly in a new business, you probably won't want your employees deciding where your company goes! You may, however, want their input before implementing a new system.

Fictitious Business Name Statements

In Chapter 9, we talked about how to get and file an FBN. What do you do, though, if your name isn't taken locally but you want to expand nationally? Your FBN does not protect you. So how do you protect your name nationwide? It varies greatly by many things, including who had the name first, who can show it is essential to their business, who is willing to relinquish rights and name, if it's available for sale, who has imminent domain over a name, and if a person has expanded a business. It also varies greatly by the jurisdiction, court, county, and so on.

State-by-State Issues

The big issue when expanding from one state to another is going to be your business name. What if you are moving from one state to another, and come to find out that someone in the city you just purchased a home in already has an established business and is using the same business name that you are currently using? Who gets the right of use for that name, once you move into town? Which one of you gets to continue business under the same identity that you have been previously? All good questions, although the answer may not be to your liking (or in your favor).

Let me preface this section by letting you know that there are actually a couple of ways this could go. I will briefly discuss each one.

If you are moving to a new state and there is already an established business under the same name that your current business has, the general rule is whoever had the name first gets to continue using it. You could, of course, get around this by buying the other guy out (if the business type was the same) and acquiring his business. You could take him to court and see what a judge has to say on the matter, although the judge will usually find in favor of the owner with the longest use of the name, which is usually considered to be imminent domain over the name itself.

There are other aspects that are taken into consideration as well, such as company size, customer base, notability, and "recognizability," etc. An example of the premise of these issues would be if you owned a fast-food restaurant named McDonald's that has been in your family for 100 years, you would most likely still not win if you went up against McDonald's. They are more widely recognized, have a larger demographic, etc. The overall thought behind using these criteria is that the business that would suffer the most from losing its name gets to keep the name. If both businesses make out to suffer an equally negative impact, it will likely come down to tenure.

On a positive note, if you are moving, you could always change your business name, or the spelling of your business name. This would allow for both you and "Business B" to coexist without any of the aforementioned hassles. If you are not moving to another area, and are expanding your business, you will likely fall into one of the scenarios I just detailed.

Where to Go for Help

If you get stuck with all of these difficult decisions, you need to go to specific attorneys for help. There are patent and trademark attorneys that the SBA can refer you to, or you can ask others for counsel on who they use. You can also do a search online, but you run the risk of getting the attorney paying the most for advertising, and not necessarily the one that does the best job.

Deciding If You Need to Hire

In your first year, you may grow rapidly and feel the need to hire as you get more and more overwhelmed. Remember that there are many costs associated with hiring, so while it feels like the business is growing rapidly and you're buried in work, this may need to remain the case for awhile. If you truly cannot do the job, consider a part time assistant until you can afford one full time, or consider a contractor. Remember that if you hire an employee you will have a new set of headaches: payroll taxes, deductions, and so on. While many larger banks now handle payroll for you online (and many small business software products do too), it is still a new area to research and understand. In general, if you cannot serve your customers without hiring, it's time to bite the proverbial bullet.

Be sure you hire the right type of person, too. Personality does matter! If someone is answering the phones, you don't want someone with a poor "bedside manner" and a grumpy voice representing your business. It reflects on you.

Remember that, regardless of how close you get with your team, you are still the boss. You must always act like one or risk losing control of your business.

Try to figure out what people are good at, too, and then hire them for appropriate jobs. If someone hates a portion of her job, she may just have to deal with it if you don't have the funds to hire another person. Explain this to the employee; most of us don't like some aspect of our job. That is life.

SURVEY SAYS

What about our survey respondents? 52 percent were a business of 1! 32 percent had 1–2 employees; 85 percent had 3–4 employees; 8 percent had 5–10 employees, and 2 percent had 31–100 employees. In terms of contractors, 56 percent had no contractors. 28 percent had 1–2; 6 percent had 3–4; 6 percent had 5–10; 2 percent had 11–30 and 2 percent had 1,000 or more contractors.

Costs

Among the costs of hiring include payroll taxes and, of course, the salary or hourly wage that you are paying to your employees. Deciding what to pay can be tough, but salary should be commensurate with value add, how much you can afford (you may not be able to afford the best right now), education level, experience, prior job experience, and number of hours required by the employee.

Other costs may include: healthcare, uniform costs (if applicable), payroll service costs (if you don't want to deal with calculating payroll yourself), the cost of training new employees (both in training materials as well as time spent), additional insurance needed to cover your employees in the case of an accident or injury while on the job, etc.

Benefits

Of course, there are many benefits to hiring employees, too: delegating some of the busy work, expanding your business more rapidly, feeling that great sense of progress, feeling as though your business is a true business now, supplying a job for another human being (a great sense of pride for many of us), having someone to bounce ideas off, and gaining a feeling of camaraderie (particularly if you have been working alone for some time). Unfortunately, no one will ever care about your business as much as you do, but you can find people that care enough to get close.

Amount of Work Initially

Be sure you give responsibility commensurate with what you've seen an individual be able to perform. It might be a great feeling to dump lots of work on your new colleagues, but a bad move on their part can be highly detrimental to your business. Dole out responsibility based on capability and a proven record, not because you don't want to do it. Be sure that you train employees thoroughly, and give them only what they can handle initially.

SURVEY SAYS

What did our survey respondents say with regard to the number of hours they work? 43 percent indicated they work 41–60 hours, and 20 percent work more than 60 hours per week. 16 percent work 31–40 hours, 10 percent work 21–30 hours, 6 percent work 11–20 hours, and 4 percent work under 10 hours. One respondent noted that while she works more hours, she is "2000 percent happier than in Corporate America!" I hear that!

Growth Rate

Look carefully at your growth rate; don't over hire and don't under hire. You don't want to have to hire under the gun when you badly need someone or risk making a bad hiring decision that will cost you in many ways. At the same time, hiring too prematurely can cause incredible financial distress and can make you feel resentful toward that team member—which is unfair to you both.

Keep in mind that taking on an employee doesn't automatically mean that you hire someone full time. You may only take on a part time employee or a per diem employee (Latin for "by day", commonly synonymous with "as needed" or "on call").

A general rule of thumb to go by is that if you have the time and energy to do the work yourself, you don't need another employee (unless you can financially afford to hire someone to allow yourself additional "you time"). If you are finding yourself having to constantly carry over tasks to tomorrow and the next day, chances are it's time to take a look at your finances and determine what you can afford to pay someone, as you are in the position to take on an employee.

Contractors Versus Employees

When you first hire (particularly in the first couple of years), it's a good feeling to know you have a team. It makes you feel somehow legitimized as a business owner. But contractors may actually be the way to go. There are rules, though, based on IRS tax regulations, for contractors.

Did you know that under the common law, a worker is an employee if the hiring firm (that is, the person or persons for whom services are performed) has the right to control and direct the way he or she works, not only with regard to the final result, but also with regard to the details of when, where, and how the work is done? This is important because you don't want to get into trouble with the IRS.

According to Uncle Sam, it is not necessary that the employer actually directs or controls the manner in which the services are performed; it is sufficient if the employer has the right to do so.

The IRS now investigates the status of independent contractors in all business audits they conduct. The burden of proof is always on the hiring firm to demonstrate unequivocally that an independent contractor is *not* their employee. (IRS.gov)

There are two resources for this section that are very important for you to use:

> The first is a summary of legal issues related to the hiring of independent contractors: "Independent Contractors: A Manager's Guide and Audit Reference," published by the California Chamber of Commerce, PO Box 1736, Sacramento, CA 95812-1736, 916-444-6670.

> The second is a resource when considering hiring independent contractors: "The Employer's Legal Guide," by Stephen Fishman, published by Nolo Press, 1997. An in-depth and comprehensive discussion of employee vs. independent contractor legal issues is available online at Fenwick & West: Publications.

The pros to bringing on help in the form of contractors include:

- No costs of benefits.
- No responsibility to continue contracting with them if you cannot afford it (though in at-will states, this isn't an issue anyway because employers and employees can sever their contract at any time without cause).
- The ability to cut back or increase hours easily (of course, you risk losing the contractor if he or she is unhappy).

The cons are as follows:

- Many contractors though don't feel as settled or as loyal to a company if they are not "real employees." Since the IRS requires you not treat a contractor like an employee, contractors often report feeling like outsiders, particularly in mid- to large-sized businesses.
- There is little control you can take with a true independent contractor. If you even mandate a single hour that a person must be in the office, the IRS can consider him an employee. If you tell contractors when a task needs to be completed, how it needs to be completed, when they need to start, or pretty much anything for that matter, they are no longer an independent contractor and are officially (according to the IRS and many state legal systems) employees.

Setting Up for Business

One vital decision you must make in year one is how you will set up for business. If you are going to have a back-end business that doesn't literally see customers, like a retail store would, you have more options than if you do have a retail center or will be meeting clients regularly.

Office Space—Work from Home or Not?

This may sound all too familiar. You are sitting in traffic, it's 6 P.M., and you're no closer to home than you were 15 minutes ago. Your family is calling, warning of the impending coolness of your home-cooked meal and the kids' bedtime rapidly approaching. Your clients are e-mailing you on your BlackBerry about a 7:30 meeting that you feel no more like going to than you did the business dinner last night, which kept you from the nightly bedtime story routine. Gas is expensive; the $100 per week you spend going to your own office is getting on your nerves—and hurting your wallet. You and your husband have contemplated his return to work for additional income, but the kids would be taken care of by a nanny—so you're willing to sacrifice. The thought of working from home enters your mind, and many are doing it these days—as many as 30 percent of entrepreneurs are working from home.

Every single business you ever decide to create can be run at home or in a business center, office, or retail site—but it should be dictated by the type of business you have.

So what are some pros to working at home? You definitely save money on gas, dry cleaning, and car maintenance. I only have dry cleaning costs for my television clothes; otherwise it's just laundry for my gym clothes, worn 95 percent of my working day. I drive about 5000 miles per year, down from 20,000, which has reduced my insurance and car costs—and allowed my car to maintain its value. I am stuck in traffic about 30 minutes per week to go to personal appointments, instead of 2 hours per day.

You also have the benefit of no dress code, which many of us aren't delighted with—particularly those of us from the X and Y Generations. You also get the opportunity to work during your most creative times, not the times set by your manager. If you want to exercise in the morning, take your kids to school, start work at noon, and work until midnight, so be it.

In Corporate America, everything is fairly regulated for us. When a boss piles on more work you really have two options—speak your mind and risk getting fired, or say, "Thank you Ma'am, may I have another?!" What about the alternative … selecting which projects you will undertake by balancing your desires and need for income, and then making your own decision? This is what entrepreneurs get to do. The tasks that need to get done can be left to subordinates and contractors. When you have your own business, all of this changes and you are setting the ground rules. You may have some worries or some concerns; and you may feel isolated at times, too. These are all normal things and have solutions, but you must be actively involved in the answers.

Many people also report being able to add and delete jobs from their workload as they see fit, which is a great benefit. You can turn down contracts with people you don't enjoy working with if you can financially afford to do so. The flexibility is really a great advantage.

Another big worry, particularly in the early stages of a new business, is the inability to have a regular paycheck, or the pressure of living project-to-project or client-to-client. This was very stressful for me, too, in the beginning. Eventually you will have more consistent work, and this may require you to load up slowly and transition once your income is stable. You will need to be incredibly disciplined to manage your finances. Also remember that you should stick with what you're good at, because taking on lots of extra work (particularly if the pay isn't so hot) will stress you out to no end. Many of you will choose to work from home also, which will create an entirely new set of issues or concerns.

There are of course financial benefits even if you have a business losing money in the first few years. You may also find incredible tax write-offs in home-based businesses. If an area of your home is dedicated to your business, talk with your tax accountant about how to write this area off, including utilities and maintenance prorated by the percentage of square feet dedicated to your office.

Another great advantage for many is solving the childcare issue (although working from home and taking care of children should be done at your own peril!) and gaining more time with family, particularly because of less commuting. This can be offset, though, if you work long hours like I do. I'm simply in another part of the house!

You may find yourself more invigorated and healthier if you work from home. I have suffered for many years from severe primary insomnia, often going an entire week with less than one night's sleep. Getting up in the morning for mandatory 8 A.M. meetings at my day job was grueling, not to mention taxing on my health. In my case, if I have a bad night of insomnia and work from 2 P.M. until 2 A.M. in order to get rest in the morning, that is my decision. That pressure of knowing "I must fall asleep *now*" is no longer there. I have many friends who have left their day jobs for health reasons—to allow themselves more flexibility with when and how they work.

You also of course have fewer costs when you work from home: you are not paying for expensive office rent, office furniture, business phone lines, and business Internet access. This lack of overhead will free up money for advertising and marketing.

As with anything, there are downsides. Like online workers and people that work for companies remotely (particularly home-based), you may find yourself craving human interaction. Most of my interaction now comes from travel and speaking engagements and trips to my local studio for live shots, rather than from colleagues who I develop relationships with. It takes a genuine effort on your part to create those relationships and to make time to interact with people. It is easy to hole yourself up in your house and just work all day. Sometimes the only "interaction" you get is with your online chat buddies, which can be tough and frustrating at times.

There are ways to help you out of the feeling of isolationism. For example, meeting friends for lunch and creating a real office feeling environment in the home can help. Making certain you maintain a routine, get up (take a shower!), and put on "real people" clothes before you begin working can help make you feel a bit less isolated. Going for a real lunch break outside of the home, even by yourself, feels a bit more like "normalcy," too. I personally find that going to the gym in the middle of the day and then coming back to work also gets me out of the house and driving my car in the sunshine.

You may also find yourself distracted by the very reason you decided to work from home—your family. For people lacking self discipline or feeling torn between home and work responsibilities, or for those with young children, finding time undistracted by everything from laundry piling up to a sick child can be tough.

It might sound so nice at first! Not having to deal with co-workers and being able to wear your pajamas most of the day! Taking web calls with PJ bottoms and a dress top—ah the freedom! But there can be some loss felt without human interaction and without a team environment, so that is something you need to prepare for.

A common complaint or critique I hear from individuals who leave Corporate America behind for a home-based business is that they don't have a clearly defined boundary between home and work. When they walk into their office area, are they officially back at work? Setting work time boundaries are critical to feeling successful and feeling as though you have control over your work—you need to set your "office hours" even if you are at home with your family. Others need to respect those boundaries so you can get your work done. You won't ever "go home," leaving work completely behind, unless you create that for yourself, which is not easy to do.

Retail Space

If your dream is to own a retail business and work with clients at a place like a boutique or a tanning spa, you will need retail space. Chances are, unless you are independently wealthy, you will be leasing this space for a period of time.

Find space adequate for your needs but accommodating for what your plan shows will be your requirement in two to three years. Changing a business location, particularly in a retail establishment, is not a good idea unless it's a poor location. Also, be prepared to pay a pretty penny for prime real estate.

Laws and Regulations

There are of course laws and regulations that we've discussed a bit already that you need to take into consideration. Aspects that need to be analyzed when searching out your piece of the American dream include access to your target demographic, location relative to major freeways or thoroughfares, location relative to your competition and complementary businesses, applicable laws and regulations (e.g., an adult bookstore in many jurisdictions not only will require special permits but must be a certain distance from any registered or recognized school or day care center, and most areas take it one step further, requiring surrounding businesses and residential neighbors to "approve" of this type of business setting up shop), hours of operation relative to surrounding businesses, security issues, age and condition of the building, and more.

Commercial Property

Your business may require substantially more space than you had originally allocated, in which case your search will be directed toward commercial property: a strip mall or major shopping center, enclosed retail mall or outdoor retail mall.

If you wanted to open a large retail store, let's say the size of a Target store, you may end up needing to search out a piece of land and build from the ground up.

Technology Needs at Home

You will need technology regardless of where you house your business—though depending on what you do you may not need much. You absolutely do need dedicated office space. I have been on hundreds of conference calls where I constantly hear other participants' dogs barking, kids crying, and husbands yelling. It is distracting for both you and your colleagues and can create stress that you didn't have before—and even cause discord in your relationship. To get around this, set aside very specific work areas, and make it clear to everyone in the house that this is your office—your work! Install phone lines if you need to, buy more computers—whatever you need to be sure that your kid isn't hanging out in the same room where you're trying to write a business proposal. You may also have to teach children and spouses not to answer your business line and to stay away from your cell phone. If you need to meet clients in person, consider renting office space, which is usually available at everything from Kinko's to large office complexes that rent conference rooms for that professional look. You may wear your pajamas all day but you can't meet clients in them!

Computer Necessities

You first need to determine the reason why you would be using the computer and then determine which resources would be optimal. For instance, if all someone is doing on the PC is surfing the web, accounting, word processing, and presentations using PowerPoint, there really is no need for investing in a huge hard drive, two gigabytes of memory, and dual processors. If you plan to use your computer to store large files like pictures, images, audio files, or video files, or if you plan to do audio, video, graphics, or multimedia production, then yes, the computer upgrades are going to be needed.

Your computer must be powerful enough to handle the many tasks that you may want to accomplish simultaneously—like checking e-mail, opening multiple browser windows, word processing, running malware scans in real time, and listening to music—if this would make you more productive throughout the day. This requires a powerful processor (at least two gigahertz) and enough memory (at least a gigabyte). Whether you have a Mac or PC really does not matter unless you intend to do heavy graphics or audio and video productions, in which case a Mac might prove better. Other than that, any affordable PC will do the trick. And instead of having a computer consultant build one for you, buy from the manufacturer; it may prove to save you a lot of money in support costs in the long run and preserve your business continuity.

When buying a computer, try not to get caught up in hype. Computer sellers tend to sell you computers that far exceed the power that you will need. If your business requires you to be mobile, you may want to invest in a laptop with docking station and monitor; otherwise, a regular desktop computer would do the trick. If you are going to spend a great deal of time online, it may serve you well to invest in a bigger monitor and an antiglare screen for it. I recommend a 22" LCD monitor, and they run for less than $300. Do invest in disaster recovery plans to ensure that even if you suffer a hard drive or software crash, you will be up and running again within an hour.

In some instances it may even be a good thing to get two video cards and two monitors—especially in instances where you also have a web presence and you must constantly monitor your website. This can make it easier to multitask. For example, on one monitor you can have a browser open with your online support desk and on the other you can have the website up—but you are still running it off one computer and it is very easy to set up. It makes life easier for one person to manage two separate tasks. So this is a good scenario for a one-man show.

Another option is to have one monitor and two computers—especially if you are hosting your own website. Then buy a keyboard video monitor (KVM) switch— a good one won't cost more than $50. This will let you connect to two different computers with one monitor, keyboard, mouse, etc. I use this all the time and it is very convenient—it all depends on what it takes to make you the most efficient while you are in your office.

Communications

You cannot completely depend on the Internet to handle all of your business needs, as used to it as many of us are. People still want to call and speak to someone about customer service, billing, or support issues. Having a reliable phone service is therefore important. Based on the type of business you are starting, you may decide if you want to use your cell phone as the main contact phone number, invest in a dedicated business line, employ the use of an auto attendant to answer your calls (whether or not you are available), or hire a company to answer your phones for you. But people need to speak to a live person in many instances, so be prepared to accommodate that should the occasion arise. Another option is voice over Internet protocol (VoIP), which can be done through cellular providers (check out Sprint's AIRAVE system) or through systems like Skype or Vonage.

Electronic Requirements in Today's Internet Age

There are many options out there in terms of Internet access: dialup or accelerated dialup (significantly slower than other options), DSL, cable, satellite (high speed). T1 lines, in the past reserved for highly profitable businesses, are quite affordable these days as well, and something you should look into through major telecommunications companies. In selecting a high speed Internet service, remember that speed isn't everything; reliability is also important. It is a good idea to go with the more reputable providers, which can offer you a dialup account as backup in case there is a failure on your data line. Try not to skimp, and test out the upload and download speeds once you get your new connection. If you aren't happy, move on. I recommend you always have a backup line, even a phone line you can use with a modem, in case something goes wrong and you still need to handle orders. Or consider a full scale backup provider—if you are using say, cable, then you might want a backup DSL line.

Web Presence from Day One

You will want to have a web presence from day one, which means you need to hire a developer at least six months in advance. Seek out sites you like and e-mail the owners to see who they use for development. You can usually look up the information of the owner by going to www.namesecure.com and using the WhoIs information button, or by going to www.WhoIs.net.

Be sure your website matches your business—if your business model is simple, keep it simple. If you are a jack of all trades, selling everything under the sun at wholesale, make the site easy to navigate, but get it all up there. Be sure that your legal disclaimers are easy to find, as well as your security and privacy policies. You also want to make sure anyone who visits your website knows how to contact you. This is where keeping your "Contact Us" links visible and easy to find comes in.

Hire a web designer who uses Web 2.0 techniques so you are using the most current technology, include a blog and customer review and testimonial area that you check often, and ask your web developer to create your site to W3C compliance. The W3C is the World Wide Web Consortium, the group that is responsible for defining standards used in web design, like HTML and CSS.

Hiring Basics

You want to hire the right people—after all, they represent you and your company! Like many of us, you may be used to interviewing for jobs at a company you don't own, and suddenly you find yourself being hypersensitive to answers you hadn't thought twice about in the past, because now it is *your* company. This is okay and normal! You will want to be sure to do a complete background check of possible employees, and in some states and counties it is legal to do a credit check, too. A credit check might help indicate the level of responsibility that an individual has taken in his or her personal life, and could potentially be an indication of how he or she will treat your business. I hire a lot based on instinct and always have. It hasn't let me down; but your instinct needs to be based on experiences.

Skill Sets

Determine and write down what skill sets are absolutely essential, which are nice to have, and which are icing on the cake. Then assess those strengths in each candidate, first by screening resumés and then by interviewing. You must align skill sets and the individual's desire to do a job with your needs.

Time

You may have found the perfect candidate with an excellent skill set and education, but she wants to work part time and you need full time. She must leave at 4 P.M. to pick up a child, but you need someone to cover evenings. This isn't a good fit. Time must be assessed as part of your interviewing process.

What You Offer Versus What They Need—"Life" Fit

Find out what prospective employees want in a job. Is it just a job? Do they want a place to grow? Do they prefer environments and managers that let them run with things, or do they prefer a set direction and set list of tasks? Be sure that what makes them happy and what you need is aligned.

Personality

I made mention earlier in this chapter of someone with bad phone manners (and who may not even realize it!) taking a job where he or she needed to answer phones. But there are numerous other areas where personality plays a role. The mood of one upset or generally irritated person can upset the entire office and make for what we call a hostile environment. If you want a happy place to work, hire happy people. If you need intense seriousness, hire intense, serious people.

Dedication

Be sure that the individual has the time and interest to dedicate to your business what you truly need. If they don't, you need to move on.

Final Thoughts

You have so many decisions to make as a business owner. Do you want to start off working at home? Do you want to start off in a small mall type shop? Do you want an online only business? What kind of personality will your business have and what role do demographics play? These decisions, while vital, must remain fun. It is important to think about them, but get the advice of others, remember to try to maintain some resemblance of a life in the process, and enjoy this time. You are creating something and once it is created, you go into growth and maintenance mode—often simultaneously or alternating among them. While this is a lot of fun, this creation stage shouldn't be glossed over; enjoy it while it lasts!

8

Money Basics

Money is the cornerstone of your business, giving you the ability to grow, expand, and create a life for yourself. Many of you, on the other hand, may have the ability to feel successful in your business regardless of the money that you make. Everyone has a different feeling as to what success means to them, but for many of us, our bottom line at least indirectly affects how we feel about our level of success.

In this chapter we'll discuss the basics of managing your business money, from checking accounts to the impact of your DBA, from handling payroll to contractors and bill pay services.

Business Checking Accounts

One of your first tasks as a new business owner is to obtain a checking account. I remember my very first business and the feeling of seeing my company's name printed on an official document that had the means of actually paying for something. Today it doesn't offer quite as much excitement, but is nonetheless an essential step to making your business legit and providing it financial viability.

You have many options; most banks, even small ones, offer business checking. Find free accounts—almost every bank offers one. Don't get caught up in the duplicate check copies for a fee and the printed statements—the more electronic your business becomes the more efficient you'll find yourself. The key is to get a checking account with a major bank that offers the ability to assign multiple employees different credit or debit cards. This allows you to let others in your business make deposits and handle other things you may not always have time for. One word of caution, though—make sure those whom you provide access, even depository access, are thoroughly trust-worthy!

Most banks today offer online banking as well, but only some offer online payroll. I use Bank of America and use their features, which they are constantly adding to, to the max.

Requirements to Open a Business Checking Account

To open your business checking account, you need: Two forms of photographic personal identification, a statement of incorporation (articles of incorporation, for instance), your Employee Identification Number (EIN) or DBA (Doing Business As) statement if you're using your personal Social Security number, and documentation showing you have a business license as well as the ability to use the business name you selected. Also, if others can sign on the account, be sure you bring them with you to the bank to sign the signature card. (Yes most banks still use this antiquated method!)

As a quick note, with regard to your articles of incorporation, make sure you bring the ones that you received back from the state—the set that has been stamped with your state's approval. The bank will need the "official" articles to open a business checking account when using this method. If you use a DBA statement and incorporate at a later date, your bank of choice will be able to switch the account records to reflect your business's status, so you don't have to worry that you will lose your account should you legally restructure your business at a later date.

Fictitious Name Statements and Banking

Many new business owners ask me why the bank harassed them over not having their Doing Business As (DBA) or fictitious name statement (FNS) completed yet. Banks need proof that you are allowed to operate under the new business name.

A fictitious business name statement provides this legitimacy. Take it with you to the bank. With a fictitious business name statement, you can take it to the bank and then get the ability to cash checks with your DBA name.

Unless you are operating your business under your own name or have completed the steps to be a corporation (incorporated), LLC, Limited Liability Partnership (LLP), etc., you will be required by your state or county to apply for a DBA. This legitimizes your business and establishes that you are doing business as (get it? DBA?) XYZ Company.

In most situations that I am aware of, a DBA is as simple as completing the DBA form within 30 days of completing your first transaction and following through on each county's rules with regard to publication, although I always advise you do so prior to conducting business. Completing this step will allow you to establish a business checking account prior to "opening your doors." Most states also require that you notify the public of your newly established business by posting an announcement in local newspapers and then submitting proof of publication to the state.

To learn more about your state's requirements, check your state's official website and search for "DBA."

"Doing Business As" (DBA)

If you are doing business as another name, you will need your proof of the DBA to opening a business checking account. For instance, one of my businesses is my own name and Social Security number, doing business as … my company name. Many sole proprietors do business this way, particularly in the beginning.

It is an important side note that if you are using a DBA (which includes, by the way, your previously used names if, for instance, you are recently married and want to be able to cash checks made out to you, your previous name, or your business's name) you need to bring proof of this.

Best Banking Deals

Seek out the best deal; compare checking accounts. Here are some things to look for:

- Fees (initial and recurring)
- Minimum balance requirements
- Automatic credit cards
- Overdraft options
- Number of ATMs
- Nonbank ATM fees
- Ability to manage the account online
- Ability to get debit and credit cards in others' names (with set limits, or deposit-only cards)
- Fraud responsibility—if your card is stolen, how does the bank handle it?
- Maximum number of checks you can write in a month (many still have limits!)
- Miscellaneous fees, like if a client bounces a check on you
- Merchant service capabilities, specifically those that integrate with your website
- Online banking tools
- Online payroll
- Downloadable information into QuickBooks or Quicken

If a bank meets your minimum needs, it's time to sign up! Expect an hour or so at the bank. I recommend asking for a business line of credit at the same time, and even walking away if they say "no" to your request. Usually they will want the new account badly enough to offer you something.

Merchant Accounts

A merchant account is a bank account set up with a payment processor to allow for the acceptance of credit card payments. Most banks offer this service, although keep in mind that it is a fee service. This means that you pay for the transactions the bank processes for you. Going through your local bank will often result in your having a physical credit card terminal, which is great if you have a brick-and-mortar establishment or are willing to enter credit card information each time you accept an order.

There are also merchant account providers online, the most notable being PayPal. In my opinion, PayPal is really a strong choice today. The fees are minimal (they can afford to keep fees low due to the amount of customers they have and the streamlined process between PayPal and eBay) and through their service you can accept PayPal transfers, credit card transactions, and online checks. They handle everything, literally, even protecting you in the event of fraud or declined charges, just as they protect you as a consumer of goods and services online. Visit PayPal.com, and go to "Business—Merchant Services" for more information on available services, fees, etc.

Choosing a Merchant Vendor

Chances are your bank will offer merchant services, but they may not offer the best deal on them. You can use one bank for your checking and another for merchant services, but you may not get a fee advantage by doing this. One reason I recommend inquiring about this before you sign up for checking is so you can compare the banks you're evaluating.

What should you look for when evaluating a merchant account vendor? Start with this list:

- Transaction fees
- Ability to handle a virtual terminal (see the rest of this section for more information)
- Online website integration for credit card processing
- Security
- Protection in case card numbers are stolen
- Reporting to you in case security is breached
- Monthly routine costs and any associated "maintenance fees"
- Integration with American Express or Discover, should you wish to accept them now or in the future
- Dispute resolution practices—Do they automatically side with the consumer? With you? It isn't unusual for the burden of proof to be on the business, even though the merchant might say it's the consumer's burden.

> You will have many options in merchant services. What you need depends on how often you will use the credit card system, how most of your consumers will pay, and how much you want to incur in costs each month. Don't let banks upsell you because you can always add services on later, depending on your need.

Online Integration

Be sure your merchant account has online integration. For instance, you want to be able to hand your web developer the plug-ins for handling transactions online in any form, whether through Google Checkout or your own website.

Web Transactions for Credit Cards

Most merchant services offer you the ability to run a credit card through a virtual terminal. You will want this capability if you take phone orders. Much like with an old credit card machine, you go to a website, type in the payer's credit card information, the last three digits on the back of their card, and their billing address. This charges the buyer and deposits the money into the account that you have linked to that service, which will most likely be your business checking account.

Alternative Payment Options

In today's Internet environment, you have more than traditional merchant accounts available to you. Numerous online sources offer systems that allow your consumers to pay for items online. Versions 1-4 of my primary website at www.drdaniellebabb.com offered nothing more than PayPal as a payment option, using their shopping cart. Not knowing how this was affecting sales, my www.teachonlinetraining.com site offers integrated merchant services, and my new version of www.drdaniellebabb.com next year will offer credit card payments without the use of PayPal, too. This is discussed more in a few paragraphs.

Google Checkout

Google Checkout provides a fully complementary merchant service that is directly linked to your website. It is literally as simple as a customer shops on your site and "checks out" through Google Checkout. If you advertise through Google, Google Checkout is provided to you free of charge. Companies like Linens-N-Things and Aéropostale are even starting to use Google Checkout within their websites.

Some additional benefits of Google Checkout, according to their website (which you can check out at checkout.google.com):

Guaranteed Payment: Checkout's Payment Guarantee protects 98 percent of Checkout orders on average—when an order is guaranteed, you get paid even if it results in a chargeback.

Free Protection: While merchants are typically charged for fraud protection services, Google's comprehensive protection is free.

Lower Fraud Costs: Checkout's fraud detection systems reduce fraud and manual review costs by proactively filtering out fraudulent orders.

More Sales: The same systems also help increase sales by identifying legitimate orders that you might otherwise mark as fraudulent.

Fair Treatment: Unlike other services that immediately deduct funds from you for "chargebacks," Google does so only after a decision has been made as to who is at fault. (Note that a chargeback is when a customer files a dispute and wants their money back because they feel as though you haven't satisfactorily completed the transaction. Also note that some customers do this as a form of fraud, so you need a helpful, reputable merchant that will handle these types of situations.) (Google, 2008)

PayPal

Getting its start as the primary payment option for eBay and then later becoming an eBay-owned business, PayPal has been and remains sufficient for many business owners. Of course, PayPal payments must be initiated by those with PayPal accounts, possibly turning many users off or creating too much of a hassle for some buyers. However, it does have basic invoicing capabilities, the ability to transfer funds to accounts and easily handle payments from any source (including checking accounts), and provides security and low fees—as well as cash back when you use it as a credit card.

In summary, PayPal's website notes that they offer five ways to get paid online: Website Payment Standard, Website Payment Pro, E-mail Payments, Express Checkout, and eBay Payments.

Website Payment Standard is the most basic service that you can sign up for, allowing you to accept credit card payments quickly and easily. There is no application process, no fancy programming that you will have to do to include it on your website. PayPal will provide you with simple HTML code "buttons" that you can use throughout your site, allowing your customers to "Buy Now," "Add to Cart," and "Donate." All that is required to use this option is a PayPal account.

Website Payment Pro is a highly upgraded version of Website Payment Standard—so much so that you will need to either have a fairly thorough understanding of web programming or the ability to hire a website developer. As the criteria and standards are fairly involved, visit PayPal.com for more information. You will find the option for Website Payment Pro under the main "Business" tab.

E-mail Payments is a highly efficient and simple way of invoicing your customers. This option is geared more toward invoicing a client for services than a customer for a product, which is better accomplished through live or real time payment acceptance. With E-mail Payments, you enter the e-mail address of your client, the amount that you are invoicing, and the reason for the invoice, and click "send invoice." Your client receives the invoice in his or her e-mail inbox, with a direct link to PayPal to make the payment. The only requirements of you and your client is that you both have active PayPal accounts. This is an issue for some business owners who find that their clients want to use a credit card without PayPal. If your client does not have an account, he or she will be prompted to sign up for one, which is both free and quick.

Express Checkout is a system that integrates your customer's PayPal account information with your website. If your customers are PayPal customers, they can login to Express Checkout with their username and password, auto filling out all billing and shipping information. They can of course alter the shipping and billing information should they need to. This option is quick and simple for both you and your customers. Remember, keeping your customers' experience simple is one way to keep them happy, which means they will likely return!

eBay Payments is a fantastic option for anyone who is setting up an eBay Store or who will simply be conducting many auctions. With eBay Payments, you will be able to accept PayPal as your primary payment method, with automatic PayPal logo insertion in your auctions or store.

Other Available Systems

There are other competing systems with PayPal and Google payment options that are purely online. Two of the leading companies, along with a notation about each, are as follows:

Authorize.net. Authorize.net is a simple service provider that will allow you to accept credit card payments online, on your web-enabled mobile device (like your BlackBerry), through mail order and telephone sales, and even within a retail establishment (meaning you can utilize their services even if you run a traditional brick-and-mortar establishment). This is the company that I use on my teachonlinetraining.com website that has easy integration with lots of tools.

MerchantExpress.com. Merchant Accounts Express has been providing online merchant services since 1998, and like the others that I have already mentioned, offers both quick and easy solutions for accepting credit card payments online. Merchant Accounts Express also handles physical acceptance of credit cards with point-of-sale (POS) terminals and service using an online card processing system as well.

As a reminder, fees and services for merchant accounts vary. Feel free to shop around and weigh all available options before signing up!

Handling Payroll

Payroll is daunting to many business owners; in fact, it is a top reason that entrepreneurs prefer to use contractors rather than hiring employees. As a business owner, you have to be careful not to cross IRS lines with regard to who is a contractor and who is an employee, and equally important, when a contractor really becomes an employee based on job requirements.

There are many tools out there today, thankfully, to help you with payroll. Automatic Data Processing Inc., or ADP, is known for their payroll and human resources services, and offer many options for small businesses all the way up to Fortune 500 corporations. From preemployment services (background checks, substance abuse testing, identification, etc.) to time and labor management to payroll services, 401(k) services, and benefits administration, ADP is truly a one-stop shop for all of your businesses management and operational needs.

To find out more about what ADP has to offer, visit www.ADP.com or call 1-800-Call-ADP.

Intuit, the same company that brought you QuickBooks, also offers payroll services. Visit Payroll.Intuit.com for more information.

There are other options, too, for online payroll services to help you handle this requirement with ease. Most banks will allow you to process payroll through your online business account. For example, my Bank of America online login allows me to pay employees directly from the home page, set up routine payments (including taxes), handle withholdings, and so on.

When you hire employees, you have to have them fill out different paperwork. An employee fills out a W4 for withholding, and then a state withholding form, which varies by state. You can find your state's withholding form at www.irs.gov/formspubs.

Contractor Payments

If you are paying a contractor, the rules are easier and the hassles lessen. You simply get an invoice from the contractor; be sure you have his or her Social Security number and current address on file, and submit a 1099-MISC form at the end of the year. The box for nonemployee compensation is what you complete for payments to contractors. Contractors are required to pay their own taxes, relieving you of the burden of calculating withholdings and sending W2s at the end of the year. Several online companies make 1099 submissions easier. A couple of the most notable ones are FileTaxes.com and eFileForBusiness.com, both offering online completing and filing of the 1099 (and even W2 forms) at very reasonable rates—a couple of bucks per form.

If you have any contractors in your business that you paid more than $600, you need to file a 1099. This will be written off as contractor payments (submitted on Form 1099) on your Schedule C, or on your corporate tax file. Generally you have 30 days to pay contractors unless you agreed to another time period. It is important to remind contractors that you have this right, particularly if you usually pay weekly or bimonthly; they may get used to that, and if you need additional time you'll have unhappy contractors despite working within your rights. With contractors, I do not ever recommend paying ahead of time for work. Pay after work has been completed.

Employee Payments

How and when you pay employees is based on your employment contract. When you hire employees, you will provide them with information on when and how you will pay them, if you offer direct deposit, and so on. One reason I recommend using an online company is that they handle direct deposits, withholdings, and employee payments all for you, with easy-to-read reports and simple end-of-year reporting.

When you make a payment to an employee, you can select when and how—and you can change whether you offer direct deposit and when you pay, but you must provide adequate notice of any changes. A few of my employers, for instance, have changed from every-two-weeks to bimonthly pay schedules. Give your employees enough time to plan on their end. You can begin or end direct deposit at any time, too. If you are writing manual checks and you aren't going to be in town on pay day, be sure you have a plan to handle this. You are now responsible for your employees.

Automated Online Payments

You can automatically pay your employees or contractors online. For some of my contractors, I use transfers initiated in Bank of America's transfer system. This allows the contractor to receive payment same-day (sometimes same-hour) with near-immediate clearance of funds. You can also use services to pay based on a specific time period. You really should do what is easiest and best for you, and make it clear to employees that anything you do electronically is a bonus to them—it is not a requirement of any sort.

Handling Taxes for Employees

Taxes for employees aren't fun—from paying them to filing them. As a business owner, you are responsible for withholding payroll taxes, including:

- Social Security at 12.4 percent (6.2 percent split employer/employee)
- Medicare at 2.9 percent (1.45 percent split employer/employee)
- Federal withholdings (dependent on completed W4)
- State withholdings (dependent on completed W4)

- Any employee-paid costs for healthcare (varies by plan and other factors)
- Any pretax offerings, such as a flexible spending account (FSA) or health spending account (HSA) (varies)

So what do you do with the federal and state withholding money? In short, you are paying the money to the IRS under the employee's name.

As you can imagine, these matters are highly sensitive and legally binding—if you mess up, you're going to have to pay! As I am no tax expert and will never claim to be, it is my most sincere advice that you contract with a payroll service, either a local or national firm, such as ADP, to handle this aspect of your business. The last thing you need to worry about is the IRS coming after you for not dotting your Is or crossing your Ts.

Remember that you have to offer employees the ability to adjust their withholdings. How they calculate their numbers isn't your call—they can withhold (or not) as much or as little as they want. The tax burden at the end of the year is their responsibility, provided you withheld the amount that they asked you to (which you are legally obligated to do).

Many business owners also ask about overtime. You do not need to pay a salaried employee overtime, as long as certain common criteria are met. These issues do vary by state, field of work, etc. EmployeeIssues.com provides a detailed yet succinct explanation of the complications with overtime. You can view their full explanation at www.EmployeeIssues.com/overtime_pay.

The basic explanation is that one workweek consists of 7 consecutive 24-hour days. Overtime is monetary compensation for all hours worked in one workweek above 40 hours. The current overtime wage is 1.5 times the normal hourly rate, which is what you would pay for all hours worked above 40. For example, if the hourly wage of an employee is $20, the overtime rate would be $30 per hour.

EmployeeIssues.com notes that, "Employers may pay eligible employees by some other method than hourly, such as by piecework or annual salary. But in any case, employers must still calculate overtime pay based on the hours eligible employees work per workweek."

Here are the general criteria regarding overtime, again according to EmployeeIssues.com:

"Overtime pay is due on the regularly-scheduled paydays for which employees earned it. For example, if an employer pays regular wages every Friday, then every Friday the overtime pay employees earned in the same workweek is also due and payable.

"Non-management, 'blue-collar' hourly, and salaried employees who perform manual labor for the types of organizations listed below are eligible for overtime pay. 'White-collar' hourly and salaried employees who work for the types of organizations listed below and earn less than $455 weekly (or less than $910 biweekly or $1971.66 monthly) are also broadly eligible."

- Any engaged in interstate commerce
- Any that gross $500,000 or more annually
- Federal, state, and local government agencies
- Hospitals and other institutions engaged in the care of sick, aged, or mentally ill people
- Educational institutions

EmployeeIssues.com also notes that job titles have no relevance when determining eligibility for overtime pay. Overtime eligibility is determined based on "occupations, wages or salaries, and job duties," although they note that exceptions may apply.

Breaking down the overtime law even further, the information on EmployeeIssues.com continues with the definition of those who are exempt from overtime pay—those employees who do not receive overtime pay. They state that:

"Generally, employers may classify the following types of employees as exempt from (not eligible for) overtime pay:

- White-collar executive, administrative, and professional employees who earn more than $455 per week and regularly exercise discretion and independent judgment with respect to matters of significance.

- Employees who earn $100,000 or more per year, and also customarily and regularly perform any one or more of the exempt duties or responsibilities of executive, administrative, or professional employees.
- Certain computer professionals who earn more than $455 in weekly salaries or $27.63 in hourly wages, depending on their specific job duties." (EmployeeIssues.com, 2008)

Now of course, the list of variables that are taken into account with regard to who is and who is not eligible for overtime is long, and gets longer with each passing revision of the tax code. The information provided above by EmployeeIssues.com is a general overview of the federal tax laws that relate to overtime issues. Please note that state laws may vary from those listed above and may supersede federal tax law, as well. When in doubt, consult with financial or legal counsel for additional information and guidance.

Social Security Taxes

The Social Security Administration splits up who pays what between the employer and employee. Each party pays 50 percent of the total percentage noted in the withholding list above (12.4). The current cap for Social Security withholdings is $97,500 annually, according to the Social Security Administration's website. If you are considered "self employed," you are required to pay the full amount, as you are both the employer and employee. (Social Security Administration, 2008)

Social Security taxes, while currently paying for those withdrawing the money, were designed to be used to ensure that each individual, upon retirement, would have some income and not be left without money when they're unable to work. In recent times, due to lack of money in the Social Security coffer and the ability of many of us to invest better than the government does, some people have called for employees to have a choice as to whether to invest in higher-yield funds or traditional Social Security benefits, while still paying into the system for those who will need it soon.

Bill Pay Services

Bill pay services are yet another aspect of business checking and payroll services. Many of us use bill pay services, like Bank of America's "e-bill" service, to pay everything from utilities to credit card bills. But businesses have the same options to pay their bills online. Be careful of companies now putting corporate credit cards into "corp accounts" that must be paid instead of the credit card company (I recently ran into an issue here myself). You should use a banking organization that allows you to set up bill pay, and not just if your company accepts electronic payments but also if it requires mailed cashier's checks. Let the bank handle all of this. Since most online banking systems don't show you pending payments in your balances, I always recommend using a secondary system that also allows you to categorize payments for tax purposes and for expenditure tracking and allocation.

Financial Management

Everything we have talked about so far rolls up under the umbrella of financial management. You will need to manage all aspects of your finances, and you need to plan for the costs of each.

Payroll Taxes

We already noted that having employees is costly. If you create a business plan that doesn't assume you will have employees in year two and then you need them, revise your plan to include the new costs you will incur as a result of this decision; for instance, the cost of training your new employee(s), the cost of payroll services, uniform costs (as applicable), additional taxes that you as the employer must pay (Social Security, Medicare, etc.), and additional insurance costs (workers' compensation, etc.). More information on this is available in Chapter 7 as well.

Some business owners worry that as employees change their withholdings, it will impact their bottom line. It won't, because you either pay the government or the employee. There is no need to make adjustments based on withholding changes.

Budgeting

It seems daunting to think of everything you need to budget for your business. One thing you can do is ask other business owners what they didn't budget for that they learned later was a mistake—particularly the most costly ones. Of course, not all of these will apply to your business.

Some items to budget for that you may not have thought about:

- Bonuses for jobs that are above and beyond the call of duty
- Overtime
- Unforeseen office supplies (like water, or whatever you want to offer at your office)
- Healthcare
- Sick time
- Temporary workers
- Gifts (birthdays, holidays)
- Specialized training or certifications (notary training, etc.)
- Additional technology (more computers, printers, etc.)
- Additional space
- Uniforms

Corporate and Sole Proprietor Taxes

Regardless of what your business is created as (sole proprietorship, partnership, LLC, etc.), you will have to file business taxes from its inception. Be sure that you note the actual date you started business, because all costs are prorated in year one based on how many days you were in business that year.

Sole proprietors use what is called pass-through income; the income is noted on a Schedule C and passed through to the individual. Sole proprietors still take all business deductions—including depreciation, and so on—in their business, just like corporations do. Some note that the taxes can be higher because personal income tax is higher than most corporate tax, depending on the income of the business. Sole proprietors usually only need to file once per year on their annual tax return, depending on annual profit or income, though many scenarios may make it necessary to file quarterly—many sole proprietors file quarterly no matter what. Ask your tax authority on whether you need to file yearly or more often.

Corporations file corporate tax returns, often at a lower tax rate than those who file as self employed (sole proprietors). As there are many variations of legal structure, each with their own set of determinant factors with regard to taxability, consult with a tax attorney for more information on the tax implications of each.

Insurance

Last but not least of your cost and budget requirements is insurance; everything from employee insurance you provide to business insurance to disability insurance for yourself.

I recommend asking a lawyer and an insurance specialist what is necessary for a business owner. Personally, I have umbrella insurance (it covers all of my properties), I require anyone driving my cars for business to have personal insurance (something you should always do), liability insurance (how much depends on what you do and your risk level), and disability insurance for yourself should you get sick.

Some other common insurance plans include:

- Property insurance—protection for your property from damage/loss.
- Legal liability—product and general.
- Workers' Compensation—protection in case of an on-the-job accident.
- Key person loss—especially important for the small business with one or two "key" individuals, without whom would cease to exist or suffer a large loss to business.
- Business interruption—this policy pays the business, should something occur that prevents the business from operating.
- E-commerce insurance—this is a more recent trend. This policy protects the business should it suffer a great loss of its Internet presence due to hackers or other problems.

Final Thoughts

As a final note and word of caution, the information contained within this chapter is simply a starting point of reference. There is a lot that goes into your business for payroll, taxes, hiring employees, managing healthcare, and so on.

The data that I have presented, with regard to laws, regulations, tax rates, etc., can change at any point, with or without notice. Please always consult with legal and financial counsel, in addition to contacting the IRS and your local governing bodies regarding all applicable laws and regulations that you will be held to. The IRS and the government are two entities you do not want to mess around with!

9

Advertising and Marketing Your Business

Without advertising and marketing, your business may be doomed. Word of mouth is a form of marketing—it is the way that most businesses truly grow—in which people spread the word and say good things about your business. Word of mouth can make or break a company. Ask any restaurateur what happens if someone gets sick from their restaurant or a neighbor has a bad experience. There are many variations of this, but a good friend who is also an entrepreneur said it best: One unhappy person will tell ten; one happy person will tell two.

In this chapter, we'll look at what's available for you to use to market and advertise your business; and the fundamental differences between different options. We will examine the effectiveness of common techniques and the details of lesser known alternatives. We will learn from those who have been successful what works—and from those who haven't, what doesn't.

Using Online Tools

In the Internet era, we have a lot of online tools available to us to advertise businesses, many at little to no cost. Some online advertising tools are more effective than others; just as many are significantly more expensive than they were even a year ago and may not necessarily provide the bang for the buck you expect.

First and foremost, have a website! Even if it's for informational and contact purposes, testimonials, and so on—have a web presence. For many Gen Xers and Gen Yers, this can legitimize your business, particularly if you offer support (like product manuals in PDF form) or products (in an online catalogue or store) available in a purely online format. As the Internet expands (yes, it is still growing) Gen Xers and Gen Yers are starting to look at whether or not a company has a website as a credential of legitimacy—taking the standpoint of "If they don't have a website, they can't be a very good establishment."

It's important to note that most online buyers do not want to fax or e-mail an order. They want an immediate placement, an e-mail confirmation, and that item crossed off the to-do list. If you're going to only offer the option to fax in an order, don't bother offering products online. Of course, you can always offer faxing as an option, just ideally not your customer's only option.

How in depth and what type of online presence you have is highly dependent on the generation and demographic you are after. People that buy entirely or almost entirely online are usually younger or are limited on spare time. They are less afraid of giving information online, and they have credit cards or online PayPal accounts. In essence, they grew up with the Internet and it is a part of their normal daily lives. The fear factor is gone or dissipated because they intuitively know what to look for to make sure a site is secure.

What Your Buyers Are Looking For

If your target generation is Gen Yers, for instance, you will want to incorporate something more engaging on your website; product reviews, blogs, videos, and so on. If your target is the Boomer generation, offer security, convenience, and service. Understanding your target is critical here.

You need to know more than the generation, though. You need to know what that demographic—which includes age, income levels, educational levels, and so on—really wants and what the market for them is doing (it might be great for

Boomers but not so great for new parents, for instance). Participate in the public arena online if it's within your target demographic, understand through surveys and asking your buyers what they really want, read trade publications, and watch for what is hot in the demographic you sell to. Don't be afraid to try something new, either. You can test the waters pretty easily if product development isn't required. For example, if you want to know how well a new color of a handbag you created goes over, try selling 1 or 2 in a boutique store. If you want to know how many people will buy a new digital camera bag you are selling, put it online on eBay and see what happens.

Keeping Tabs on the Market

You are undoubtedly keeping tabs on the market. You are watching the competition and you are reading up on the latest and greatest in your industry. This is one of many ways to keep tabs on the market and is essential to do regardless of what business you are in. If you are in the technical business for instance or marketing to the Gen Yers you might want to read different magazines than if you are running a travel business for executives.

A great way to increase the usefulness of your website and increase the spotlight on your own business is to share the latest developments with regard to products and services within your area of choice. If, for example, you are selling bath salts, and you are constantly updating the latest information on bath salts and other complementary products, your customers (lovers of bath salts) will be more apt to visit your website to see "what's new" on the market, which in-turn will increase your website traffic, consequently increasing the chances of purchases by those visitors.

Participating in the Public Online Arena

If your demographic is online a lot, you will want to participate in the public online arena. What does this mean? Blogging yourself, responding to blogs, creating an expert site where you offer advice as a go-to person for knowledge on the subject (or want to become one to create loyal buyers and build your reputation), and asking consumers online what they think of your product or service—and being prepared to take the good with the bad.

Another thing I find very helpful is lurking. This doesn't sound nearly as bad as you think! For instance, one of my market demographics is individuals who want to be online teachers. I have subscribed to several forums where lots of online teachers hang out—and those who aren't quite there yet but really want to be. It gives me their perspective, their interests, their ideas, and their opinions—but I don't reply to anything. If I did, then the Hawthorne Effect may apply—when people modify their behavior because they know others are watching. I'd much rather lurk—I learn more that way. You can become a lurker, too.

Regardless of how you choose to do it, set aside a few minutes per day to blog, and to write, post, and answer Q&As for your customers. They will turn to you as an expert, and even if you are a bit higher priced, they will remain loyal to you if they value your expertise.

Asking Questions of Your Potential Buyers

This category goes beyond potential buyers to people who have returned product to you, too—or asked for any sort of refund. I'll go back to one of my favorite companies, Zappos. When you click the button for your automated return and free shipping label from Zappos.com, you are asked a few simple questions that are entirely optional, but many of us feel inclined to answer anyway, to thank Zappos for making our returns no-hassle. These questions are product reviews (was the product true to size? true to width?) as well as what Zappos could have done to prevent the return, and if the consumer will shop with Zappos again. The consumer feels a part of the process—as though Zappos didn't really want the consumer to be unhappy and genuinely cared about his or her feedback. My guess is they do something positive with the information, because their site and service only improves with time.

What about potential buyers? I frequently create surveys, like the one for this book, that inquire as to what my readers want to see in a book—and then ask them questions to help others in their entrepreneurial boat. I use two tools: Zoomerang and Survey Monkey. They are available respectively at www. zoomerang.com and www.surveymonkey.com. Creating and collecting surveys is super simple, and you are given URLs you can insert into newsletters, e-mails, solicitations, websites, and so on. Check out these tools and, using their templates, get some ideas on what you could survey your group about—perhaps the need for a new product or service, or how much they would be willing to pay for upgrades. I generally offer something in return for completing a survey. I want consumers to know I value not only their opinion but their time, too.

Trade Publications

Trade publications are widely varied—from scholarly peer-reviewed journals for various disciplines to magazines that those in a particular trade read regularly. You can read them and contribute to them also. For instance, I'm a contributing writer—a Business Correspondent—for *MultiHousing Professional* magazine. I started writing for Military.com as well, which has led to becoming a regularly weekly contributor and much more visibility in my discipline. I enjoy getting ideas and thoughts off my chest and into the hands of the public who need good, solid, accurate information. I also build my credibility this way.

If you don't know how to start, consider becoming an about.com writer (more information is available on their website) or writing a column for free. Most newsletter editors gladly seek out writers or columnists and will let you put your website at the end.

I also read magazines and encourage you to do so, too. Are you in the retail fashion business? See what the models and celebrities are wearing by picking up *US Weekly*. Are you into electronic gadgets? See what the Gen Yers think is the hottest new trend in *Wired* magazine. These inexpensive, tax deductible expenses can do nothing but educate you about your demographic and your business.

Watching What's Hot in the New Generations

Unless your demographic and generation is going to buy from you forever, you will need to constantly innovate for the next generation. If you are a business owner who has created walkers for the elderly, that doesn't mean you cannot find something that the new generation needs—or perhaps cool walkers that the new generation would want to buy their grandparents as a birthday gift. Try to get creative with what the new generation thinks is innovative.

The serial entrepreneur is so excited about innovating and creating businesses that often her expertise is in creating businesses and not in a specific type of business. I personally am a serial entrepreneur and proud to be!

Don't know how to tap the other generations for what they want? Try a survey on your website or conduct research into the demographic you are interested in. You can also pay for a research company to conduct the research for you.

Don't Be Afraid of Something New!

When in doubt, don't be afraid to try something new! I've had everything from 30-day T-shirt businesses to long-term real estate analysis companies. Some things stick; some don't. Some are long-term prospects; others are short-term endeavors to keep boredom from creeping in.

Advertising—What Pays and What Doesn't

You have a lot of advertising opportunities available to you. But what pays and what doesn't? You want the biggest bang for the buck, of course. But if you think advertisers are going to tell you the return on investment, think again!

Here are some common methods of advertising that seem to pay off for many business owners:

- Personal client gifts (birthdays, Christmas, etc.). Keep track of recurring clients' important information, like birthdays, anniversaries, etc. Believe me, they will notice that you remembered!
- Greeting cards on specific important days or for personal events.
- Handwritten thank you notes. If your business is product driven, consider including one with each order, no matter how large or small the order is.
- Paying attention to specific likes and dislikes. Use this information to sell complementary products and services and recommend "the latest and greatest."
- Free stuff (to a certain crowd—not everyone thinks free stuff is good … some think it waters down your brand, or consider it to be "clutter" or "junk").
- Discounts that rarely occur. If you rarely if ever discount your goods or merchandise, than an unusual sale is important. Think about Nordstrom's half-yearly sale for women and children. People wait all year for a sale that occurs every six months because the discounts apply to new merchandise and not just stale merchandise—something Nordstrom rarely does.

- Connecting with established businesses, and bouncing both ideas and customers off of one another.

- Referrals and rewards. It is best practice to reward both the referred and the referrer—get the two talking about you.

- Complimentary items ("freebies") that will keep your customers coming back for more. Every time I order from x10.com I get "x10 bucks" that expire. While I get annoying reminders about those expirations, they do entice me to get some other cool gadgets I've been wanting.

- Informative newsletters. Make sure you get consent before sending out a barrage of e-mails to your customers. Also, include an "opt-out" method within each newsletter you send; make sure it is easy to find, and don't wait the allowable 10 days to take someone out of the mailing, either.

Print Advertising

Print advertising is on a rapid descent in America. Just a few short years ago, print advertising started to see a decline as it was replaced by web-placed ads, which were cheap and effective. Today, web advertising isn't as cheap; but print advertising is even less effective.

I only recommend print if your demographic still reads the papers. Each newspaper usually has an advertising demographic section on their website or available by phone. If it's precisely your target, go for it. Otherwise, stick with something more useful and less expensive.

Phone Book Ads

Years after I have closed a business, the yellow pages from various providers still call; which leads me to wonder—if they don't know I'm not in business under that name, how much can I rely on their service as a consumer? Not so much. Some companies use online referral services on the web, like Service Magic and others. But for the most part, most individuals don't go to the phone book unless they are more traditional buyers. Most Gen X and Gen Yers use online 411 and yellow pages services, or simply Google the city plus the service or product they want.

If you think about it, a phone book is obsolete the minute it is printed. Businesses come and go on a daily, even hourly basis, but the trusty yellow pages are only updated once a year.

Microsoft founder and president, Bill Gates, provided this prediction in his annual address in the spring of 2008: "Yellow page usage among people, say, below 50, will drop to zero—or near zero—over the next five years." Internet yellow pages and telephone directories are quickly becoming the most frequently chosen methods for seeking out products and services, and even these methods could become obsolete at some point with the searching and categorizing algorithms of search giants like Google and Ask.com.

Now if you feel that you *must* be in your local yellow pages, consider the following before signing up:

Consider your demographic—traditional phone book usage is strongly age driven, with the majority of users being over the age of 50. If this is your target demographic, go for it!

Smaller may be better—if you absolutely must be in your local phone book, or if you can't decide, pay for a small ad. This way, you are still in the phone book, but aren't throwing money down the drain on a full-page ad that isn't going to bring you any revenue.

Another option to consider is giving your yellow pages a "test run." Sign up for an ad for one year. In the ad, place a "yellow pages discount" offer. When those who find you through the yellow pages call, they *will* ask for the discount! Track how many of these discounts you have to honor during your first year, and if the profit you make from these customers justifies the cost of running the advertisement, continue the ad for the following year. The minute the business that the ad contributes does not justify the cost of maintaining the advertisement, cancel the service. After you cancel, though, be prepared for the telemarketers to call for years, perhaps even long after you've asked to be put on the "never call me again under any circumstance" list.

Commercials and Infomercials

Who hasn't had a bout of insomnia and lain awake listening to the "$9000 monthly I made from sitting at home doing nothing!" advertisements or the infomercials for silly products that, at 3 A.M., seem like they might be useful? Many products have gotten their start with infomercials, but may be perceived as gimmicky. Think carefully about how this falls into your strategic plan before you embark on an infomercial.

Commercials are another story. With cable television, you can target your ad to a specific area code or zip code or county, depending on the cable company. I would recommend calling the company to find out what their costs are. That will of course be highly dependent on the station and the time, prime time obviously costing more money.

Local Networking and Publicity

Many people are still advocates of local business organizations, and sure, they can help. For a while I was a member of the Women's Business Association in my area. Did it result in business? A bit. But I felt awkward; and they weren't my demographic anyway. I did network and mingle with their group, but they were significantly older than I and I sensed distrust rather than embrace from them. I chose not to continue going, but to instead create my own seminars and invite people to attend at-cost, so that I could upsell products later.

Even major chains (like Bebe retail stores) hold local events for specific businesses. Mingle parties, with cocktails and appetizers, are not all that uncommon for retail establishments; nor are fashion shows for clothing companies, and so on. Even Home Depot has their local "how to" seminars that individuals in an area can attend. This helps to attract and retain loyal customers. Whether it will work for you depends on what you do for a living and what business your business is in.

Word of Mouth

Most marketers agree that word of mouth is still the most powerful tool available. The key is that the word needs to be good—and from the mouth of reliable people! So reliable people need to say good things about your company. Remember the old adage that numerous people will share a bad story but someone with a good story might, *might*, tell one other person. This holds true today, too, though with Internet reviews people are a bit more apt to write both negative and positive comments. The Internet has leveled the word of mouth playing field.

Be sure you address negative comments, and always thank referees for referrals. My insurance broker always sends a Starbucks gift card for a new client. While it's a small token, it says a lot to me—he values my business and he values my loyalty to him. As long as he continues to do a good job, I will continue to refer people to him.

This works the same way online. Many people will refer you to others through e-mail. Everything you say via e-mail needs to be very specific, thorough, and written kindly, with a purpose—even if you aren't happy you have to write it—like an apology letter to a customer that you think did you wrong. Remember that the forward button is just a click away. How many people have reposted bad letters to entire blogs? Many—too many to count. But enough to remember that what you say is very important—as is how you say it.

Tracking Leads

As you get any type of lead—whether through snail mail, online, etc.—you need to track it. You need to know where your customers—new and repeat—are coming from. One way to do this is to have people mention a code for a discount. Another is to ask plainly how the customer found you—or if you're online, to have it part of the checkout process. Also, if you have a presence online, be sure your web hosting company provides analytical information.

Using the Web as an Advertising Platform

The Internet is an incredibly powerful tool. Look at recent changes in the way the web is used—as a powerful political machine, as an incredible marketing system for the fastest growing and most profitable businesses in history—it's no wonder more and more people are looking to advertise on the Internet.

You will want to advertise to lots of individuals—locals who want to buy local, other web businesses, affiliates, companies (business to business), consumers (business to consumer), international, national—you name it! In times when the dollar is strong, your focus might be more on domestic sales than international; as the dollar weakens, this may shift to a more global focus.

One great thing about the Internet is that you can advertise to everyone and anyone, and you can accept online payments and ship anywhere—so your market is literally limitless. A large portion of this section is about teaching you how to advertise, where to advertise, key ingredients in the advertising recipe, and how to begin getting clients.

AdSense and AdWords—Google's Baby!

"Google" is synonymous with "search" for many folks; it is a household name— and for good reason. Everything from Google Maps to Google Earth to searching for the closest florist is done through this vast company with incredible reach that is constantly expanding and innovating. Google offers two programs that could be useful to the web entrepeneur: AdWords and AdSense. AdWords is for advertisers, and AdSense is for web publishers. If you go to the Google home page, select advertising programs underneath the Search section, and then select AdWords or AdSense.

AdWords targets people actively looking for information related to a particular product or service that your business sells; this means that those who visit your site from AdWords are targeted—prescreened if you will—genuine leads. The program uses CPC pricing, which means you pay when your ad is clicked on. There is an activation fee, then a per click fee. You tell Google how much you are willing to pay per click and per day. Ads for your business appear alongside or above results on the Google search results pages for Google, too, which is great for building your brand.

AdSense, on the other hand, is for web publishers to earn revenue from their websites. AdSense will deliver an ad that is targeted to content pages, and when Google SiteSearch (more information is at www.google.com/sitesearch) is added to the site, AdSense also delivers targeted ads to the search results page. This allows your company to make residual income when visitors click on ads that are associated with your business; which also means that the ads you're "selling" and making money from are targeted leads as well. Ads that appear are those relevant to your own company and your own business, and you can manage your AdSense account and track earnings online very easily.

Search Engine Placement—Is Paying for Hits Worth It?

In order to help search engines discover your website, you can do some of the following … the more the better:

- Make at least some of the content easy to subscribe to by using feed buttons, and make sure that the content is relevant.
- Use only one URL or web address rather than multiple addresses. Try not to have one for your blog and one for your company. Integrate as much as you can.
- Have your web developer enter your site into a search engine optimization (SEO) tool. This will help get your site noticed faster with the right keywords.

In general, search engine placement is worth it if your site is extremely important to the success of your business. Be sure you research which companies are going to offer guarantees and are most competitive, and ask a qualified web designer for assistance.

The Role of Web Design

The design of your website plays an incredible role in the type of business and clients that will visit your site. A Web 2.0 enabled, engaging, friendly, and easy-to-follow site will give your audience a great experience—very important for success.

You will want to find a designer who doesn't necessarily understand your business—but understands his or her own business and how to design current, modern sites. You will also want someone who makes changes quickly without wasting time. When something needs to be updated, it needs to be done immediately.

The design of the site should be friendly to persons with disabilities and the visually impaired, and should offer the visitor the ability to do simple things like change font size and display colors on the fly. The more customized the users can make the site, the more often they will visit. Integrate the Web 2.0 things we have been discussing—like blogging and networking and reviews—directly into your site, too. Users should not have to go to a separate site for this information.

Social Networking and Web 2.0

There is a pre-Web 2.0 era and a post-Web 2.0 era. Web 2.0 is dynamic, customer driven, and consumer and community focused. It doesn't stay static and is constantly changing based on user content. Blogs, MySpace, Facebook, even Amazon with its current strategy, are all Web 2.0.

But the way we advertise in these spaces, pre- and post-Web 2.0, is different. In the pre-Web 2.0 era, people still promoted their websites through newsgroups instead of blogs. Now with Web 2.0, we do what is called social broadcasting, social networking, social blogging—notice a key phrase here? You need to be sure you hire a web architect or developer who understands how to do this!

The Web 2.0 Internet generation lives in an ever-changing, online social world where they associate engagement with being able to contribute to a blog or share a video or a file or comment—they don't like being fed information with no method of remarking. They want to synchronize their cell phones and bookmark their PDAs, and their way of living revolves around this low attention span that will eventually be your consumer. This is the group spending an hour a night answering MySpace bulletins to learn more about their "top friends," and they don't have a phone at home because they are entirely mobile because they use their cell phones as their primary lines.

The Impact of Generation Y on Business

The Y Generation is having an incredible impact on business. We already know that teenagers make up a vital part of the economy in terms of spending, but Gen Yers make up a vital component of the Internet. This is this group asking for social networking, for the ability to not be "fed" information but to respond to everything, and for information to be incredibly current.

You will want to develop for this crowd even if they aren't your target market. Chances are, one day they might be—plus, this will keep your site fresh and modern.

Responding to Negativity on the 'Net

Good marketing entrepreneurs know that having bad information out there unresponded to is far worse than bad information you do respond to. Rather than deleting negative posts, respond to them based on what you are doing—or have done—to rectify the situation and follow up with a personal response to the person posting also. This goes a long way in the online community.

Many business owners, especially hoteliers and restaurant owners, are inclined to post fake reviewers glorifying their food or their hotel rooms. Not only do others see right through this, but one glowing review amidst a bunch of bad ones will not help anything and may make the situation worse if others perceive that the owner may have posted it. Keep the online marketplace honest. Respond to negative posts so that those reading the posts know that you take pride in your business and you care about your consumers—and that the good reviews probably aren't bogus. We often learn more from negative feedback than we do from knowing what we're doing right.

Blogging

Blogging is one way to share information with the world, and it's read and picked up by lots of different engines that are constantly seeking out your specific topic. Often content for other blogs is reposted by blog originators, so your material becomes "viral" very quickly—a good thing for public relations and marketing for any company! I ran into this myself when I posted a controversial post on my blog about real estate agents hindering the market recovery. It was reposted on thousands of blogs—mostly by angry real estate agents (they aren't my target audience anyway!). As a result, hundreds of for sale by owner and investor sites also picked it up as an article that validated their message, and my website hits doubled over the following week. If you run a blog and use an RSS feed (meaning the material can be automatically fed into other blogs) it can be an incredibly rich and powerful marketing tool for your business.

A blog has multiple elements in play, each one making the blog special, unique, and perhaps most importantly, identifiable to the blogging community and to the individuals that post on there.

One element is the title, which is the headline of the post. Next is the body of the blog post, which contains the content you want viewers to read consistently, and this is often referred to as the element that is "pushed." (Babb & Lazo, 2007) The post has a date and time, and it may optionally include comments, categories, and/or trackbacks that refer to the original entry. (Wikipedia, 2006) The interactivity is what sets this apart from traditional newspapers.

> You are not allowed to post copyrighted material in your blog without first obtaining permission from the original creator or the person who owns the copyright. Sure, First Amendment rights can come into play with regard to the fair use doctrine, but this does not give anyone free reign in posting. After learning this lesson the hard way and having my own material copied, I now put a copyright notation on anything I don't want replicated out there on the Internet.

Blogs are often seen as a way for nonmainstream media to get around the "filter" that exists in the mainstream today. Recently mainstreamers have also joined the "blogosphere" (the community of blogs and bloggers) and have created blogs themselves. A published blog software comparison chart available at www.ojr.org/ojr/images/blog_software_comparison.cfm shows you lots of various options for bloggers to host and maintain their web logs. Blogs are a great way to market your expertise and your services, to share your knowledge with others, and to build a sense of loyalty if you're offering great information. I see this happen all the time on my car site forums. The shops that do work take pictures of how to do repairs and modifications yourself, share them online for free, participate in car rallies, and give away product, and they build an incredible base of followers who buy even if their prices are higher than their competition!

Just as with the web in its infancy, there really are no rules for how to decide to set up and host your own work. As noted in my coauthored book on blogs and podcasts, "Keep in mind that blogs and podcasts are tools, not solutions. This means that if you have something meaningful to say, they can help you say it in an exciting and innovative way. However, if your words are not of much value to start with, they probably will not add value to them." (Babb & Lazo, 2007)

Online Advertising That Works (and Some That Don't)

There are two major types of advertising online. The first is cost-per-click advertising, or CPC. This is the most common method of advertising on the web, and when you think of buying online ads, this is what most have in mind. Since many users are frustrated with banner ads and since they're relatively invisible to most people now (think ad overload), this method allows you to only pay when the person actually clicks on the ad, which is a benefit. Some have even called for boycotts against sites that have too many ads because they are annoying to users, so you don't want to pay for an ad no one wants to click on.

Generally you can expect to pay more for a CPC ad campaign, but it's targeted and more effective. You also set a price ceiling—a maximum amount you will pay each month—so that you can balance and protect your fees each month or year. This will help you with budgeting as well. Your ads automatically run until the number of click-thrus you paid for is reached.

In the cost-per-action (CPA) type of advertising, you pay for performance. You can either pay per impression, per click, or whatever other option is valuable to you and that the advertiser offers. CPC advertising is popular but it can be very costly; CPA-based advertising means you won't pay unless you actually make a sale from the company's referring ad. Sometimes the advertisers will charge you for registrations or subscriptions (even if subscribing is free) because it means more targeted leads for you—so read the contract carefully.

When you select this type of advertising, your ad is put into rotation and it begins to display as soon as it's added. You decide what actions you will pay for—sale, registrations, newsletters, etc.—and then budget for it. If you pay for 100 sales, your ad will continue displaying until that is reached. If the ad attracts a lot of people, you'll be paying quite a bit, but you are getting customers in the process.

You should use this method if you want to test out your ad before starting a large advertising campaign online. This will let you see how many people actually purchase your products after viewing your ad; if you want to go with bigger CPC- or CPM-based ads later, at least you'll have the ad type, graphics, wording, etc., fine tuned.

Cost-per-impressions is another effective way to reach customers. Instead of paying per click or per sale, you pay for a set number of impressions (say 2,000)—an impression being an appearance on a website. Unfortunately, though, as click-thru rates go down in general (less people are clicking on ads), this may not help you much. You need to monitor those clicks to see if this is a worthwhile method for you by asking for information from the companies you buy advertising with and by looking at statistics from your own website hosting company.

Interestingly enough, we are seeing that text-based ads often receive more attention and more click-thrus than banner ads. That probably seems odd, since banners are graphical and we assume people would prefer to click on a graphic. Data shows, though, that the average view time for a text-based ad is about 7 seconds (people have to read it!), while for a graphical ad is about 1.6 seconds. If you decide to pay for an ad, you may see if the site you're advertising on offers text-based advertising. Also, if your keywords are very popular and expensive, CPM-based methods might be better for you.

SURVEY SAYS

What do our survey respondents say about advertising and marketing? Most advertise on websites and most indicate that they had to find sites with a demonstrated need for their product. Some used websites only for advertising, but this was rare. Some used television and radio ads as well; this was also rarely noted, though, due to expense. Most noted that they relied on word of mouth and made sure to gain new clients, and that they touched base 7 to 10 times before they got new business from a current client. Some owners used networking groups and their Chamber of Commerce; others got into a business where main suppliers shut out all competition. Several owners noted that the yellow pages is a "waste of money" and yellow pages customers are "too poor to pay you anyway." Many noted they would not use their last name in the title (due to divorce and remarriage—a lesson I had to learn myself!) and others noted that sheer persistence got them good advertising. Mass-market mailings were a part of many business owners' repertoire, and others noted that it is vital to have fun in sharing your business with others, and said that research could not be understated! Most business owners noted that their high-quality product created more sales than anything else that they did. Many attended speaking engagements as a guest to get more clients and network.

Also, you should ask about having your ad appear on a page that matters to your particular customer base. Click-thru ratios improve if the audience is targeted rather than general. You should be able to find good advertising options if you ask the advertiser; they want your ad bucks and are willing to make modifications to get them. I recommend buying in low minimums first, so that you can see if the ad campaign is going to work before you pay a lot for it. Do your homework, don't pay for a large amount of impressions up front, and be sure you are very clear on your budget! Make sure the contract clearly states your maximum amount paid out monthly. You don't want any large surprises on your credit card bill.

Marketing Hooks

We have lots of marketing hooks out there to help us be successful—everything from mottos to slogans to advertising campaigns to bumper stickers! The goal is to get your name synonymous with the product or service for your area or region, but not so much so that you become a commodity (think Rollerblade or Xerox).

Here are some quick tips for a successful marketing campaign:

- Keep the message consistent
- Maintain your "sound level" consistently (the amount of info your customers receive about your company)
- Don't be afraid to get creative
- Turn negative feedback into positive experiences for individual consumers
- Encourage honesty with your customers
- Don't overwhelm customers with junk of any sort
- Make every contact with the client worth their while

There are differences between advertising and marketing. Marketing is the positioning of a business; it's a strategy that encompasses advertising campaigns, public relations, and every other tool you use to get word out about your company and its capabilities.

Advertising stems from ads—whether online or more traditional—and includes items like phone book entries, billboards, etc. You can advertise your business in general, a specific promotion, a specific product or service, or everything at one time.

The 1,000-Pound Gorilla

I'm not referring to the SEO or job search sites! I'm referring to the difficulty in handling events that are unexpected—like a large credit card bill or the death of a loved one. Sometimes these thousand-pound gorillas, known as T-P-Gs, can overwhelm and even destroy a company. This is why it's so important to have contingency plans. Some suggest that you can market your way through them and many people can and have. From a financial perspective, you need to plan for the unexpected and the unplanned—have savings, or as some call it, a failure fund. It isn't fun to think of failing before you even begin, but we must contingency plan to have enough peace of mind to focus full time on our business.

From a marketing perspective, if you're going to use any aspect of guerilla marketing, make it a big one!

What Guerilla Marketing Can Bring to Your Business

Essentially, guerilla marketing is using unique tactics to market your business—some would even suggest that it is a way to shock your buyers with unique or unexpected information or advertising to your client by unique means. The term was originally coined back in 1984 by Jay Conrad Levinson in a book titled *Guerilla Marketing*, suggesting that by focusing all of your time, energy, and creativity on unconventional promotions on a very low budget was better than big marketing plans for many businesses. The term has come to mean general unconventional marketing methods.

This method was specifically engineered by Levinson for small businesses or entrepreneurs, and is based on psychology. Your investment isn't so much money as it is time and creativity. If you're not creative, you might have to hire this out—or use another method. In this technique, you concentrate on how many new relationships are made in a given period, and work toward bigger sales with existing clients rather than getting new clients. The idea is that, ultimately, those existing customers will refer you to more clients and your business will boom. Levinson also suggested that you forget about competition and concentrate on your core, and on cooperation with other businesses—partnerships that make both businesses stronger.

How to Use Guerilla Tactics

So what can you do right away to employ some of these guerilla techniques? They sound good right? Well for starters, you can use viral marketing on the Internet through social networks. Create a Facebook page and a MySpace page for your business, and get on LinkedIn. Send great deals to existing clients to upsell; pay for referrals or incentivize those who refer others to you. Some start grassroots marketing campaigns, with others marketing on their behalf. Some use more subtle product placement to avoid having their products get stale or their ads go unheard. If your target audience needs a bit of a reminder that you exist (maybe your product line is *routine* or a commodity, or you have a difficult-to-reach demographic) you might employ some of these tactics to get your small business going.

> Remember that creating press releases, blogging, and putting up a MySpace account is all free! E-mailing your friends about your new business and asking them to tell 10 of their closest friends about it is free as well!

Try some alternative marketing techniques, like posting videos or round table events with some humor on YouTube, or throwing a beach ball around a ballpark with your company's name on it.

Get creative and give it a shot. It's time consuming, but if you're in the early phase of your business, you probably have more time on your hands than you do money.

Final Thoughts

Marketing online and using the Internet is no longer an option even for more traditional companies; it is absolutely mandatory—a requirement even. A web presence, whether intricate or simple, allows you to add another demographic to your mix. Advertising online and partnering with organizations and businesses that share similar customers is a very effective way to help get your business moving and buyers coming your way.

10

Grow, Baby, Grow!

By this point, you've started your business, you're moving along nicely in your business plan, and you're trying to figure out what to do next.

Obviously you want to meet your financial and personal objectives for this business. You don't want to go back into your unemployed or underemployed Corporate America status. You don't want to go back to working for someone else.

But at the same time, you also recognize that without forward progress, your business will stagnate. You need to begin to think about how you want to grow your baby, although it is possible that it is growing rapidly on its own.

In this chapter, we will discuss many of the growth opportunities that small businesses have, and many ways they can expand not only their target market but their reach within already existing pathways.

Moving Your Business Ahead

You want to move your business ahead—but what that means to you might differ based on your plan. Moving ahead might mean expanding your existing service offerings. It might mean tapping into a new demographic. It might mean taking a brick-and-mortar business online in a supplementary fashion, or vice versa. It might mean dismantling your online store altogether for a more traditional store, based on your clientele. One thing is certain, and that is that change is imminent. The sooner you embrace it, the better.

In our survey, the percentage of people who said their business was growing as expected or slower than expected was identical—each with 43.8 percent. The other 12.5 percent noted that their business was growing faster than expected. Some of those who noted slower growth indicated that they blamed the economy; others indicated that their own expectations were inaccurate. One insightful participant noted that education and experience were very important to growth, as well as producing high-quality, consistent results.

Evaluating Competition

To get started with your advance into new markets, your changing demographic, your modified business practices, and your new products and services, you need to do another evaluation—take a fresh look at your existing products and services and at your competition. What do you want to offer and where is that market base currently going to get it? Are they going to existing competitors or new ones? Document your findings carefully. You may need to go through the funding process again, after your business is established, to get additional income for your added growth potential. If you have earned income you can reinvest in the business, you will want to get another accurate assessment of your new market and new opportunities so you can hit the ground running with the best information. Even if you don't find yourself having to seek out additional investors and funding, it is advisable that you update your business plan to reflect your change in goals and update the section on where you are starting from. This will also help you figure out where you're going—which is essential to actually getting there. It also helps to motivate you when you look back and see where you've been.

Knowing Your Market

One traditional way to "know your market" and know your business is with an "old school tool" we call a SWOT analysis. SWOT stands for Strengths, Weaknesses, Opportunities, and Threats. First described in the 1960s (I told you it was antiquated!) by Edmund Learned, C. Roland Christensen, Kenneth Andrews, and William Guth in *Business Policy, Text and Cases*, the SWOT analysis became more popular and widely used when the General Electric Growth Council used a similar assessment in the 1980s. Notably, according to NetMBA. com, experts indicate that it has the most impact when you have very little time to analyze a very complex problem or situation, so you should use it when you need to grow rapidly and foresee or notice a problem or issue standing in your way.

Taking it at its simplest form, you would do the following for a SWOT analysis:

First, look at the internal workings of your business. Identify the strengths and weaknesses of your company—your particular business operation. Think about your desires to move forward, too, and consider whatever might hinder that growth as a weakness. Then look at the external environment. Look at opportunities for your business, and threats to your company. This makes up the SWOT profile.

When you do an internal and external analysis, I highly recommend that you bring your team together—your partners, colleagues, and those people you trust—to give you honest advice. This process can produce a lot of information, and much of it may not be relevant. Part of your job is to sort through what is and what isn't.

Now here is the key—use the strengths to build on from a foundational perspective; use them as your competitive advantage. Look at those internal weaknesses that may keep you from realizing this full benefit, advantage, or competency in the marketplace. When you identify weaknesses, it is vital that you determine their threat level. If they are a significant threat, it is time to brainstorm

This SWOT analysis has to have purpose—it needs to lead into your strategic plan. Now that you have a solid business plan, your strategic plan will be an update to that—a road map for moving forward! Excited yet?

with your team and trusted partners on how to avoid disaster. If it is minor, you can probably move through it with small modifications to your business plan or product.

Look at the potential threats as well as opportunities; minimize the threats by taking a proactive approach and capitalize on all opportunities. This is a good time to revisit your business plan and verify that the fundamental assumptions you documented haven't changed.

When you do the internal (strengths and weaknesses) analysis, you are going to want to focus on many things. Here is a list from NetMBA to get you started:

- Culture
- Image of your business
- Your key staff
- Natural resources you have access to
- Experience
- Efficiencies
- Brand awareness
- Market share
- Resources—think of everything from human to financial
- Exclusivity—contracts, patents, trademarks, trade secrets, and so on
  (I highly recommend going through the NetMBA.com website for more information on a variety of these topics.)

Now you move on to the external analysis. You want to understand everything that could be not only a threat, but a perceived threat—often equally, or even weighted more importantly as you grow your business. This is where you look at things like the external environment, taxes, market conditions, technology that may change your business, political climates, regulation and legislative practices (those in effect now and those expected down the line), partners, societal changes (including generational differences), and so on.

Flexibility

When you decided you wanted to be an entrepreneur, you probably knew you'd need to be flexible. Just how flexible you can be is dependent on a number of things—your human and capital resources, your current efficiencies and capabilities, the marketplace in which your business is operating, and so on. To determine how flexible you can be, you will need to assess many things, including:

- How much available capital you have
- The amount of resources you can spend on your business's advancement
- How much of your profits you can pour into new ventures
- Your cash reserves
- How conservative you wish to be in your advancement
- Your understanding of the areas you want to expand into
- The knowledge of your team—and if you don't have one, whether you will need one to grow
- Your personal situation, individual or familial needs, and what you want out of your work

Once you assess these components, you can create a strategic plan that will allow you the flexibility as well as the growth path to be successful.

The Role of the Global Markets in Today's Economy

Global markets have had a significant impact on all businesses in the United States and abroad; there is a good possibility that whatever business expansion you are planning will involve an overseas market that is as yet untapped, a new area for you, one that builds on increasing sales, or one that stems from a weaker dollar.

Throughout 2007 and 2008, as interest rates decreased or stalled, we saw the value of the dollar fall (with some months as exceptions) compared to the British pound and the euro, as well as most other currencies. As a result, overseas demand was a major factor in keeping GDP up for the 2007 and 2008 government reported numbers.

Some consider this to be frightening and damaging to their business; others know how to capitalize on it. I want you to be in that latter group—so here is how you do it!

First, realize that the value of the dollar will rise and fall based on a number of factors. These include, but are certainly not limited to: interest rates set by the Federal Reserve (the Fed or FOMC), interest rates set by other world banks, expanding demand in other nations, and the global demand of commodities. Know that today's well of wealth could dry up tomorrow and we could be back to a U.S.-based market, so you should be constantly reassessing where you are strategically and where your demand is coming from.

> It is important to watch not only demand from other nations, but demand from various states or even counties. The more demographic information you have about your clients, the better. Watch where your sales and website hits are coming from. If you are a computer reseller, for instance, you may find that computer sales in Midwestern states is higher than the South—and then you need to find out why. You might discover, upon asking your customers, that a large Internet service provider just offered bulk high-speed Internet discounts and people are cashing in—generating demand you had not expected. You will then want to begin an immediate marketing campaign to that segment.

Once you begin to expect the unexpected, as the saying goes, you'll be better prepared for whatever growth strategy you decide to move forward with.

Demand from Overseas

Demand from other nations has been consistently rising for many years; some economists say decades. This is bound to continue as many countries become more capitalistic and democratic. I recall visiting a small farm town in China three years ago that had state-of-the-art computers, but illness-invoking food and water. It was a dichotomy of all dichotomies. They had relatively quick Internet access, great computers, but I couldn't drink the water. This is an example of how much these areas are growing in the demands for commerce, and trade with the United States.

Many of these nations are not only experiencing record demand for U.S. products (and our dollar dropping in value increases this demand because it makes our products cheaper), but they're experiencing incredible inflation within their own countries. Strong global demand is coming from China, Brazil, Russia, Mexico, Asia, South America, and the Middle East among many others.

In November 2007, *BusinessWeek* had a fantastic article written by James Cooper about this foreign demand helping U.S. businesses just when they needed it. The demand helped turn around a trade gap we had been experiencing for years. You need to be prepared for and take advantage of this.

How do you do that? Good question! Answers will follow!

Working with International Clients—No Matter What

The first thing you need to realize is that you will probably be working with international clients no matter what you do. Whether you are a wood supplier or a farmer or a supplier of office printers, global demand will impact you.

If your company is offering products, you need to be able and capable of fulfilling and handling overseas clients and customers. To do this, you need to be able to ship to their countries. It seems simple enough, but many U.S.-based small businesses feel that overseas customs and shipping requirements are daunting. Thankfully the USPS, UPS, and FedEx have made this much easier by providing online forms for small businesses. Don't let shipping deter you.

Next, you need to be able to accept credit cards. You also need to ask your bank how they calculate foreign exchange rates, and then decide what your pricing will be for international customers based on that exchange rate. For instance, if the value of a peso to a dollar is 11:1, the bank may give you 13:1 or use a different index altogether. Find out what they're using, and find a different merchant to process international orders if you aren't getting a decent price.

Remember that Canada and Mexico are the United States' two biggest trading partners, and small businesses are no exception. Shipping to these areas and working with these clients may mean developing a Spanish version of your website, too. Think globally!

What is selling overseas? Primarily products that have an American stigma, such as Coca Cola, Nike, Levi's, and so on. But the service sector is rising fast, and particularly in business services, education, and medical treatment. These are strong areas for businesses in the United States to grow internationally.

International Customs and Cultural Expectations

When you work with anyone internationally, you will need to work within their culture and expectations. Rather than get a feel for this on the fly, I recommend that you read up on each particular country you intend to market to or do business with, and make an educated determination as to how you will handle these clients' expectations. You can do this in advance, or as the need arises. Here are some tips on common international business etiquette that will help you realize just how sensitive you need to be to other cultures, and how different it is doing business abroad than doing business in America.

When doing business in Germany, meetings are always formal. Greet your fellow attendees with a firm handshake. Titles are very important and require a high level of respect, particularly for those high up on the food chain. You should always greet people by using their title, followed by their surname, unless you are invited to address them otherwise by their first name.

Moving on to Thailand—much of the etiquette and traditions of doing business in Thailand are products of Buddhism. The Thai culture traditionally uses first names over surnames, with "Khun" placed before the first name, which is a formal address for both men and women alike. There is also a formal bowing, with how low you bow being dependant on your status in relation to the other person. You should always wait for your host or hostess to introduce you to all other parties present, allowing time for everyone to understand your status, and you theirs, based on this formal greeting. Some of these rules, like the name usage, even apply to online correspondence.

Business conducted in Australia is generally very relaxed. A simple handshake and a smile will often suffice when meeting. Nonnatives should refrain from using "G'day" or "G'day mate." A simple "Hello" or "Hello, how are you?" is more appropriate.

Want to know more? A fantastic resource for many countries that you could potentially need information on can be found on the Kwintessential Cross Culture Solutions website, at www.kwintessential.co.uk/resources/country-profiles.html.

Using the Internet to Grow an International Business

One question I hear from entrepreneurs a lot is "How the heck am I going to let those international customers know I'm out there?" Walk on stage—get on the Internet! The Internet is your friend in growing your business internationally. Consider creating a multilingual site, supporting multiple languages via e-mail (you can hire out for translation if it's a big area of business for you), and accepting credit cards from all countries.

Of course, we already discussed shipping—working internationally means you need to build your shipping rates into your website, too. One way to do this is similar to the eBay method—you input the dimensions and weight of an item, and then the buyer can enter their ship-to information, which then generates an accurate shipping price and delivery date. It also allows the buyer flexibility with regard to pricing and delivery.

Checks and Balances

In the strategic planning process you will go from your original mission and objectives to a new understanding of your current situation and the strategy you wish to implement going forward. Ultimately, this all leads to control of your business and movement forward.

Remember that your objectives will be fairly static—they should not change much over time. They need to challenge you and your business but should be stable enough to serve as a checks-and-balances routine for your new endeavors. If you measure a new opportunity against your business objectives, you can decide if that move is right for you or not.

In the implementation phase, you may need people. You will certainly need marketing, you may need public relations assistance and production or service expansion help, and you will need information systems. Consider all of these when looking at how to implement your new business endeavors.

Evaluating Your Progress

When do you evaluate your progress? Continually and through the control mechanism of strategic planning. Once you go for a specific strategy, you need to be sure you're meeting your own standards and taking any action necessary to realign your business for success. You can do this by evaluating your critical success factors, such as:

- Profits
- Pace of growth
- Interest from your new target market
- Your competitors' success compared with yours

> Be careful when you scenario-plan because your bias about what you think may occur or what you've seen in the past may skew results, so bring as many people as you trust in on this action!

Another way to plan for progress is to plan for specific scenarios. In this model, you try to determine each possible deviation from your expected end result and goal, and then determine what contingency plan you will enact as a result. You will want to identify every possible event—macro and micro, large and small—to build into your planning process.

What is a macro event? Something that affects more than just you—economic downturns, taxes, and so on. What is a micro event? Losing a key employee or having a supplier raise prices on your products.

When you do plan for specific scenarios, you will need to assign a probability of the event occurring. I like to keep it simple and use a 1 to 10 scale. Focus on those events that are most likely or most probable first, and then decide how you will or want to handle them, should they occur. You also need to determine what the impact of each occurrence will be on your business, and what you will do to compensate for that impact should it occur.

Goal Realignment

You may notice that what you thought would occur as you advanced your business in fact did not. When that happens, it's time for goal realignment. To do this, you must identify where you currently are and where you want to be, and then figure out if the new opportunity you thought was there in fact is. If it is, then look at what is standing in your way. Is it capital? Revisit Chapters 6 and 7. Is it human resources? Revisit our sections on staffing. Is it a lack of ideas? Consider hiring a marketing firm. The key is to make goal realignment a continuous improvement process.

Some entrepreneurs don't find this area of the business very fun. Unfortunately, that is what happens when we feel our creative sides are stifled by business decisions. Nonetheless, in order to get back to the creativity, this analysis must occur.

This planning process is only one of many you may go through. For instance, you may go through the scenario-planning method discussed briefly above, in which you note multiple contingencies and how you will react to each. All of this is important, because when an event occurs, you need to be acting and not just reacting. You need to consider everything—from losing key staff to losing valuable efficiencies, from new entrants into the marketplace to legislation that dampens your company's capabilities and profits.

Outsourcing Opportunities Even for Small Businesses

Even small businesses have outsourcing opportunities. What does this mean? It means two things—you have the capacity to be the company others outsource to, and you have the capacity to outsource work if you get overwhelmed and need help fast. It also means you may be able to outsource product assembly and supply to other nations and take advantage of the same benefits that larger companies offer.

From automotive parts to retail products, if you need it manufactured or assembled, chances are you will find a company that can handle your order in China, no matter how small or large it is.

Manufacturing China is one such company. According to their website, www.ManufacturingChina.com, they are a family-owned business with factories in Fuzhou and Ningbo. They have worked with the smallest of business owners in the production of children's toys, all the way up to working on progressive tooling with companies like GM and Honda.

If you want to search for products or services by category, visit www. B2BChinaSources.com. With products and services categorized by genre, you can pick and choose from thousands of options. On this site you can literally sift through hundreds, if not thousands, of manufacturers in China. Don't see the product that you need? Find a similar product and contact the manufacturer. Inquire as to whether or not they would be willing to be contracted for a new product.

> You have probably heard the stories of small business owners who went to China to get the dolls they wanted to sell on eBay reproduced for pennies on the dollar; or the small business owner with an idea who got a patent and shopped it to other countries for a cheaper manufacturing price. This is fairly common today and if you are in manufacturing, I recommend you consider it unless "buy American" is part of your company objective.

You may also find yourself taking on work as an outsourcing supplier. For instance, say you are an accountant running a firm. No doubt many bigger companies need accountants, but cannot afford to hire any more. They turn to outsourced partners—much like companies have done with information technology for years. Another potential area for growth is marketing yourself as a solution to larger companies that need added hands for less money.

Here are some statistics from our study that might be useful for putting your potential income and your methods of growing your business into context. In the survey, the following was the income breakdown of the participating businesses in gross revenue, in U.S. dollars:

- 26 percent make $10,001 to $30,000 (many noting they were in startup phase)
- 17 percent make under $10,000 (most noting they were in startup phase)
- 15 percent make $30,001 to $50,000
- 11 percent make $150,001 to $300,000
- 8.7 percent make $70,001 to $90,000
- 6.5 percent make $120,001 to $150,000
- 2 percent made $1 million to $3 million, 2 percent made $3 million to $5 million, and 2 percent made over $5 million. Way to go!

Final Thoughts

Throughout your business, you will need to assess where your product or service fits into the marketplace, who your competitors are, what your potential business risks are, and how you can create the most efficient business model possible. It's entirely feasible you will enter into your new business without efficiencies; partly because there is a rush to get out there but in part because you won't yet have discovered *what* the efficiencies are that you *can* create. Watch out for them; they may be overseas business partners that you can join forces with or even outsourcing production.

Service Demands

11

If your business is a service-oriented one (and whose isn't?), you need to be prepared for very demanding customers. Even if your business is product based, the service you provide is getting your product to your customer in the time you promise and in great condition. In essence, no matter what business you set up, you need to be prepared for the worst case service scenario.

Studies have shown that companies skimping on customer service—like airlines, for instance—are getting bad reviews that spread like wildfire. Returning customers are going back to them only because they have no other choice. When alternatives come along that offer service-oriented products (like Virgin America, keeping with the airline example), customers that aren't price driven flock to those businesses as fast as they can.

You do not want to be on the side of the aisle where you have to improve service later on to keep existing or acquire new customers to replace those who are leaving. It's important that you assess what customers want and need right from the beginning and build that into the model you decide on for your company. As the general public's wants and needs are constantly changing, you will have to be vigilant, constantly analyzing and adjusting as needed—and before the market dictates that you must do so.

Studies also show that, even if the price is a bit higher, individuals tend more often to resort to companies that they know will offer superior service, particularly if it would make their lives uncomfortable or add unnecessary time to their day should the company not come through with its product or service.

Customers Are Demanding—And They Should Be!

Customers are generally demanding—and they should be. There are millions of companies out there competing for their dollars. Every family and individual has only X dollars available for discretionary spending. That means that if your product or service is optional, you need to fight incredibly hard to keep your service factor up, thereby increasing your chances for success.

> Companies that have a truly unique, niche product or service, one which is unavailable elsewhere or with very limited competition and very fixed pricing throughout the industry, often believe that they have fewer requirements placed on them for superior service. This is simply not the case. Those companies also have to provide service, or another company will come along, see the niche, and fill it for them.

If you are offering a product or service that would be considered a staple—a need; nonoptional—service is equally important. The Internet, which we will discuss more in the section that follows, plays an increasingly important role in setting customer expectations and overall demand for products and services.

The Role of the Internet in Customer Demands

With the Internet lowering costs and creating a strong demand for low prices to allow for more of that discretionary spending, you will need to provide not only low cost but superior service to keep and grow your client base.

In many cases, the Internet has created what economists call a "perfect market." A perfect market is one in which a buyer sells a product or service for exactly the price it is worth at a given moment. eBay is the leader in this type of thinking.

With traditional businesses, there is a lag in time. For instance, if I release a product, the price consumers really place on it often isn't reflected in actual price until I realize my product isn't moving off the shelves. I determine this based on resell information (which is often late and behind the curve), and then I make adjustments to price or product differentiation accordingly. However, the news of my adjustment takes time to work itself into the minds of the general public, meaning it will still be a while before my alterations make a difference.

With "perfect markets," though, the value of any object or service is real time. For instance, around gift-giving holidays, demand for products is up and eBay and other real-time auction sites find that final selling prices are higher—demand is higher. If a particular item is difficult to get via traditional means, then anything available on eBay will go for more money than it would when supplies return to normal.

If you are running any sort of online business, you will want to watch all online competitors, including stores and auctioneers on eBay, because they will directly impact your price. If the name of your product is XYZ, a simple weekly or daily search for XYZ on sites like eBay will return what is currently available.

> Did you know that although the original "Tickle Me Elmo" carried a suggested retail price of $28.99, during the Christmas buying season of 1996, "Tickle Me Elmos" were being sold for $1,500 and higher by those consumers who had already gotten their hands on them and were offering them for resale?

You will also want to build feedback mechanisms into your own website, even if you have a traditional brick-and-mortar store. More today than ever before, consumers are relying on other consumers to give them honest opinions and feedback. Check out Amazon's book reviews or Zappos's shoe reviews. Do you read those before you buy a book or buy a shoe? Chances are high that you do. These are considered higher in validity because they are from a random sample of actual buyers rather than a magazine review or an editors' choice award where one or two individuals are looking for specific things that they find important.

> You can use the Internet to your advantage particularly when it comes to service. Offer super fast, easy returns, near-immediate support, live chat, highly detailed catalogues, easy payment, and the capability to store information for future return visits to help consumers make an easy transition to your business.

Expectations—Even If You Are the "Low Price Leader"

Many entrepreneurs and business owners wrongfully believe that if they are the low price leaders, service won't matter as much. This is true for a certain segment of the population that has far more time than they have money. We see this as a trend with the unemployed, for instance, and with extremely low-wage workers who work below the poverty line. However, in general, this doesn't hold true for most Americans.

Have you noticed that even the king of inexpensive retail, Wal-Mart, is service oriented? They tout service; they keep smiling people at the door to hand you carts and they train their employees to watch checkout lanes for long lines and open new lines immediately. They make certain individuals are available for each major area of the store, and they make it easy to get a hold of a manager. They have even made returns easy by keeping information on hand so that returns without a receipt are not difficult—a service that the majority of large chain and department stores (Target, Macy's, Nordstrom, etc.) are adopting.

Even if you are the low price leader, people still want a minimum level of service. Any time you create hassles or difficulties, time delays or inefficiencies for your consumer, they are more likely to pay a few pennies or even a few bucks to go elsewhere and get minimum customer service levels. Don't make this vital mistake.

Service Demands

We have gone through demands on product organizations, but what about the outlook in the service sector? More companies than ever are outsourcing, but that is mostly cost related and not because companies here in America are offering poor services. There is a labor shortage in America, and a capital shortage overseas. This makes it logical that we'd exchange with other country's labor and capital.

If you are a service-oriented business and want to keep your customers, you need to stay focused on core competencies and provide quick, reliable information, near-immediate access to data, and fast responses to clients.

Change in Service Outlook

America is, more than ever, a service-sector environment. Many manufacturing plants are closing up shop and going overseas where products can be made more cheaply, increasing profit margins and stock prices and impacting shareholder value. However, as we discussed in Chapter 10, a large portion of growth in exports is in services. Americans are providing everything from management consulting for the Chinese, where they have few managers and lots of workers due to strict hiring requirements, to information technology workers for South American companies looking for Americans with an education in technology to build their infrastructure.

The service outlook for American businesses is growing stronger by the day. Even if your business is product- or commodity-based, which is often price sensitive, you may find yourself growing your business into a service sector related to your product offerings.

Profitable Versus Unprofitable Companies and Service

It is a modern myth that if you are a service company and you provide good service, you won't make any money. Many highly educated professors in business schools across the nation cite the airlines in America as an example of the worst of the worst—service providers not offering what they supposedly do best, which is provide a service. As a result, they're not profitable.

But what about the myriad companies out there that are both service oriented and profitable? What about even those specific airlines that have remained relatively profitable, given the high cost of oil in recent times and poor consumer sentiment about the industry in general? I'm talking about Southwest Airlines, for one, and Virgin America, a relative newcomer with high expectations in the U.S. markets.

When you are a service-oriented business, not providing what you are supposed to can quite literally kill your business. Once you get a tarnished reputation of not providing excellent, top quality service, you will find yourself having a very hard time recovering.

Many companies have gone as far as to change their names to disassociate themselves with negatively performing companies; same management, new techniques and new name. A university that I work for recently changed its name because they were attempting to become re-accredited and didn't want to be associated with their old name. Spare yourself that grief—besides, people see right through it.

Learning from the Best and the Worst

MSN Money released the 25 companies where customers come first, reprinted from *BusinessWeek*. So who made the grade and what can you learn from them? (These are not in order of highest to lowest, but instead separated by industry—you will see some patterns here!)

- Southwest Airlines
- JetBlue Airways (remember what I said about airlines?!)
- Washington Mutual
- Toyota Motors
- Cabela's
- T-Mobile
- Apple
- Home Depot
- Nordstrom
- Four Seasons
- Marriott International's Ritz Carlton
- USAA

If you want to see the complete list, you can visit the MSN Money website, which shows you the top 10 and their grades, both in processes and people (note the delineation there—it is hard to be top notch without both great processes and great human resources): articles.moneycentral.msn.com/News/25CompaniesWhereCustomersComeFirst.aspx?page=1.

What about those companies that didn't do so well? They are trying to learn from the best through training. One popular training method is to have the employee go through what the customer goes through. For instance, if your customers tend to be military personnel, this might consist of making employees go through training with military meals, military-like schedules, and so on. While simulating a combat environment is tough, some elements can be re-created with ease—the benefit, of course, is being able to view the situation through your customer's eyes.

Another thing to remember is that customers want to talk to humans. They do not want voice mail and they do not want to be routed through 15 menus to get a live person! In fact, there is an entire MSN Money blog devoted to reaching a human when you call customer service. You can find it at blogs.moneycentral. msn.com/smartspending/archive/2008/01/15/reach-a-human-when-you-call-customer-service.aspx. I suggest you check it out and see what customers are saying about what they want. Make it easy for a caller to get to a supervisor, too—even if that supervisor is you.

To avoid putting consumers through unpleasant processes and unpleasant people, hire right and allow people to get right to you through e-mail or phone. While customer service people usually aren't paid well and have to handle lots of complaints all day, you need to be sure that the people you hire for these roles genuinely enjoy working with customers and righting wrongs. You can do this through personality profiles and reference checking. I personally use scenario-based interviewing techniques to see how an individual might handle a specific customer issue.

Listening to Your Customers with Open Ears

So what are some things you can do to make sure you beat the customer service game?

One thing you can do is learn from the best. Even companies like Starbucks, Disney, and Lexus send their executives to leadership training, where the executives from that top 25 list have gone to learn from the best.

We know that customers like it when employees show empathy. There is a correlation between consumers feeling understood and feeling content and satisfied with service. Having primary insomnia and being on the road a lot, I can personally testify to this. If the hotel I'm staying at doesn't care that my room is next

> All of the partners you work with and all of the employees you hire reflect back on you. If any of them don't fit the model you want and the image your business needs, cut them loose.

to a noisy elevator or ice machine, I will probably not ever stay at that hotel again. On the contrary, one particular hotel I stay at every couple of months has remembered me so well that when I step out of the car from the airport, my room keys are handed to me. That company happens to be on the list of top service-oriented companies.

You should also take the potential outsourcing of customer service-related activities very seriously, too. Having a customer call an offshore service division for support can be aggravating and can result in negative feelings toward that business. Watch closely what you decide to outsource and what you don't.

Spotting Potential Problems Before They Threaten

With the power of the Internet, consumers are taking their complaints global, and fast! There are many websites devoted to noting consumer opinions about nearly everything. One such site is epinions.com, and I have personally used it many times to get opinions on lots of companies and products, prior to becoming a customer of theirs and purchasing certain products.

I recommend scouring these sites and spending some time each week Googling your company—even set a Google Alert so that you know if and when your company is mentioned in blogs. If anything pops up, handle it right away by contacting the customer directly and setting things right. Usually the customer, of their own accord, will take the time to note that the issue was corrected. If not, feel free to respond to the post or blog entry, explaining what you did and reinforcing your commitment to service.

If you start to see customers play the loyalty card ("I come to your hotel every six weeks!"), this is a sign that they may not feel they're being treated fairly for their consistent patronage, and may feel desperate for someone at your establishment to help them.

Soliciting Feedback

When you solicit feedback from customers, you are showing them a level of concern about the service they received and their perception of that service. When you get their feedback, you need to act on it—and not react to it. When you get negative feedback, realize that it is an opportunity to keep a customer and to create something positive out of a negative. It is also a chance to reward employees when they have done something that improved service perception and quality at your business. Sometimes the smallest things that your employees or contractors do can really go a long way in making your business successful.

You can get feedback through phone surveys, online surveys, follow up e-mails, or mailers. This depends on the type of business you have and how personal you need or want to be. For instance, if your company is entirely online, then it would make more sense to have a web-based survey or an e-mail survey. If you are a highly specialized boutique, then a store gift card in a gold wrapped envelope with a personalized note and a solicitation of feedback might be far more appropriate.

How to Get Honest Feedback

Let me start this section with what not to do: do not barrage your customers with so many surveys and customer forms to fill out that they feel you are disrespecting their time. No matter how great the service, this tactic often leaves a bad taste in the mouths of consumers. Ask for feedback once, and if you don't get it, move on. No news is usually good news, particularly if you don't see sales numbers dropping. It may just mean that the customer is happy—and busy! Calling and then e-mailing follow-ups is just plain annoying and could end up shifting a customer's perception from a good one to a negative one.

Acting on What You Learn

We all know the reputations that airlines have in today's climate. But why do Southwest and JetBlue rank high in customer service? An example in *BusinessWeek* showcases how to take a bad situation and turn it around into a customer service advantage.

In an article printed in 2007, a Southwest Airlines passenger found himself delayed for many hours before takeoff—five hours delayed, in fact—due to a required pilot change and a plane de-icing regimen that lasted too long.

How did Southwest handle it? Not by leaving starving customers with inoperable restrooms, but by having the pilot walk up and down the aisles, explaining the situation to customers and offering information and updates. Flight attendants kept passengers appraised of connecting flight information, and Southwest, on its own, acknowledged the problem by sending two free ticket vouchers to the passengers affected. Southwest notes that it isn't something they "do," but something that consumers "deserve." (McGregor et al., 2007)

Many business owners argue that some of their customers are just plain old bad customers. Many of us have had to "fire clients" or downsize our workload because the customer was simply being unreasonable. You need to assess whether it's you or the client that is the problem. Here are some great tips from Liz Weston in an MSN Money column, with regard to how some companies are handling "bad customers," and whether or not it is actually the company's fault.

If the client consistently asks you for advice but buys elsewhere, move on.

A client constantly returns most of their stuff to you, particularly after it is worn, used, far outdated, or well past the return policy. What is recommended? Remove the client from mailing lists, and discourage him or her from coming to you again.

Weston also recommends restricting returns, which is easily done through a company called The Return Exchange, based in Irvine, California. This company helps other businesses refuse shoppers that abuse store policies. This is monitored through driver's license numbers and then sent to The Return Exchange's Verify-1 device, which records the consumer's name, address, age, and details of the transaction, then the information is aggregated and stored. Be careful though—don't let any system automatically turn away a good client! (Weston, 2008)

There are also flat out bad customers! Who are they and what do they look like? Bad customers are those who return purchases after mailing them in for a rebate; customers who return items so that they can buy them again at a discount; customers who return or want to exchange used goods.

Some business owners don't like to sell to companies or people who only buy loss leaders, either. A loss leader is an item that you advertise extremely cheap, at a loss, so that you can get customers into your store with the hopes of convincing them to buy more in the process. You might find you don't value these customers because the intent of the loss leader is to get people to buy more expensive goods as well, or to be able to upsell that client.

Permeating Your Organization with Your Business Attitude

You may have the right customer-focused attitude, but what about your partners, colleagues, outsourcers, business associates, contractors, and employees? If you don't set the right customer-first tone from the top down, those working with and for you won't take it seriously. You are responsible for setting the service-oriented tone in your business. Do so, and enforce it—even with yourself.

You also want to figure out who your most prized clients are, and treat them exceedingly well. Airlines do this through elite frequent flier programs, giving their best customers perks, shorter lines in security, free upgrades, and so on. Take a cue from them and treat your prized clients very well.

What customer service mostly comes down to is doing what is right, what is fair, and what you would want done, if you were the customer. Put yourself in your customers' position. Look at the situation through their eyes. Do as much as you can to ensure that, at the end of the day, those customers have something positive to say about your business, and about you. Remember, although good news doesn't spread quite as quickly as bad news, bad news is not the news you want spreading. Also, don't forget to lead by example with regard to ensuring that your employees are following the guidelines you have set. It is up to you to set the proper tone for your business, in everything from how phones are answered to how customers are treated when they complain. You can do this through modeling the behavior you want others to live by and rewarding them when they do.

There are other things you need to be sensitive to in the workplace as well. How you react to unethical behavior within your company sets the expectation level for your employees and contractors, and sets the ethical tone for your customers as well.

You will want to train your employees periodically on core values; those who aren't listening may need to find someplace else to work. Take action against violators, whether they are business partners or team members. Stay true to your philosophies and don't compromise your boundaries or your dedication to your business or customers.

Allow customers and employees to tell you what they are thinking and how they feel through genuine open-door policies. Make sure all communication sets the tone you want in your business—notwithstanding, of course, any disciplinary notes, which may have to take a more aggressive tone. Set the code of acceptable conduct, and have employees sign off on the rules (a form for this can be found in the Fast Forms appendix). Set expectations during interviews—not after someone is hired. Remember, perhaps above all else, that fear-based management rarely works and rarely creates the customer service-based outcome that you desire.

Final Thoughts

As a business owner, you will have to discern between the constantly complaining, previously identified bad customer, and those offering genuine advice that can make your business better. One of your jobs as a business owner is to not just listen to your customer, but listen *actively* with the intent to change what has to be changed and fix what is broken. Your customers can be your biggest ally; and they can be the first to dismantle demand for your business. Treat them like royalty because they are.

12

Watching Out for Scary Monsters

Scary monsters in business? Indeed! There are many scary monsters that can destroy your business if they get their hands wrapped around your company!

What are the scary monsters in businesses? Rising costs, decreased productivity, decreased efficiencies, a decrease in demand for your product, less consumer spending, higher jobless rates, unforeseen competitors, competitors that get big quickly, and too many loose barriers allowing new entrants into the marketplace.

These factors—and others—need not destroy your business. You just need to keep a watchful eye out for them, stay on top of any potential issues, and immediately take action should something not appear to be going well. Better to look into a potential problem than have to chase after a known one that is quickly getting out of hand.

There are quite a few tools that we use to monitor and protect businesses. Among the time tested, established, and proven is Porter's Five Forces model, developed by Michael Porter to help understand a business's competitive advantage. Some argue it doesn't have much to offer in the Internet era; but I believe much of it can help us at the very least assess where we are today.

Porter's Five Forces

So who is Porter, and what the heck do his five forces have to do with your business? Just about everything! Michael Porter of the Harvard Business School developed the five forces model in 1979 to help determine the competitive intensity of a specific market. In turn, he believed that this model also identified how attractive a specific market is to enter into. Attractiveness, of course, leads to potentially more entrants into the market—more competition for you as you work to maintain your existing clients and grow into new businesses through expansion.

In the true sense of the entrepreneurial spirit, attractiveness refers to an industry or market that can turn a good profit; an unattractive market is one in which profitability is poised downward or is currently down with limited chance of revival. For instance, in 2008, Blockbuster was deemed no longer a good model, as online rivals took over and cable companies offered on-demand access to movies. On the contrary, Virgin Money is a new up-and-coming business model that uses the Internet and the need for consumers to borrow to afford businesses, cars, and houses—while still giving those that lend the feeling they have borrower accountability. One uses old-school methods and technology and relies on a dying business model, while the other embraces everything about the Internet, Gen Yers, and the older generations that want more security—everything that embraces positive change in almost all demographics.

> By knowing your business's advantages, you can get a more firm grasp on its disadvantages in the market, which is essential to strong growth and riding the tide in uncertain times. Where you are not strong, you are most likely weak—knowing these both will highlight where you need the most growth.

Porter, like many before and after him, refers to both the micro and macro environment. As we discussed in Chapter 10, the macro environment is the environment at large (legislation, economic prosperity, taxes, job rates, etc.—the bigger picture) and micro deals with the specific things related to your industry, like rising cost of goods, production rates, and so on.

Many strategists—in fact some would argue most strategists—use Porter's Five Forces in their arsenal of weapons to help assess any given company—and many venture capitalists will use it to determine your business's potential attractiveness.

Keep this specifically in mind when you are preparing to approach any VC or angel investor. If you have already prepared a thorough analysis based on Porter's Five Forces, you will be in a better position to demonstrate your knowledge and understanding of the business you are looking for help financing.

These are the five forces in Porter's model:

- Supplier power (the power that suppliers have over you and your costs)
- Threat of substitutes (substitute goods or services)
- Barriers to entry (into your market)
- Buyer power (the power your customers have over you)
- Rivalry—this is at the center of everything!

Taking each one independently, first we can examine the variables that go into supplier power. In general here we refer to the power that suppliers have over you, the business owner. The more power they have over you, the worse your position.

> Wal-Mart is an excellent example of a business in which suppliers have very little, if any, power. In fact, many suppliers have been tossed out of business by failing to live up to Wal-Mart's requirements on everything from Radio Frequency Identification (RFID) chipping to coming down a few pennies on the cost of the products that Wal-Mart resells. Wal-Mart is in the position of power because of the volume it purchases and suppliers not wanting to lose their contract. Should the suppliers gain more power over Wal-Mart, it may quickly find itself in a weaker position, unable to offer bargains to customers.

Supplier power also refers to the costs the suppliers have to create a product or supply raw materials, the costs they can pass along to the buyer (you and your business), how high switching costs are within the industry (how easy it is for you to switch suppliers—the harder it is, the more leverage they have over you), and what alternatives you have (if you have few substitutes, they again have more leverage over you—one reason that competitiveness is so healthy and necessary to keep prices low and the marketplace healthy).

We know that the supplier is weak if, among other things ...

- They have competitors to supply goods.
- They have weak customers. Customers that are at risk of going out of business cannot afford higher prices, so the suppliers feel threatened and keep prices low to keep business coming into them.
- They purchase commodity products.

The above conditions are what you want to look for when you hunt for suppliers—they are to your benefit!

We know that suppliers are powerful (which we don't want) when ...

- There is a significant cost for buyers to switch suppliers. (That locks you, the business owner, into that one supplier.)
- There is limited competition in their market; they're a single source or one of only a couple of sources to supply what you need.
- They collude—while illegal, any suppliers fixing prices hurts competition.
- They have powerful customers—like Wal-Mart—that can dictate what they want because they bring so much business into the company.

Barriers to entry is also another big force playing into competition and rivalry. In the section that follows, we will discuss their impact on your business and how you can use them to your advantage to put a protective ring around your business circle.

For now though, we will discuss a fundamental of the model—buyer's power. Buyer's power isn't what power you have over your customers. It is what your customers have over you. If your customers have leverage over you, then you are in a position of weakness.

Buyers—the customers—are powerful if they are concentrated or if they buy a lot. Government contracts are a great example here because the government spends so much in contractors that they have the upper hand in many negotiations (whether they use it or not is another story!).

Buyers are weak if there are a lot of them with no influence over the product or price, or if they cannot affect distribution in any way. From a purely strategic sense, this is where you want to keep your buyers.

Just to make sure that I haven't lost you, I will provide you with an example that demonstrates everything that we just discussed, using Wal-Mart again as the main player.

Wal-Mart's customers are powerful in the sense that they are large in number and loyal because of what the company offers them. Wal-Mart would not be nearly the giant they are without them, which means that they can't afford to lose those customers; which in turn means they will typically do what the consumer demands for fear of alienating their client base.

In order to maintain the contentment of their customers, they provide large amounts of products at extremely discounted costs, which they create by demanding low price-per-unit costs from their vendors. Being that Wal-Mart places such large orders to keep their shelves stocked, their vendors and suppliers are in a position to oblige their demands for a lower unit price in order to keep the business. Some vendors complain about literally making a penny on each item that they sell to Wal-Mart because of the force that they have in the marketplace.

In Wal-Mart's case, their vendors are weak, their customers are powerful, and Wal-Mart themselves are both powerful and weak, depending on which side of the coin you look at. You probably won't be Wal-Mart—there are only a few in each generation—but you can still look for these same qualities and positions of leverage with your suppliers. In the section below on retaining the clients you have, we will go into this in detail. In that section, too, we will discuss the threat of substitute goods and how to keep them off of your business's scary monster list.

All of this centers around rivalry. For most industries, your rivals in the marketplace will determine your profit margins, your customers' options, and the barriers to entry. The things that affect rivalry include: the number of competitors, how diverse the competitors' product offerings are, how expensive it is to advertise, how easy it is to get out of the market or business (should you choose to or need to), the number of still other competitors, and the growth rate of the industry as a whole.

The more firms there are competing, the more the rivalry intensifies. We often see companies, like banks and airlines, taken over, bought out, or merging with competitors.

The higher the costs are in obtaining supply to sell, the more a business must sell large quantities of it to make a reasonable profit, unless the profit margin is very high. This leads to a fight for market share among rivals or competitors. Market share is the percentage of the potential market that your particular business has captured and maintained. If a business loses market share, it is losing business to others, as a percent of total sales in that industry. If it is increasing market share, it is selling to more of the potential client base than it has in the past.

Remember also that low switching costs will also create more rivalries because consumers can easily move from one business to another without much sacrifice. The less differentiated your brand is, the more rivalry will take hold and try to take away what business you do have. And of course, not least of all, the more profit there is to be made the more you can expect new entrants (new competitors) into the market! All of this leads you to do one major thing and that is—protect your business!

Protecting Your Business

Many companies are quite concerned, and rightfully so, about knockoff products. Louis Vuitton and Tiffany have both sued eBay because of their volume of knockoffs for sale—but courts have overturned the rulings and have found eBay not responsible for what buyers put up for sale on the auction system.

Knockoffs tarnish a company's brand image and water down the brand, making its worth—which is partly dependent on its value as a status symbol—less worthy. These are the sorts of things you want to watch out for in the marketplace. Competitors get tricky—often naming products similar names and even making similar patterns on products to those of the known brand. If you are that known brand, do your best to protect your company's image and reputation. You need to be sure you have filed for copyrights and patents if you have a product or service that is extraordinarily unique. High-end luxury items deal with this all the time with people selling knockoffs particularly on eBay, and it's damaged the business of big companies like Louis Vuitton, Tiffany, even Stuart Weitzman, the shoe company. Many are finding themselves creating exceedingly unique products just to keep the knockoff creators on hold a bit longer.

Keeping Competitors Out

There are lots of entities and individuals that create barriers to entry. The government creates barriers even though one of its mandates is to preserve competition (by using antitrust and antimonopolization practices and legislation). Regulation can help create barriers into new marketplaces. For instance, in 2007 and 2008 it was nearly impossible to become a mortgage broker because of the regulation required for new entrants.

Patents also help to create a barrier to entry. If you have a brilliant idea—or just a unique one—a patent can help keep new entrants out of your market. Provisional patents are good for one year, which gives you time to file a full patent, but note that they cannot be renewed, contrary to popular opinion and urban myth. Note that any witnesses must have reviewed and understood your patent; they cannot merely sign without that understanding. Generally family members are considered disinterested parties and lawyers are considered biased, so as you file for patent, keep these tips in mind. Friends or colleagues that are distant but educated on the topic are good selections. Also note that in this country, we award patents to the "first to invent," not the "first to file." This can be tough to determine, though, without proper documentation.

> Contrary to popular belief, there is no such thing here in the United States as the "poor man's copyright" or "poor man's patent." It is a common myth that writing down your idea and mailing it to yourself, as long as you don't open the envelope, protects your idea from the date the envelope is postmarked. Fiction, not fact! Even the document disclosure program ended in 2007, allowing for a patent for $10 for two years.

Internal efficiencies are those things that are built into your business that make it efficient. It might be the equipment that you purchased or the technology that you use, or even your calendaring system that you require your staff to contend with. Internal efficiencies help create barriers for new entrants, too. Every time you increase the amount of product you buy (and the more you buy from a single supplier), the more efficient you become—to a point.

Remember, it is easy to enter a market if you have common technology, very easy access to channels of distribution, and an unknown and unbranded name (lack of name recognition). It is difficult for a new company to enter a market if an existing company (hopefully yours!) has patents or trademarks, if it will cost customers a lot to switch to their product (high switching costs), and if channels of distribution are restricted. This is why some buyers that have large purchasing power require suppliers to sign noncompete agreements. When this occurs, the buyer requires that the supplier not sell to competitors, or that the supplier not offer competitors the same price that they get.

Retaining the Clients You Have

No doubt you want to grow your business—but do you want to lose the clients you have in the process? Probably not—since at this rate, you are merely "standing still"! (Unless they are considered "bad customers," as we discussed in Chapter 10.)

You have the power over your customers if your customers are …

- Not sensitive to price.
- Not affected by economic downturns.
- Unable to bargain with you.
- Needing your product, regardless of price.
- Offered incentives to come to you.
- Offered different or unique products than your competitors'.

You also have the power if there are no substitute products available, which will help you keep your existing clients while you grow your client base for new ones. Anytime there is a close substitute potential, it increases the likelihood that customers can go elsewhere and that someone else can run with your idea or product or service. Anytime you are able to increase the costs to the consumer of switching providers, the more secure you are. (The happier the customer? Not necessarily.)

High switching costs are why phone companies fought the "phone number portability" requirement, where consumers could take their phone number to any carrier. Not being able to do so kept many consumers with one carrier because it was too much of a hassle to switch numbers. We saw costs go down substantially once consumers could take their number with them.

Developing Relationships

Developing strong relationships is another thing you can do to help keep entrants out and customers in. The stronger the relationships you have with suppliers and the stronger your relationship with customers, the more likely you are to retain both. When negotiations come for new pricing strategies, both will be more willing to work with you if you have a good relationship going in.

Perhaps equally important is your relationship with like-minded or similar business partners. When new competitors come onto the horizon, "attacking them" with more than just your own resources can prove beneficial, so strategic alliances are very important to your success.

Creating Ways to Keep Competitors Out

Another vital facet in the Porter model is barriers to entry—many say it is the most important force of them all.

Generally a specific business has unique characteristics that keep consumers buying, and that helps to create a barrier to entry for those that might try and enter your market space. The more unique your business—the more competitive advantage your business has—the harder it will be for competitors to take away your customers. This is the heart of the barriers to entry component of Porter's Five Forces.

Any time there is a possibility that more entrants or competitors will be coming into the marketplace or the industry, this is going to increase competition. This is great for customers—not so great for you!

Here are some things to look out for to protect your business as you evaluate your company and look to the Porter model for evaluation:

- The profitability of your particular industry going up substantially. We saw this with the "green movement"—suddenly anything green was getting VC money hand over fist, and companies offering green products or clean energy saw their stock prices soar on nothing more than speculation.
- Startup costs becoming lower. When startup costs are higher, there are fewer new entrants into the market. When costs are lower, more will come into the market.
- Certainty in the market. The more certain the market is, the more competitors. The more uncertain, the fewer competitors—everyone likes a "sure thing."

In your business, you want to keep the barriers to entry high to lessen competition. You can do this by investing in such high-end technology to create efficiencies that it becomes very expensive to enter into your market space or to copy you—at least for a while. You can do this by having incredible access to exclusive distribution, and by selecting a business that has a steep learning curve so that others require time, which will then be on your side, to be successful or to enter your market. You do this by making it very expensive for customers to go with the "other guy," and by creating brand equity—perceived differentiation that your product is simply better. You can also do this through government lobbying and policies.

Review Your Five-Year Plan

Periodically, as you move through your business, you should review your original plan and consider future plans when you wish to expand (discussed further in Chapter 13). As you review your plan and take account of where you're headed, be prepared to identify changes, determine where you need to be flexible, where your potential areas for growth are, where your business as an industry is headed, and step it up wherever you need to.

Identifying Changes as Needed

The first of these is identifying your business changes. First, examine the industry as a whole, and then examine your consumers. Are you finding that they are moving toward a specific brand? Is yours no longer as trendy as it once was? Think about Nordstrom and the trouble it went through in the 1990s. It had to rethink its entire branding strategy by hiring new, more trendy buyers because it was becoming associated with boring, outdated clothing. Now a hipper, trendier Nordstrom is hitting new marks in profits and finding new, younger life-long buyers.

All industries will change; all consumers will change—it is simply a fact of life. It is rare that an individual will stay brand-loyal throughout their entire lives. I think back to my teenage years, admittedly dating myself here, when Guess jeans were the hot item. I was unable to afford a pair but wanted them so badly that my best friend would give me her clothes when she was done with them, a year outdated and five or six sizes too big. I would wear them with safety pins all over the waistline because I wanted the brand—Guess. Today, though, I am not in search of Guess jeans; my age and income bracket hunts out True Religion and Antik Denim, for instance. If you are the company selling Guess jeans, you can either continue to market to new young people and figure out what they want, or you can look at it from the other side—how to keep those same junior high and high school kids from buying other brands, creating perhaps a more "grown up" line from the same brand.

Flexibility

Your business has to be flexible to sustain its growth! Just like the Nordstrom example, businesses must understand when need is changing or when their demographic is changing, and then maintain their flexibility to grow at the pace they wish to grow at.

In many cases, flexibility is easier when you are an online business. You can hire a web developer and, within a few weeks, transform how you do business, the portal your consumers go to for information, and the method that consumers use to purchase your product. If you check out the online store shopbop.com, you can see their brand-driven menu on the side. Why? One can guess (and as a frequent shopper there, I can speculate with accuracy) that the change to a brand-driven menu was due to the brand-conscious consumer.

This is an example of being very flexible and understanding what your customers want. At the core, of course, is what we discussed in Chapter 11—sampling your customers and knowing how to take feedback and use it to make positive change.

Flexibility, particularly if you have limited income, can also refer to your work and interactions with your team, suppliers, contractors, and employees. Often times small businesses don't have the money to mandate to others how things will happen, so they offer flexibility in lieu of money to those who find it most important. Everything from your customer relationship management (CRM) software to your enterprise resource planning (ERP) tools to your management philosophies will need to be flexible enough to manage your business the way you want to.

Growth Potential

The key here is to identify growth threats and new areas of potential growth. One of the worst things that can happen to a small business is if one day a new entrant pops up into the market space you play in, offering a new type of product that could have been a great growth business for you!

So how do you identify growth potentials? First, be sure that you cast a broad net into the marketplace. Try to capture as much of the market as you can in your surveys, your consumer data-driven information, and your potential new customers. Next, determine if the new product or service has strategic value for your business. Will it help you grow in the long run? Will it help profits in the short run, but need to be transformed to adhere to new business endeavors in the long term? Then look at your existing offerings and what the "next phase" is for those offerings.

You want to look at all of the potentials of each area of growth:

- Lifetime value of that particular customer, product, or service
- The potential problem your new growth area can solve in the long run
- The change in demographic in the marketplace and in your market space
- What the media is covering and exposing, and patterns that you notice
- Sales potential for your new product or service (and profit potential, too, of course)

Stepping It Up When You Need To

When you determine there are untapped areas for growth, or as happens to me often, you think of something at 2 A.M. that you'd like to go for and give a whirl, a key to success is stepping up and trying it! During the 2008 presidential race, I opened an online T-shirt company. Was it successful? Not by my profit requirements. Was it worth it? Yes, because it kept me from always wondering "what if" later on down the road; a lesson I have had to learn numerous times the hard way.

When you think of something—a new source of revenue or a new avenue for your existing market, product, or consumer, go for it if the numbers make sense.

To do that, you may very well need capital. Often it is easier to raise capital for an existing business adding a new product or line than it is to raise capital for the opening of your new business. If you go to the bank you established your merchant account and/or business checking with, you may find it easier (assuming your company has a good credit and bank rating) to get money for your new ideas than for your initial business.

Knowing When You Are Off Course

A big risk to all entrepreneurs is not identifying—or not identifying fast enough—that they are veering off course when the macro environment isn't going favorably in their direction.

One example of this occurrence would be if your business sells low efficiency air conditioners; chances are the market isn't headed favorably in your direction. When you find consumer tastes and your product going in opposite directions, you need to identify it quickly, and either change direction or add product offerings more in line with the strategic moves and demographic (macro) changes in the market.

In addition to the changing of demographics, you could also find yourself directing your efforts toward a fading demographic—your target audience may be diminishing altogether. An example of this would be if your target demographic was customers who owned compressed natural gas (CNG) vehicles. If the government started mandating the phasing out of production of CNG vehicles, you would not want to wait until the last CNG car or truck drove off the assembly line to alter your business model. You would need to shift focus as soon as you got the word that your target demographic, and your profits, were jeopardized. In Chapter 13 we go into further detail on business expansion and what to do when your buyers diminish, which will come into play before your business is in jeopardy, if you are doing your job of monitoring your business and market sector.

Yet another way to lose market share is when your products/services are simply no longer "the fad." Many businesses experience great amounts of success providing popular products and services that are simply a phase for the general consumer base. Examples of this would be "pogs" (do you remember those?), the hula hoop (although it did make somewhat of a comeback), the pet rock, etc. Jumping on this bandwagon is a great move, should you be interested in it, but recognize the looming and ever-present downside—the fad will end. Tracking the life of these fads is imperative to being successful in riding the wave that they create. Waiting too long to get out could mean the difference between quick and easy money and ending up with a year's worth of stock that you will never be able to see off for what you paid for it all.

Managing and Identifying Risks to the Business

As you move forward, you have to manage and identify any potential risks to your business and not just find new growth areas. You can find all the new growth areas possible and imaginable, but one risk that you hadn't identified can take years of hard work away very quickly. The goal here is to avoid costly mistakes, particularly those that sacrifice any portion of your business, your profits, your customers' loyalty to you, your brand identity or awareness, or your business model.

One of the risks that is often overlooked is the risk of disasters, and how to plan around them and for them. In information technology, we refer to both business continuity planning, or BCP, and disaster recovery planning, or DR. Disaster recovery deals with the process of recovering from a disaster, while business continuity planning helps the business stay functioning even if its continuity is broken. Both BCP and DR involve all areas of your business, and not just technology (though many large companies have had a hard time grasping this concept!). Something as simple as protecting your consumers' data online or storing offsite backups can help you protect your company from disaster.

Other risks to you and your business include: breaking government rules or laws; breaking legislative rules or laws; stepping on another business's trademarks, patents, or copyrights; improperly filing tax returns; hiring the wrong people; using a low cost supplier that has poor quality products; using a high cost supplier that has mediocre quality products; and so on. The list of potential risks is huge, but these are a few of the ones that carry enormously large repercussions.

One of the best ways to hedge against risks is to keep in contact (not to the point of annoyance, but enough to get information you need) with your customers— stay in touch wherever they stay in touch online, and keep in close enough contact with suppliers, business partners, contractors, and employees that you know what your customers are asking for and can identify trends before they identify your business—as a potential target for their competitive nature.

Final Thoughts

You have a unique product and service; and you must protect the heck out of it! If you don't create barriers for others to enter into your market space, you only have time to be profitable and become a market leader before others realize what you have and try to copy it. You can fight this through innovation, watching your market share closely, and looking constantly for new advantages that you can use to solidify your business.

13

Success!

Ah, the wonderful feeling of success. Is there anything sweeter? Of course, what you decide or determine is success ultimately depends on what success means to you. I told a story early in this book about a friend who quit most of his contracts because success meant more time with his family; for others of us, it may mean buying the family a "McMansion," or having more disposable income, or paying off personal debts.

Once you have determined what success is to you, chances are it will become a moving target. I know personally that each time I begin to feel successful (which is a rarity), the definition changes and once again I feel like I'm far, far away from that point. I believe that many of us thrive on that constantly moving target; why else would we continually go back to it?

Feeling Successful and Loving What You Do: The Ultimate Payoff!

What is the ultimate in business success? In my view, and in the view of 98 percent of those surveyed who are existing entrepreneurs, it means meeting goals for the business and also loving what you do. If you are highly successful but dread going to work, you might as well have stayed in Corporate America! You really want to enjoy each component of your job, just as you want to be able to enjoy each component of your life. As the time required to run my business increases and as the resources available to me increase, I find myself outsourcing more and more of the work I don't like to do and spending more time on the coaching side of my business, which is what I enjoy doing. If you don't have many resources, try to think outside the box. Are there neighborhood kids who would like some extra cash for some of the labor? A family member or friend you wouldn't mind mingling business and pleasure with?

Even though most of our survey respondents are working long hours, 49 percent said that their business is taking the amount of time they anticipated when they planned, 45 percent said it is taking more time than planned, and 6 percent say their business takes less time than they had anticipated. Some noted that their learning curve was so steep that it was tough early on, but is getting easier as time goes by. Others indicated that the reason for the large amount of time spent is because they set their own bar very high, and others said they enjoy their work so much that they have stopped worrying about how many hours they spend on it.

Rewarding Yourself

Most people who run their own business prefer to put capital back into the business to grow it, although there are those who spend the profits immediately, never having a second thought about reinvesting. Many others feel that bonuses should first go to their team—the people who fueled the success in the first place—and while I don't disagree, you also have to keep yourself motivated through personal rewards. What would you want from a boss? Why not give that to yourself?

Here are some creative ideas to help you reward your own success, essentially keeping your head in the game.

First, don't forget about where you started from. This is very easy to do; I admit I do it all the time myself. In my case, it's easy to fall into the mindset of "one more interview" or "one more course," but I have to remember that a year ago there were no interviews and only half the number of courses in my business.

It's easy to lose sight of your own success. I try to count on family and friends to keep me in check; when I beat myself up over lack of success, they catch me by gently reminding me what I started with. Reminding yourself where you started from should provide you with a clear view of how far you have come, even if it's not as far as you eventually want to go. By the same token, don't allow yourself to revel in all your glory, as doing so can easily take your focus off continued success and you could find yourself sliding backwards.

Personal Merit Increases

If you are successful, you can certainly adjust your own compensation—and you should! Many of us have had people work for us who want to know what we get paid, or what our contracts pay us—it is none of their business! If you are close to your team it's sometimes hard not to share that information, but remember that your team is there to do a job—they didn't take all the risk of starting the business.

Moreover, what you pay yourself need not be something you are ashamed of. It certainly shouldn't be increased because of others' inquiries—tell them to mind their own business and do their job! For most of us, these questions are uncomfortable, but employees who are too comfortable in their work tend to feel it's okay to ask. Remind them that it isn't. Often they're trying to assess if they feel they're being paid fairly. Remember, as a business owner, you have the right and obligation to make a profit on everyone you hire. If you didn't, there would be no point in hiring anyone. It's one thing to have your staff feeling like they work with you and not for you—it's another for them to be asking questions that make you uncomfortable or are outside acceptable bounds. Many business owners in the survey for this book expressed concern over it, and I have felt it myself, too.

We know from many surveys that money alone isn't enough to motivate our workers, so it most likely won't be enough to motivate ourselves, either. However, you need to pay yourself for your own successes, your new ideas that do well, and your new risky ventures that paid off; or just for trying something new—for stepping outside the boundaries of safety and taking a leap of faith, no matter how it ends up. This is similar to what you'd expect if you worked for someone else.

One thing you can do for yourself is be sure you are still building your nest egg, even if you're not paying yourself a ton of cash (at least, not yet). A nest egg can give you a sense of security and can alleviate the feeling of being "stuck" if you're no longer happy with your current business. Of course, don't get so trapped in the mindset of building your nest egg that you forget about growing your business.

Also, be sure that you always take care of your healthcare needs. Going without healthcare policies can ruin your business, because one major illness can wipe away years and years' worth of profits. As we noted in previous chapters, joining professional organizations can often lessen the cost burden. If you find health-care costs enormous, consider raising your yearly or per-visit deductibles or searching out other providers. Going through an insurance agent can alleviate many hours of searching for the best option—let them do the work for you, you have a business to grow!

Separating Business and Personal Funds

On the flip side, some business owners are tempted to take pay increases or merit increases too far. This can utterly destroy a business in no time flat. At a very young age, I worked for a very successful small business owner—very suc-cessful until about two years into each business, when he filed for bankruptcy. Ultimately—about nine companies later—he created a company and sold it to Microsoft and retired early. In the meantime, though, he damaged great busi-nesses by frivolously spending money on his own personal things. This is one of the many reasons that it's vital that we keep our personal money separate from that belonging to the business, notwithstanding those funds required by the IRS.

Remember, too, that unless your income passes through to your own personal return, the IRS has rules about separating business income. Even if it does pass through, most accountants (and some IRS PDFs available online) note that you must keep funds separate anyway. If you don't have your business set up that way, discuss any ramifications with a tax planner, and always keep receipts so it's clear what purchases were spent specifically on your business. If it's not clear that the item was used for business purposes, the IRS could require you to pay back taxes on that amount in the event of an audit.

Expansion

One surefire way to get yourself excited about your business again is to expand. Toward the end of this chapter, we'll talk about expansion with a different twist—overcoming common obstacles, particularly for small businesses. If you find yourself lacking enthusiasm for your work, consider expanding into new territories and see if that lights your fire again! I know for myself and many of my self-employed colleagues, finding new ways to grow my business is so motivating that I *want* to work until midnight again rather than feel drained in doing so.

Your Personal Definition

As you reward yourself and expand your business deeper into existing territories or broader, into entirely new ones, don't lose sight of your personal definition of success and where you want to be. One thing I find to be a common "complaint" among successful entrepreneurs is that their business grew so fast (oh what a problem to have!); they didn't expect the time commitment that was ultimately required, nor the level of responsibility that would be needed on their part. Try not to lose sight of those core competencies, or you risk doing what my friend did—drastically cutting back your workload to balance your work and home life again. I also have many friends who have lost families and good marriages because their spouses felt that they were more committed to their business than to the relationship. Keep your priorities in check. I make my attempts at doing so (though I'm not always the best at it) by asking very close, trusted friends to tell me when they see that I'm "out of whack." They tell me—I don't always change, but they keep on telling me anyway, and I am glad that they do.

Knowing If You Want to Take It to "Another Level"

Obviously you need to do some assessing before you take your business to another level—whether it is in the depth of what you offer along the same lines, or in breadth, in terms of expanding the opportunities and capabilities of your products or services. As with anything, there are pros and cons, and you need to evaluate the market before taking a plunge.

Pros of the Next Level

There are some obvious pros to expansion:

- Potential for more profit
- Diversification, and lessening risk to one market or demographic as a result
- Excitement over new possibilities
- Motivating the team you hired because of the new areas they get to learn about and be a part of
- Meeting new customers, bringing on new clients, and understanding a new business sector
- Eliminating things you don't enjoy in your work

Sometimes, by growing into areas we do enjoy, we're able to slowly remove those elements from our business that we don't—or those that have become unprofitable.

Cons of the Next Level

There are also cons, of course, to expansion. Some of these include:

- Potential risk and profit loss
- Upsetting existing customers
- Upsetting business partners who don't like you in their space
- Too much diversification leading to too little focus on core competencies—losing focus on what is important and necessary
- Going back to the beginning again in many respects—finding new sources of capital, new revenue streams, and new clients
- Rebranding if necessary
- The risk of diversifying to the point of not having brand identity anymore

Evaluating the Market

Before you decide to expand or not, you must evaluate the marketplace or space that you wish to enter into. For instance, if you sell products to Boomers and have a new spin on an old product for Gen Yers, evaluate what the interest level might be. We've discussed many ways to do that in Chapters 4 and 5.

Try to mitigate risk and unknowns by evaluating how the market will react to your new product or service. One quick way to do that is to ask existing customers.

Deciding to Expand

Often, the time to expand is when business is slow, whether it is due to macro or micro issues. As you expand your business and identify potential new areas, try to identify each obstacle and a way around it.

Identifying common obstacles is a good place to start, but you should identify obstacles within your particular market, as well as in your business sector, for the best opportunities and the least risk. While most potentially highly beneficial endeavors involve the most risk, that isn't always the case.

One big obstacle to expansion is fear; fear of the unknown or fear of failure, or fear of losing money that you fought so long for and worked so hard (through long days and late nights) to earn. You may be risk averse, not wanting to take much risk regardless of how great the reward. It can be exceedingly hard to change this particular personality trait. The best thing you can do is create a nest egg, and calculate your risks as much as possible. Usually for people who are risk averse, putting every contingency and possibility on paper can make them seem less daunting and more predictable, lessening anxiety along the way. Some people of course have the opposite problem—they are big risk takers, sometimes taking uncalculated risks with lots to lose and not much to gain.

Another possible obstacle is if you lack in the self-discipline department or tend to be a procrastinator. Both of these can kill any expansion efforts. As your own boss, you will need self discipline to be successful, and at a level you've probably not experienced to date. Every day, something will compete for your attention— your spouse, your children, all the ideas floating around in your head, expansion versus maintenance of your existing business, customers, employees, contractors, suppliers—you name it! The more you stick to your principles, set specific hours, and be disciplined in your time (for example, try to avoid surfing the web at work, even though you can), the more successful you will be. Try to remove office distractions, too, just like you would if you were working in an office for someone else.

Another expansion killer is lack of confidence. You need to have confidence in yourself, your business, your employees, your contractors—everyone you work with. If someone in the chain is not performing up to standards (yourself included), he or she may need a kick in the pants. Any area of your business you lack confidence in needs a second, third, nth look, until it meets your satisfaction and you are confident that it can work well. This may mean restructuring parts of your business, removing employees who aren't performing up to snuff, or revising product offerings. Try to remember that you got this far on your own, and remember that you can trust yourself. This can get lost along the way sometimes, particularly if something unexpected happens or doesn't go the way we would have liked or hoped. That is just par for the course.

Once you decide that expansion will work or you want to give it a shot anyway (as I often do), here are some things to do to get ready:

- Send information about your expansion to existing clients through e-mail or snail-mail, informing them about new opportunities with you and, of course, offering coveted discounts and referral bonuses.
- Update your website to reflect your new business endeavors and be sure that your meta tags for search engines are updated, too.
- Consider new advertising strategies and what marketing techniques will be needed.
- Survey existing clients and potential new ones to be sure you're covering the bases in terms of what they want in your new offerings.
- Determine if existing staff, suppliers, and contractors can handle the new avenues, or whether you need to make changes.
- Scope out who the new target market is and what changes will need to be made between your old business and the new one.

- Form strategic alliances both with people you can help and those who can help you—and preferably, they will be the same people!

- Assess staffing needs.

- Promote like crazy!

Financial Implications

There will be financial implications for whatever methods and practices you use to expand into your new business growth opportunities. For one, you will have additional costs that perhaps you hadn't planned for at the beginning of your fiscal year. You will also have financial implications by way of less time to dedicate to existing lines of businesses that are profitable, potentially hurting existing revenue streams.

The Need for Additional Revenue

Many businesses decide to expand because they quite simply need to find additional avenues for revenue or capital raising. In the next and final section of this book, we talk a bit more about raising capital for expansion. But first you need to identify what kind of potential revenue increases you will see as a result of your new endeavors. Any bank or investor will want this information, and you will need it for your own peace of mind.

You have to outline in very precise detail how much money you will raise as a result of your new expansion, much in the same way that you did when you created your business plan. In many respects, when you expand you go back to basics in terms of planning, leading, organizing, and controlling your business. If the need for additional business revenue is the main reason you are expanding, be sure that the return on investment will be there or you may wind up in a worse position than you were when you began.

> Get a handle on current expenditures and what is costing your business, and make necessary cutbacks to fund and supply money to your new business avenues.

Raising More Capital

Any time you wish to expand, you will need resources—both monetary and human resources. First, evaluate whether you have the right people and the right contractors and suppliers in place to handle your new lines of business. Also evaluate how much money will be required to promote and market your new idea, get the word out, and then sustain that part of the business until you have vetted its viability. Don't be afraid to back out if you realize this course of action isn't going to have the net result that you thought. Better to stop the bleeding and rebuild while you can than to bleed out, so to speak.

Should you decide you need to raise capital, you should revisit Chapters 6 and 8 in this book on raising capital for your new business because much of the same applies here. There are a few sections of the business plan that will of course be different than in the first attempt. For starters, you will have to update items such as:

- History of successes
- Methods of handling and mitigating failures
- Potential risks to the existing business by engaging in a new one
- Required capital for expansion
- Profits and losses of the existing business
- Documentation of all needs for expanding into the new business space
- Potential risks
- Potential upsides (including money, but other things as well, like new sources of business for existing product or service lines)

Final Thoughts

It is tough to end a book like this—there are thousands more concepts and ideas we could discuss, including strategies and goals, ways to keep yourself sane and ways to make your business the best it can possibly be. Of course I have many more stories and input from survey respondents to share—ideas and experiences from those who, like us, are out there becoming and creating what we want and running our own businesses and creating our own pathways in life.

What about final thoughts from our survey respondents? Among the things noted as the most difficult aspects to owning your own business were some of the following:

- Controlling the volume of work
- Uncertainty about the future
- Economic conditions that are not controllable
- Finding new contracts
- Managing personal time and finding a work/life balance
- Irregular income
- Monthly expenses without having a chance to save
- New entrants driving down the value of your business
- Finding good employees
- Finding patience
- Interruptions
- Business development
- Self discipline and procrastination
- Managing expenses
- Networking
- Growing the business
- Turning off the mental switch
- Long hours

On the other hand, one person indicated that the only downside to starting a business was not doing it sooner!

What about the most rewarding aspects?

- Building something you own
- Flexibility
- Freedom
- High profits

- Pride and success
- Autonomy
- Low transportation costs
- Money
- Time to allocate as you wish

A very important note is that over 70 percent mentioned flexibility in their write-in comments.

Another aspect of this book is the resources and glossary section. I encourage you to read through the resources section, and to use the forms as guides to check and to help you be sure you are including all that you should in your own work. Be cautious out there, but have fun. Be excited, but remember your checks and balances, and continually assess where you're at and where you're headed. Embrace technology, but don't forget about your core business and your clients—keep your customers first, but don't forget to take care of yourself, too. Enjoy life as an entrepreneur!

Glossary

There are many great glossaries that you can find and use online and many books that have nothing but glossaries for business owners. There is an outstanding glossary available to you online, with additional small business resources to help you in your journey. The Small Business Taxes and Management website, available at www.smbiz.com, provides lots of great information for business owners, including practical tips, highlights on legislation, and lots of great tools for doing taxes and managing your business. I highly recommend you check out the website!

Another great resource is the Small Business Administration, which prints its glossary at www.sba.gov/smallbusinessplanner/plan/getready/serv_sbplanner_gready_glossory.html.

General Business Terms

This excellent glossary of general business terms comes from the website www.isquare.com. isquare.com has numerous articles about starting and operating a business, marketing a business, websites, business tips, stress tips, and tradeshows. They also have excellent technology archives and product reviews. Check out their terrific site!

accounting period   A period of time, (month, quarter, year), for which a financial statement is produced.

accounting rate of return   A method of computing the profitability where the total cash inflow over the life of the project is reduced by expenses. This amount is divided by the estimated life of the project to arrive at an annual return. That's then divided by the investment's cost. The result is an average rate of return. (See *discounted cash flow*.)

accounts payable   This represents what a business owes to its suppliers and other creditors at a given point in time.

accounts receivable   This represents the amount due to a business by its customers at a given point in time.

accrual accounting   A method of bookkeeping in which income and expenses are allocated to the periods to which they apply, regardless of when actually received or paid. For example, when an invoice is rendered, its value is added to income immediately, even though it has not been paid. (See *cash accounting*.)

angel investor   Someone who invests his or her own money in startup businesses or expanding existing businesses.

audit   Verification of financial records and accounting procedures generally conducted by a CPA or accounting firm or, if you're really unlucky, the IRS.

balance sheet   Financial statement showing assets and liabilities at a specific time.

bond   A third party obligation promising to pay if a vendor does not fulfill its valid obligations under a contract. Types of bonds include license, performance, bid, and indemnity and payment.

break-even point   The point at which sales equal total costs.

capital asset   An asset that is purchased for long-term use, such as machinery and equipment.

capital expenditure   The purchase of or outlay for an asset with a life of more than a year, or one that increases the capacity or efficiency of an asset or extends its useful life. Generally, such expenditures cannot be deducted as of the date of writing this book for tax purposes (or expensed for financial accounting purposes). Instead, they must be depreciated or amortized over their useful life.

capital gain (or loss)   A category of gain or loss under the tax law, resulting from the sale or other disposition of specified property such as stock or bond investments, real estate, etc. It does not include property used in a trade or business. However, special rules apply in certain situations that can result in similar treatment for business property.

capitalization rate   The rate of interest used to discount the future income from a property to arrive at a present value.

cash accounting   The simplest form of accounting in which income is considered earned when received and expenses are not taken into account until paid.

cash-on-cash return   Usually reserved for real estate income properties, it's the annual cash flow from the property divided by your cash investment. Sometimes called return on equity or equity dividend rate, it's a quick and dirty way to evaluate an investment.

caveat emptor   "Let the buyer beware."

certified lenders   Banks that participate in the SBA's guaranteed loan program.

collateral   An asset that can be sold for cash and which has been pledged to a creditor to secure a future obligation. For example, if you finance a car it is the collateral for the loan.

compound interest   Interest earned on previously accumulated interest plus the original principal. Most spread sheets can calculate this easily for you, but for the curious, the formula is $C = P(1 + r/n)n$, where C = compound amount, P = original principal, r = annual interest rate, and n = total number of periods over which interest is compounded.

contract   An agreement between two (or more) parties in which each promises to perform in some way. Contracts can be complex and should always be reviewed by an attorney. A contract may not be binding if not correctly drafted and executed.

credit report   A listing of an individual's or company's history of repaying past loans and other liabilities.

debt financing   This is financing in which you get a loan from someone or somewhere and go into debt. You are obligated to repay the money at some predetermined interest rate.

depreciation   Decrease in the value of equipment over time. Depreciation of equipment used for business is a tax-deductible expense.

discounted cash flow   The application of a factor, based on the cost of the company's capital or prevailing interest rates (with a possible adjustment for risk), to the cash inflows and outflows from a project or investment. (Also called net present value analysis.)

drop shipment   A shipment directly from the manufacturer to the end user.

DUNS (Data Universal Numbering System)   A database maintained by Dun and Bradstreet that is used by the government to identify each contractor and their location(s). This number is required to register with the Central Contractor Register (CCR) that is used by the government's electronic commerce/electronic data interchange (EC/EDI) system called FACNET. You can obtain a DUNS number at no cost by calling Dun and Bradstreet at 1-800-333-0505.

Employer Identification Number (EIN)   A number obtained by a business from the IRS by filing form SS-4. If you are a sole proprietorship, your EIN is your Social Security number.

entrepreneur   Someone who is willing to assume the responsibility, risk, and rewards of starting and operating a business.

equity financing   This involves "selling" a portion of your company to an outside investor. You have no obligation to repay the funds. In general, venture capital firms provide this type of funding.

escrow   Temporary monetary deposit with an independent third party by agreement between two parties. The escrow money is released when certain agreed conditions have been met.

ESOP (Employee Stock Ownership Plan)   A plan where employees have a vested interest (stock ownership) in the company.

factoring   The buying and selling of invoices or accounts receivables.

fiduciary   A person or company entrusted with assets owned by another party (beneficiary), and responsible for investing the assets until they are turned over to the beneficiary.

fiscal year   Any 12-month period used by a company or government as an accounting period.

fixed cost   A production cost which does not vary significantly with the volume of output. An example would be administrative costs. (See *variable cost*.)

franchise   A franchise is a form of licensing. The franchiser provides his or her services through a series of franchisees. Before investing in any franchise, check with the International Franchise Association at 1-800-543-1038 to see if the franchise is a member in good standing.

free on board (FOB)   Commercial term in which the seller's obligations are fulfilled when the goods reach a point specified in the contract.

grace period   Time allowed a debtor in which legal action will not be undertaken by the creditor when payment is late.

guarantee   Pledge by a third party to repay a loan in the event that the borrower cannot. A special case is a *personal* guarantee, in which you personally guarantee an obligation.

guaranteed/insured loans   Programs in which the federal government makes an arrangement to indemnify a lender against part or all of any defaults by those responsible for repayment of loans. An example is a small business loan guaranteed by the SBA.

indemnity   Obligation of one party to reimburse another party for losses which have occurred or which may occur.

job sharing   Arrangement in which the responsibilities and hours of one job position are carried out by two people.

lien   Legal right to hold property of another party or to have it sold or applied in payment of a claim.

liquidation   Sale of the assets of a business to pay off debts.

marginal cost   Additional cost associated with producing one more unit of output.

MLM (multilevel marketing)   A way of selling goods or services through distributors. These plans promise that if you sign up as a distributor, you will receive commissions—for both your sales of the plan's goods or services and those of other people you recruit to join the distributors. This is called "pyramiding" and is illegal in many states.

OSDBU (Office of Small and Disadvantaged Business Utilization)   These offices offer small business information on procurement opportunities, guidance on procurement procedures, and identification of both prime and subcontracting opportunities with the United States government.

overhead   Business expenses not directly related to a particular good or service produced. An example would be utilities.

power of attorney   An agreement authorizing someone (generally an attorney) to act as your agent. This agreement may be general (complete authority) or special (limited authority).

preferred lenders   Banks which have a special written agreement with the SBA which allows them to make a guaranteed SBA loan without prior SBA approval.

profit and loss (P&L) statement   A listing of income, expenses, and the resulting net profit or loss. (Also called an income statement.)

Prompt Payment Act   A federal law that requires federal agencies to pay interest to companies on bills not paid within 30 days of invoice or completion of work.

SBDC (Small Business Development Center)   SBDCs are located throughout the United States and are administered by the SBA. They provide management assistance to entrepreneurs and new business owners.

SBIC (small business investment corporation)   SBICs are licensed by the SBA as federally funded, private venture capital firms. Money is available to small businesses under a variety of agreements.

SCORE (Service Corps of Retired Executives)   A volunteer management assistance program of the SBA. SCORE volunteers provide one-on-one counseling and workshops and seminars for small businesses. There are hundreds of SCORE offices throughout the United States.

SIC (Standard Industrial Classification Code)   A four-digit number assigned to identify a business based on the type of business or trade involved. The first two digits correspond to major groups, such as construction and manufacturing, while the last two digits correspond to subgroups, such as constructing homes versus constructing highways. A business can determine its SIC number by looking it up in a directory published by the Department of Commerce, or by checking the SIC book in the reference section of a local library. SBA size standards are based on SIC codes.

simple interest   Interest paid only on the principal of a loan.

sole proprietorship   The simplest (and most popular) form of business organization. The individual is personally liable for all debts of the business to the full extent of his or her property. On the other hand, the owner has complete control of the business.

sweat equity   A common form of investment. This refers to the investment in time owners make, with no salary, to a new business.

sweep account   A brokerage or bank account whose cash balance is automatically transferred into an interest-bearing investment, such as a money market fund. Use sweep accounts to earn interest on surplus cash. At the end of each business day, a sweep account would transfer excess funds into an interest-bearing account, earn overnight interest, and make the funds available the next day.

tax number   A number assigned to a business that enables the business to buy wholesale without paying sales tax on goods and products. Contact your local courthouse for additional information.

variable cost   Any costs which change significantly with the level of output. The obvious example is cost of materials.

venture capital   Money used to support new or unusual undertakings; equity, risk or speculative investment capital. This funding is provided to new or existing firms that exhibit potential for above-average growth.

The first set of tools in this appendix are the forms, applications, and documents you will need, from articles of incorporation to employment applications. The second set of tools are spreadsheets: examples for your use as well as the original source website where you can download incredibly powerful tools to help you with your analysis. There are many great forms online for free, or through sources like LegalZoom.com for a fee. I have done my best to compile some great forms here for you to use, but first, a legal disclaimer:

Forms and requirements from the IRS and the government change constantly. Courts change rules all the time through decisions that they make, leaving companies vulnerable if they use older forms. These forms should be used not as complete templates, but as a guide for what to expect as you fill out the forms and required paperwork to create your new business. Most forms, regardless of where you acquire them, must be highly modified to suit your purpose and business.

This first section of forms is from a great online resource, LectLaw. You should visit this site because it has excellent forms, advice, and referrals. As Jeff Liebling (president of the company) says in an e-mail to me, "Lectric Law Library is the best thing in the entire Universe—be it animal, vegetable or mineral." You can access his website at www.lectlaw.com. He also offers an important caution and warning, noted here—which goes for all forms in this book, too, although below, I am quoting LectLaw, sarcasm and all!

"Although we try to ensure the Library's holdings are accurate and virus-free, we only guarantee that it contains no intentional mistakes or defects and has no fraudulent, unlawful, or improper purpose. Otherwise there is no guarantee made or implied about the accuracy, currency, usefulness, functionality, safety, toxicity, or anything else regarding the Library or anything in it, near it, related to it, or connected with it in any way. Use it at your own risk!

This means that if you use the Library's material for whatever purpose and, due to our completely negligent and idiotic error, you are embarrassed, imprisoned, bankrupted, flunked, deported, divorced, molested, castigated, outcast, crucified, sickened, beaten, drowned, excommunicated, ridiculed, or elected to high public office—don't [paraphrasing here, complain] to us about it. —From "Ralf's Library Tour".

NOTE TO LEGAL PROFESSIONALS: You can skip this part. If you don't already follow its advice you are (or will soon be): fired, disbarred, in jail, being sued, hiding from clients, under investigation, all of the above, or serving on the Supreme Court. Important Hints for Students, Pro Ses & Other Lay People

1. Be careful in using any of our material. While we try to ensure the Library's holdings are accurate and current there is no guarantee we've always succeeded. Before using it in a real-life situation check it against a current 'official' copy at your local law library or elsewhere. And this is good advice for all legal info, no matter the source. It's even rumored that the government can screw things up.

2. The laws and rules are always changing. Don't rely on your memory or old books. Remember what our Head Librarian Ralf claims to have told Aristotle, or Plato … or Pluto: 'There's nothing more dangerous than an outdated lawbook—except maybe a pissed-off judge.'

3. Even if something is accurate—in context—it may not be as applied to your specific situation. For example, a form, procedure, or other information may be entirely accurate as it applies to Alabama but if you use it in Wyoming you'll be immediately burned at the stake. So please contact an appropriate professional or go to the law library.

4. Be aware that much legal information can only be a static snapshot of a constantly changing, growing, evolving concept. Also, with many subjects (e.g., many court procedural rules), even if you completely understand them, You Don't. For an approximation of what is really required in practice, you can start at a real law library. However, with that said, you should also realize that certain—some say all—legal questions (e.g., to whom and what do RICO—racketeering—laws apply) have no firm, unchanging answer. This is one of the main reasons judges exist.

5. Despite what some may say, a normally intelligent person can figure out the answer to most legal questions—if they spend enough time and effort. But do you want to spend six weeks learning and researching how to deal with a legal issue when a legal professional might only charge a small amount to do it?

6. Advice for lay people who will be appearing in court: Unless you're a masochist or trying to lay a foundation for an insanity defense when addressing a judge you should refer to him or her as 'Your Honor'—NOT 'Your Highness,' 'Your Holiness,' 'Buddy,' 'Sweetie,' etc., and, no matter how attractive he or she is, DON'T hit on the judge while court's in session. This may be one of the few times you should watch what the lawyers do and act like them. Just be careful you don't make it a habit! Finally, read some of the Library's transcripts, especially the ones in our News Room from the Freeman proceedings, and do the exact opposite.

7. A last bit of advice for now: If you're not sure what you're supposed to do in a given legal situation, don't just wing it. Check the laws, rules, commentaries, etc.—and if you're still not sure, Get Advice From Someone Who Knows. For procedural matters a judge's or court's clerk may be able to help, while on matters of law—understanding the difference between the two is about as easy a nailing Jello to the wall—contact a knowledgeable legal professional." (Liebling, 2008)

That said, we can move on to some of our most important documents!

```
GENERAL AFFIDAVIT

State of _____

County of _____

Before the undersigned, an officer duly commissioned by the laws of
_____, on this_____day of _____, 20____, personally
appeared _____ who having been first duly
sworn depose and say:

_____
_____
_____


Witness:_____      _____


Sworn and subscribed before me this ___day of _____A.D. 20__


_____

_____
```

General Affidavit

(Source: www.lectlaw.com/forms/f041.htm)

```
CONDITIONAL SALES CONTRACT

For good and valuable consideration, this conditional sales
contract is entered into between (Seller) and (Buyer).
Seller agrees to sell and the Buyer agrees to buy the following
goods on a conditional sale:

Sale price: [$]
Sales tax: [$]
Other charges: [$]
Finance charges: [$]
Total purchase price: [$]

Deductions

Down payment: [$]
Other credits: [$]
Total deductions: [$]
Amount financed: [$]
ANNUAL INTEREST RATE: [%]
```

The amount financed is payable in [number] monthly payments of [$] each, starting on the [day] of the month of [month], [year], and continuing on the same day each succeeding month until paid in full.

The title to the goods remain with the Seller until payment of the full purchase price, subject to allocation of payments and release of security interest as required by law. The Buyer agrees to keep the goods free from other liens and encumbrances and not to remove the goods from the below address without the written consent of the Seller.

Buyer agrees to execute all financing statements as may be required of Seller to perfect this conditional sales contract.

The entire balance shall become immediately due upon default on any installment due or other breach of this agreement.

In the event of a default, Seller may enter upon the premises of the Buyer and reclaim said goods. If the Seller retakes the goods he/she has the right to resell them for credit for the balance purchased, and Seller may reacquire same all as further defined and set forth under state law.

On the demand of the Seller, the Buyer shall keep the goods adequately insured with the Seller named as the loss payee. On request, the Buyer shall provide Seller with proof of insurance.

In the event of default, Buyer shall be responsible to pay attorney fees, collection costs, and other fees associated with enforcement of this agreement. This agreement is binding upon and inure to the benefit of the parties, their successors, assigns, and personal representatives.

The full balance shall become due on default. Upon default, Seller will have the further right to retake the goods, hold and dispose of same and collect expenses, together with any deficiency due from the Buyer, but subject to the Buyer's right to redeem pursuant to law and the Uniform Commerci
al Code.
This agreement shall also be in default upon the death, insolvency, or bankruptcy of Buyer.

Signed under seal and accepted this [day] day of [month], [year].

.

_____
Buyer

Conditional Sales Contract: Use this if you are selling something on some condition.

(Source: www.lectlaw.com/forms/f200.htm)

COLLECTION LETTER

Date:

To: [name and address of debtor]

Re: Your account with [name of company]

Dear [name of debtor]:

Your delinquent account with [company name] has been referred to my office for collection action. You are currently several payments behind on the above referenced account.

I have been instructed to bring legal action against you as may be necessary, which may result in levies against your property or other assets after judgment.

The file indicates that you have failed or refused to pay the above claim even though it appears just, owing, and correct.

You are hereby further advised that if payment is not received within 15 days of the date of this letter, suit in small claims court may be commenced against you forthwith and without further notice for the amount indicated above, together with prejudgment interest. Instead of small claims court, this matter may be referred to our attorney for suit in municipal court.

As I am sure you are aware, if this matter goes to suit, all court costs, process server's fees, sheriff's fees, attorney fees where permitted, and other post judgment costs will be added to the amount that you already owe.

You can avoid the unnecessary inconvenience and added expenses of a lawsuit by making immediate payment to us within 15 days.

Sincerely,

_____

Collections Manager

Collection Letter: Use this as an example of a letter to collect on a debt.

(Source: www.lectlaw.com/forms/f198.htm)

```
CREDIT APPLICATION (COMMERCIAL)

Date:

Business name:
Type of business:
Trade name (if different):

Address:                        City:
State:                          Zip:


Telephone:
Owner/President:[name]
How long in business:
Credit rating:

Trade references (names and addresses):

Bank references (include account numbers & addresses):




Location of financial statements:



Notice:

The undersigned authorizes an inquiry as to the credit
information of the business. In addition, credit if granted may
be withdrawn at any time. I certify the above information to be
true.


_____
Owner/President
```

Credit Application for Businesses: Use this when businesses want a line of credit with your company.

(Source: www.lectlaw.com/forms/f208.htm)

CREDIT REFERENCE REQUEST

Date:

To:[name & address of credit reference]

Re:[name of person seeking a credit reference]

Dear Madam/Sir:

The above referenced person has applied for credit with our company and has listed you as a credit reference. To assist us in making our credit decision, please provide us with the below requested information:

High credit limit:

Present balance:

Payment history:

Number of payments more than 30 days late:

Length of time account open:

Other information that we should consider:

Any information received from you will be held confidential. Enclosed for your convenience is a stamped return envelope.

Sincerely,

_____

[title]

Credit Reference Request: Require those asking you for credit to have it filled out to get references.

(Source: www.lectlaw.com/forms/f211.htm)

ARTICLES OF INCORPORATION

ARTICLES OF INCORPORATION OF [NAME]

The undersigned subscriber to these Articles of Incorporation, a natural person competent to contract, hereby forms a corporation under the laws of the State of [NAME].

ARTICLE I   NAME

The name of the corporation shall be [NAME].

ARTICLE II   NATURE OF BUSINESS

This corporation may engage in or transact any and all lawful activities or business permitted under the laws of the United States, the State of [NAME], or any other state, county, territory or nation.

ARTICLE III CAPITAL STOCK

The maximum number of shares of stock that this corporation is authorized to have outstanding at any one time is [#] shares of common stock having a par value of $1.00 per share.

ARTICLE IV   ADDRESS

The street address of the initial registered office of the corporation shall be [ADDRESS] and the name of the initial Registered Agent for the corporation at that address is [NAME].

ARTICLE V   SPECIAL PROVISIONS

The stock of this corporation is intended to qualify under the requirements of Section 1244 of the Internal Revenue Code and the regulations issued thereunder. Such actions as may be necessary shall be deemed to have been taken by the appropriate officers to accomplish this compliance.

ARTICLE VI   TERM OF EXISTENCE

This corporation shall exist perpetually.

ARTICLE VII   LIMITATION OF LIABILITY

Each director, stockholder and officer, in consideration for his services, shall, in the absence of fraud, be indemnified, whether then in office or not, for the reasonable cost and expenses incurred by him in connection with the defense of, or for advice concerning any claim asserted or proceeding brought against him by reason of his being or having been a director, stockholder or officer of the corporation or of any subsidiary of the corporation, whether or not wholly owned, to the maximum extent permitted by law. The foregoing right of indemnification shall be inclusive of any other rights to which any director, stockholder or officer may be entitled as a matter of law.

ARTICLE VIII SELF DEALING

No contract or other transaction between the corporation and other corporations, in the absence of fraud, shall be affected or invalidated by the fact that any one or more of the directors of the corporation is or are interested in a contract or transaction, or are directors or officers of any other corporation, and any director or directors, individually or jointly, may be a party or parties to, or may be interested in such contract, act or transaction, or in any way connected with such person or person's firm or corporation, and each and every person who may become a director of the corporation is hereby relieved from any liability that might otherwise exist from this contracting with the corporation for the benefit of himself or any firm, association or corporation in which he may be in any way interested. Any director of the corporation may vote upon any transaction with the corporation without regard to the fact that he is also a director of such subsidiary or corporation.

This corporation shall have a minimum of one director. The initial Board of Directors shall consist of:

[NAME]
[NAME]
[NAME]
[NAME]

ARTICLE X INCORPORATOR

The name and address of the incorporator is: [ADDRESS]

IN WITNESS WHEREOF, the undersigned has hereunto set his hand and seal on this _____day of _____, 20_____.

Incorporator: [NAME]

STATE OF [NAME]

COUNTY OF [NAME]

The foregoing instrument was executed and acknowledged before me this _____ day of _____, 20_____, by [NAME].

[NAME] Notary Public   (SEAL)
State of [NAME]
My Commission Expires: [DATE]

Articles of Incorporation: Use this as an example of incorporating. You can get actual forms sent to you from legalzoom.com.

(Source: www.lectlaw.com/forms/f163.htm)

ARTICLES OF INCORPORATION FOR A NOT FOR PROFIT ORGANIZATION WHICH IS
NOT A PRIVATE FOUNDATION.

ARTICLES OF INCORPORATION OF [NAME]

The undersigned, acting as incorporators of a corporation under the Not
for Profit Corporation Act of the State of [NAME], adopt the following
articles of incorporation for such corporation:

ARTICLE I

The name of the corporation, hereinafter referred to as the
"Corporation" is [NAME].

ARTICLE II

The period of duration of the Corporation is perpetual.

ARTICLE III

The Corporation is organized exclusively for charitable, religious,
educational, and scientific purposes, including for such purposes, the
making of distributions to organizations that qualify as exempt
organizations under section 501(c)(3) of the Internal Revenue Code, or
corresponding section of any future federal tax code. The Corporation
may receive and administer funds for scientific, religious, educational,
and charitable purposes, within the meaning of Section 501(c)(3) of the
Internal Revenue Code of 1986 and to that end, the Corporation is
empowered to hold any property, or any undivided interest therein,
without limitation as to amount or value; to dispose of any such
property and to invest, reinvest, or deal with the principal or the
income in such manner as, in the judgment of the directors, will best
promote the purposes of the Corporation, without limitation, except
such limitations, if any, as may be contained in the instrument under
which such property is received, these Articles of Incorporation, the
By-Laws of the Corporation, or any applicable laws, to do any other act
or thing incidental to or connected with the foregoing purposes or in
advancement thereof, but not for the pecuniary profit or financial gain
of its directors or officers except as permitted under the Not-for-
Profit Corporation Law.

No part of the net earnings of the Corporation shall inure to the
benefit of any member, trustee, officer of the Corporation, or any
private individual, except that reasonable compensation may be paid for
services rendered to or for the Corporation affecting one or more of
its purposes, and no member, trustee, officer of the Corporation, or
any private individual shall be entitled to share in the distribution
of any of the corporate assets on dissolution of the Corporation. No
substantial part of the activities of the Corporation shall be the
carrying on of propaganda, or otherwise attempting, to influence
legislation, and the Corporation shall not participate in or intervene
in, including the publication or distribution of statements, any

political campaign on behalf of any candidate for public office.

Upon the dissolution of the Corporation or the winding up of its affairs, the assets of the Corporation shall be distributed exclusively to one or more charitable, religious, scientific, testing for public safety, literary, or educational organizations which would then qualify under the provisions of Section 501(c)(3) of the Internal Revenue Code and its Regulations as they now exist or as they may be hereafter amended, or to the federal government, or to a state or local government, for a public purpose. Any such assets not so disposed of shall be disposed of by the Court of Common Pleas of the county in which the principal office of the Corporation is then located, exclusively for such purposes or to such organization or organizations as said Court shall determine, which are organized and operated exclusively for such purposes.

ARTICLE IV

The qualifications for members and the manner of their admissions shall be regulated by the by-laws.

ARTICLE V

The initial street address in the state of [NAME] of the initial registered office of the Corporation is [LOCATION], and the name of the initial registered agent at such address Is [NAME].

ARTICLE VI

The territory in which the operations of the Corporation are principally to be conducted is the United States of America and its territories and possessions, but the operations of the Corporation shall not be limited to such territory.

ARTICLE VII

The initial board of directors shall consist of at least three (3) members, who need not be residents of the state of [NAME].

ARTICLE VIII

The names and addresses of the persons who shall serve as directors until the first annual meeting of members, or until their successors shall have been elected and qualified, are as follows: [DESCRIBE]

ARTICLE IX

The names and addresses of the initial incorporators are as follows: [NAMES]

```
IN WITNESS WHEREOF, the undersigned have made and subscribed to these
Articles of Incorporation at [LOCATION] on [DATE].

[NAME]
[NAME]

STATE OF [NAME]
COUNTY OF [NAME]


The foregoing instrument was acknowledged before me this [DATE].

[NAME] Notary Public            (SEAL)
State of [NAME]
My Commission Expires:
```

Articles of Incorporation for Nonprofit Organizations

(Source: www.lectlaw.com/forms/f164.htm)

```
Certificate of Transaction of Business Under Fictitious Name - By
Corporation


Certificate

That the undersigned corporation hereby certifies that it is
transacting or proposes to transact business in the State of
_____, under the fictitious name of _____;
and that the principal place of business of said corporation in the
State of _____ is located at _____, in the City
of _____, County of _____.


Dated: _____       _____
                                [Name of Corporation]


[Corporate Seal]           By _____
                                [/S/ Corporate Officer]

[ACKNOWLEDGMENT]
```

Fictitious Name for Corporations

(Source: www.lectlaw.com/forms/f042.htm)

SAMPLE CORPORATE BYLAWS

BY-LAWS

"COMPANY"

ARTICLE I -- OFFICES

Section 1. The registered office of the corporation shall be at:

"Address"

The registered agent in charge thereof shall be: "Name".

Section 2. The corporation may also have offices at such other places as the Board of Directors may from time to time appoint or the business of the corporation may require.

ARTICLE II -- SEAL

Section 1. The corporate seal shall have inscribed thereon the name of the corporation, the year of its organization and the words "Corporate Seal, "State".

ARTICLE III -- STOCKHOLDERS' MEETINGS

Section 1 Meetings of stockholders shall be held at the registered office of the corporation in this state or at such place, either within or without this state, as may be selected from time to time by the Board of Directors.

Section 2. Annual Meetings: The annual meeting of the stockholders shall be held on the 3rd Wednesday of February in each year if not a legal holiday, and if a legal holiday, then on the next secular day following at 10:00 o'clock A.M., when they shall elect a Board of Directors and transact such other business as may properly be brought before the meeting. If the annual meeting for election of directors is not held on the date designated therefore, the directors shall cause the meeting to be held as soon thereafter as convenient.

Section 3. Election of Directors: Elections of the directors of the corporation shall be by written ballot.

Section 4. Special Meetings: Special meetings of the stockholders may be called at any time by the Chairman, or the Board of Directors, or stockholders entitled to cast at least one-fifth of the votes which all stockholders are entitled to cast at the particular meeting. At any time, upon written request of any person or persons who have duly called a special meeting, it shall be the duty of the Secretary to fix the date of the meeting, to be held not more than sixty days after receipt of the request, and to give due notice thereof. If the Secretary shall neglect or refuse to fix the date of the meeting and give notice thereof, the person or persons calling the meeting may do so.

Business transacted at all special meetings shall be confined to the objects stated in the call and matters germane thereto, unless all stockholders entitled to vote are present and consent.

Written notice of a special meeting of stockholders stating the time and place and object thereof, shall be given to each stockholder entitled to vote thereat at least 30 days before such meeting, unless a greater period of notice is required by statute in a particular case.

Section 5. Quorum: A majority of the outstanding shares of the corporation entitled to vote, represented in person or by proxy, shall constitute a quorum at a meeting of stockholders. If less than a majority of the outstanding shares entitled to vote is represented at a meeting, a majority of the shares so represented may adjourn the meeting from time to time without further notice. At such adjourned meeting at which a quorum shall be present or represented, any business may be transacted which might have been transacted at the meeting as originally noticed. The stockholders present at a duly organized meeting may continue to transact business until adjournment, notwithstanding the withdrawal of enough stockholders to leave less than a quorum.

Section 6. Proxies: Each stockholder entitled to vote at a meeting of stockholders or to express consent or dissent to corporate action in writing without a meeting may authorize another person or persons to act for him by proxy, but no such proxy shall be voted or acted upon after three years from its date, unless the proxy provides for a longer period.

A duly executed proxy shall be irrevocable if it states that it is irrevocable and if, and only as long as, it is coupled with an interest sufficient in law to support an irrevocable power. A proxy may be made irrevocable regardless of whether the interest with which it is coupled is an interest in the stock itself or an interest in the corporation generally. All proxies shall be filed with the Secretary of the meeting before being voted upon.

Section 7. Notice of Meetings: Whenever stockholders are required or permitted to take any action at a meeting, a written notice of the meeting shall be given which shall state the place, date and hour of the meeting, and, in the case of a special meeting, the purpose or purposes for which the meeting is called. Unless otherwise provided by law, written notice of any meeting shall be given not less than ten nor more than sixty days before the date of the meeting to each stockholder entitled to vote at such meeting.

Section 8. Consent in Lieu of Meetings: Any action required to be taken at any annual or special meeting of stockholders or a corporation, or any action which may be taken at any annual or special meeting of such stockholders, may be taken without a meeting, without prior notice and without a vote, if a consent in writing, setting forth the action so taken, shall be signed by the holders of outstanding stock having not less than the minimum number of votes that would be necessary to authorize or take such action at a meeting at which all shares entitled to vote thereon were present and voted. Prompt notice of the taking of the corporate action without a meeting by less than unanimous written consent shall be given to those stockholders who have not consented in writing.

Section 9 List of Stockholders: The officer who has charge of the stock ledger of the corporation shall prepare and make, at least ten days before every meeting of stockholders, a complete list of the stockholders entitled to vote at the meeting, arranged in alphabetical order, and showing the address of each stockholder and the number of shares registered in the name of each stockholder. No share of stock upon which any installment is due and unpaid shall be voted at any meeting. The list shall be open to the examination of any stockholder, for any purpose germane to the meeting, during ordinary business hours, for a period of at least ten days prior to the meeting, either at a place within the city where the meeting is to be held, which place shall be specified in the notice of the meeting, or, if not so specified, at the place where the meeting is to be held. The list shall also be produced and kept at the time and place of the meeting during the whole time thereof, and may be inspected by any stockholder who is present.

ARTICLE IV -- DIRECTORS

Section 1. The business and affairs of this corporation shall be managed by its Board of Directors, _____ in number. The directors need not be residents of this state or stockholders in the corporation. They shall be elected by the stockholders at the annual meeting of stockholders of the corporation, and each director shall be elected for the term of one year, and until his successor shall be elected and shall qualify or until his earlier resignation or removal.

Section 2. Regular Meetings: Regular meetings of the Board shall be held without notice, at least quarterly, at the registered office of the corporation, or at such other time and place as shall be determined by the Board.

Section 3. Special Meetings: Special Meetings of the Board may be called by the Chairman on 2 days notice to each director, either personally or by mail, fax or by telegram; special meetings shall be called by the President or Secretary in like manner and on like notice on the written request of a majority of the directors in office.

Section 4. Quorum: A majority of the total number of directors shall constitute a quorum for the transaction of business.

Section 5. Consent in Lieu of Meeting: Any action required or permitted to be taken at any meeting of the Board of Directors, or of any committee thereof, may be taken without a meeting if all members of the Board of committee, as the case may be, consent thereto in writing, and the writing or writings are filed with the minutes of proceedings of the Board or committee. The Board of Directors may hold its meetings, and have an office or offices, outside of this state.

Section 6. Conference Telephone: One or more directors may participate in a meeting of the Board, or a committee of the Board or of the stockholders, by means of conference telephone or similar communications equipment by means of which all persons participating in the meeting can hear each other; participation in this manner shall constitute presence in person at such meeting.

Section 7. Compensation Directors as such, shall not receive any stated salary for their services, but by resolution of the Board, a fixed sum and expenses of attendance at each regular or special meeting of the Board PROVIDED, that nothing herein contained shall be construed to preclude any director from serving the corporation in any other capacity and receiving compensation therefore.

Section 8. Removal: Any director or the entire Board of Directors may be removed, with or without cause, by the holders of a majority of the shares then entitled to vote at an election of directors, except that when cumulative voting is permitted, if less than the entire Board is to be removed, no director may be removed without cause if the votes cast against his removal would be sufficient to elect him if then cumulatively voted at an election of the entire Board of Directors, or, if there be classes of directors, at an election of the class of directors of which he is a part.

ARTICLE V -- OFFICERS

Section 1. The executive officers of the corporation shall be chosen by the directors and shall be a Chairman, President, Secretary and Chief Financial Officer. The Board of Directors may also choose a one or more Vice Presidents and such other officers as it shall deem necessary. Any number of offices may be held by the same person.

Section 2. Salaries: Salaries of all officers and agents of the corporation shall be fixed by the Board of Directors.

Section 3. Term of Office: The officers of the corporation shall hold office for one year and until their successors are chosen and have qualified. Any officer or agent elected or appointed by the Board may be removed by the Board of Directors whenever in its judgment the best interest of the corporation will be served thereby.

Section 4. Chairman: The Chairman shall preside at all meetings of the stockholders and directors; he shall see that all orders and resolutions of the Board are carried into effect, subject, however, to the right of the directors to delegate any specific powers, except such as may be by statute exclusively conferred on the Chairman, to any other officer or officers of the corporation. He shall execute bonds, mortgages and other contracts requiring a seal, under the seal of the corporation. He shall be EX-OFFICIO a member of all committees.

Section 5. President: The President shall attend all sessions of the Board. The President shall be the chief executive officer of the corporation; he shall have general and active management of the business of the corporation, subject, however, to the right of the directors to delegate any specific powers, except such as may be by statute exclusively conferred on the President, to any other officer or officers of the corporation. He shall have the general power and duties of supervision and management usually vested in the office of President of a corporation.

Section 6. Secretary: The Secretary shall attend all sessions of the Board and all meetings at the stockholders and act as clerk thereof, and record all the votes of the corporation and the minutes of all its

transactions in a book to be kept for that purpose, and shall perform
like duties for all committees of the Board of Directors when required.
He shall give, or cause to be given, notice of all meetings of the
stockholders and of the Board of Directors, and shall perform such
other duties as may be prescribed by the Board of Directors or
President, and under whose supervision he shall be. He shall keep in
safe custody the corporate seal of the corporation, and when authorized
by the Board, affix the same to any instrument requiring it.

Section 6. Chief Financial Officer: The Chief Financial Officer shall
have custody of the corporate funds and securities and shall keep full
and accurate accounts of receipts and disbursements in books belonging
to the corporation, and shall keep the moneys of the corporation in
separate account to the credit of the corporation. He shall disburse
the funds of the corporation as may be ordered by the Board, taking
proper vouchers for such disbursements, and shall render to the
President and directors, at the regular meetings of the Board, or
whenever they may require it, an account of all his transactions as
Chief Financial Officer and of the financial condition of the
corporation.

ARTICLE VI -- VACANCIES

Section 1. Any vacancy occurring in any office of the corporation by
death, resignation, removal or otherwise, shall be filled by the Board
of Directors. Vacancies and newly created directorships resulting from
any increase in the authorized number of directors may be filled by a
majority of the directors then in office, although not less than a
quorum, or by a sole remaining director. If at any time, by reason of
death or resignation or other cause, the corporation should have no
directors in office, then any officer or any stockholder or an executor,
administrator, trustee or guardian of a stockholder, or other fiduciary
entrusted with like responsibility for the person or estate of
stockholder, may call a special meeting of stockholders in accordance
with the provisions of these By-Laws.

Section 2. Resignations Effective at Future Date: When one or more
directors shall resign from the Board, effective at a future date, a
majority of the directors then in office, including those who have so
resigned, shall have power to fill such vacancy or vacancies, the vote
thereon to take effect when such resignation or resignations shall
become effective.

ARTICLE VII -- CORPORATE RECORDS

Section 1. Any stockholder of record, in person or by attorney or
other agent, shall, upon written demand under oath stating the purpose
thereof, have the right during the usual hours for business to inspect
for any proper purpose the corporation's stock ledger, a list of its
stockholders, and its other books and records, and to make copies or
extracts therefrom. A proper purpose shall mean a purpose reasonably
related to such person's interest as a stockholder. In every instance
where an attorney or other agent shall be the person who seeks the
right to inspection, the demand under oath shall be accompanied by a
power of attorney or such other writing which authorizes the attorney
or other agent to so act on behalf of the stockholder. The demand

under oath shall be directed to the corporation at its registered office in this state or at its principal place of business.

ARTICLE VIII -- STOCK CERTIFICATES, DIVIDENDS, ETC.

Section 1. The stock certificates of the corporation shall be numbered and registered in the share ledger and transfer books of the corporation as they are issued. They shall bear the corporate seal and shall be signed by the President.

Section 2. Transfers: Transfers of shares shall be made on the books of the corporation upon surrender of the certificates therefore, endorsed by the person named in the certificate or by attorney, lawfully constituted in writing. No transfer shall be made which is inconsistent with law.

Section 3. Lost Certificate: The corporation may issue a new certificate of stock in the place of any certificate theretofore signed by it, alleged to have been lost, stolen or destroyed, and the corporation may require the owner of the lost, stolen or destroyed certificate, or his legal representative to give the corporation a bond sufficient to indemnify it against any claim that may be made against it on account of the alleged loss, 'theft or destruction of any such certificate or the issuance of such new certificate.

Section 4. Record Date: In order that the corporation may determine the stockholders entitled to notice of or to vote at any meeting of stockholders or any adjournment thereof, or the express consent to corporate action in writing without a meeting, or entitled to receive payment of any dividend or other distribution or allotment of any rights, or entitled to exercise any rights in respect of any change, conversion or exchange of stock or for the purpose of any other lawful action, the Board of Directors may fix, in advance, a record date, which shall not be more than sixty nor less than ten days before the date of such meeting, nor more than sixty days prior to any other action.

If no record date is fixed:

(a) The record date for determining stockholders entitled to notice of or to vote at a meeting of stockholders shall be at the close of business on the day next preceding the day on which notice is given, or if notice is waived, at the close of business on the day next preceding the day on which the meeting is held.

(b) The record date for determining stockholders entitled to express consent to corporate action in writing without a meeting, when no prior action by the Board of Directors is necessary, shall be the day on which the first written consent is expressed.

(c) The record date for determining stockholders for any other purpose shall be at the close of business on the day on which the Board of Directors adopts the resolution relating thereto.

(d) A determination of stockholders of record entitled to notice of or to vote at a meeting of stockholders shall apply to any adjournment of the meeting; provided, however, that the Board of Directors may fix a new record date for the adjourned meeting.

Section 5.   Dividends: The Board of Directors may declare and pay dividends upon the outstanding shares of the corporation from time to time and to such extent as they deem advisable, in the manner and upon the terms and conditions provided by the statute and the Certificate of Incorporation.

Section 6.   Reserves: Before payment of any dividend there may be set aside out of the net profits of the corporation such sum or sums as the directors, from time to time, in their absolute discretion, think proper as a reserve fund to meet contingencies, or for equalizing dividends, or for repairing or maintaining any property of the corporation, or for such other purpose as the directors shall think conducive to the interests of the corporation, and the directors may abolish any such reserve in the manner in which it was created.

ARTICLE IX -- MISCELLANEOUS PROVISIONS

Section 1.   Checks: All checks or demands for money and notes of the corporation shall be signed by such officer or officers as the Board of Directors may from time to time designate.

Section 2.   Fiscal Year: The fiscal year shall begin on the first day of January.

Section 3.   Notice: Whenever written notice is required to be given to any person, it may be given to such person, either personally or by sending a copy thereof through the mail, by fax, or by telegram, charges prepaid, to his address appearing on the books of the corporation, or supplied by him to the corporation for the purpose of notice.   If the notice is sent by mail, fax or by telegraph, it shall be deemed to have been given to the person entitled thereto when deposited in the United States mail, faxed or with a telegraph office for transmission to such person.   Such notice shall specify the place, day and hour of the meeting and, in the case of a special meeting of stockholders, the general nature of the business to be transacted.

Section 4.   Waiver of Notice: Whenever any written notice is required by statute, or by the Certificate or the By-Laws of this corporation a waiver thereof in writing, signed by the person or persons entitled to such notice, whether before or after the time stated therein, shall be deemed equivalent to the giving of such notice.   Except in the case of a special meeting of stockholders, neither the business to be transacted at nor the purpose of the meeting need be specified in the waiver of notice of such meeting.   Attendance of a person either in person or by proxy, at any meeting shall constitute a waiver of notice of such meeting, except where a person attends a meeting for the express purpose of objecting to the transaction of any business because the meeting was not lawfully called or convened.

Section 5.   Disallowed Compensation: Any payments made to an officer or employee of the corporation such as a salary, commission, bonus, interest, rent, travel or entertainment expense incurred by him, which shall be disallowed in whole or in part as a deductible expense by the Internal Revenue Service, shall be reimbursed by such officer or employee to the corporation to the full extent of such disallowance. It shall be the duty of the directors, as a Board, to enforce payment of each such amount disallowed. In lieu of payment by the officer or employee, subject to the determination of the directors, proportionate amounts may be withheld from his future compensation payments until the amount owed to the corporation has been recovered.

Section 6. Resignations: Any director or other officer may resign at anytime, such resignation to be in writing, and to take effect from the time of its receipt by the corporation, unless some time be fixed in the resignation and then from that date. The acceptance of a resignation shall not be required to make it effective.

ARTICLE X -- ANNUAL STATEMENT

Section 1. The President and Board of Directors shall present at each annual meeting a full and complete statement of the business and affairs of the corporation for the preceding year. Such statement shall be prepared and presented in whatever manner the Board of Directors shall deem advisable and need not be verified by a certified public accountant.

ARTICLE XI -- AMENDMENTS

Section 1. These By-Laws may be amended or repealed by the vote of stockholders entitled to cast at least a majority of the votes which all stockholders are entitled to cast thereon, at any regular or special meeting of the stockholders, duly convened after notice to the stockholders of that purpose.

Contributed to the Library by Richard Widrig

Corporate Bylaws—For-Profit Company

(Source: www.lectlaw.com/forms/f151.htm)

STOCK PURCHASE AGREEMENT

THIS AGREEMENT is made and entered into this ____ day of _____ , 20__, by and between _____, hereinafter collectively referred to as the "Seller" and _____ and/or assigns and/or nominees, hereinafter collectively referred to as the "Purchaser" (the term "Purchaser" shall extend to in the first instance the original Purchaser named herein and also the assigns of such Purchaser);

WITNESSETH:

WHEREAS, the Seller is the record owner and holder of the issued and outstanding shares of the capital stock of _____, hereinafter referred to as the "Corporation", a _____ corporation, which Corporation has issued capital stock of _____ shares of $ _____par value common stock, and

WHEREAS, the Purchaser desires to purchase all of the issued and outstanding capital stock of the Corporation (referred to as the "Corporation's Stock"), and the Seller desires to sell or cause to be sold all of the Corporation's stock, upon the terms and subject to the conditions hereinafter set forth;

NOW, THEREFORE, in consideration of the mutual covenants and agreements contained in this Agreement, and in order to consummate the purchase and the sale of the Corporation's Stock aforementioned, it is hereby agreed as follows:

1. **PURCHASE AND SALE: CLOSING.**

    a. **Purchase and Sale of Corporation's Stock.**
Subject to the terms and conditions hereinafter set forth, at the closing of the transaction contemplated hereby, the Seller shall sell, convey and transfer, or cause to be sold, conveyed or transferred, all of the Corporation's Stock and deliver to the Purchaser certificates representing such stock, and the Purchaser shall purchase from the Seller the Corporation's Stock in consideration of the purchase price set forth in Section 2 and Exhibit "A" of this Agreement. The certificates representing the Corporation's Stock shall be duly endorsed for transfer or accompanied by appropriate stock transfer powers duly executed in blank, in either case with signatures guaranteed in the customary fashion, and shall have all the necessary documentary transfer tax stamps affixed thereto at the expense of the Seller.

    b. **Procedure for Closing.** The closing of the transactions contemplated by this Agreement (the "Closing"), shall be held at _____, on the _____ day of _____, 20__, at _____ or such other place, date and time as the parties hereto may otherwise agree (such date to be referred to in this Agreement as the "Closing Date").

2. **AMOUNT AND PAYMENT OF PURCHASE PRICE.** The total consideration and method of payment thereof are fully set out in Exhibit "A" attached hereto and made a part hereof.

3. **REPRESENTATIONS AND WARRANTIES OF SELLER.** Seller hereby warrants and represents:

    a. **Organization and Standing.** Corporation is a corporation duly organized, validly existing and in good standing under the laws of the State of_____and has the corporate power and authority to carry on its business as it is now being conducted. A true and correct copy of:

        i. its Certificate of Incorporation and all amendments thereto to date certified by the Secretary of State of the State of _____, and

ii. its Bylaws as now in effect, will be delivered by Seller to the Purchaser prior to the Closing Date. The Corporation's minute books will be made available to the Purchaser and its representatives at any reasonable time or times prior to the Closing for inspection and will be complete and correct as of the date of any such inspection.

b. Capitalization. The authorized capital stock of the Corporation consists of _____ shares of $ _____ par value common stock.

c. Restrictions on Stock.

i. Neither the Corporation nor Seller is a party to any agreement, written or oral, creating rights in respect to the Corporation's Stock in any third person or relating to the voting of the Corporation's Stock.

ii. Seller is the lawful owner of all the Corporation's Stock, free and clear of all security interests, liens, encumbrances, equities and other charges.

iii. There are no existing warrants, options, stock purchase agreements, redemption agreements, restrictions of any nature, calls or rights to subscribe of any character relating to the capital stock of the Corporation, nor are there any securities convertible into such stock.

d. Subsidiaries. The Corporation has no subsidiaries.

e. Authority Relative to this Agreement. Except as otherwise stated herein, the Seller has full power and authority to execute this Agreement and carry out the transactions contemplated by it and no further action is necessary by the Seller to make this Agreement valid and binding upon Seller and enforceable against it in accordance with the terms hereof, or to carry out the actions contemplated hereby. The execution, delivery and performance of this Agreement by the Seller will not :

i. constitute a breach or a violation of the Corporation's Certificate of Incorporation, By-Laws, or of any law, agreement, indenture, deed of trust, mortgage, loan agreement or other instrument to which it is a party, or by which it is bound;

ii. constitute a violation of any order, judgment or decree to which it is a party or by which its assets or properties are bound or affected; or

iii. result in the creation of any lien, charge or encumbrance upon its assets or properties, except as stated herein.

f. Financial Statements. Seller is furnishing financial statements of the Corporation as an inducement to Purchaser to purchase the Corporation's Stock and accordingly, Seller warrants and represents the financial operating history or condition of the Corporation as indicated by the financial statements turned over to Purchaser. Moreover, Seller warrants and represents that at closing the Corporation and the Corporation's Stock will not be subject to any liability save and except those specifically enumerated in Exhibit "B" attached hereto and made a part hereof.

To the extent that liabilities are discovered by Purchaser after Closing which relate to events prior to Closing, Seller shall be responsible to forthwith pay such liabilities, including income tax liabilities in cash within fifteen (15) days thereof, or alternatively, if Seller objects to such liabilities in good faith, litigate the issue and indemnify and save harmless Purchaser from any claim for such liability. This indemnification as it relates to income tax liabilities of the Corporation shall terminate on the tenth (10th) day after the expiration of the applicable period of limitations on assessments and collections applicable to such taxes under the Internal Revenue Code. Moreover, the aforementioned indemnity shall not apply to any tax liability which may occur by reason of actions taken by the Purchaser including, but not limited to, the liquidation of the Corporation.

g. Tax Matters. The Corporation has timely prepared and filed all federal, state and local tax returns and reports as are and have been required to be filed and all taxes shown thereon to be due have been paid in full.

h. Litigation. The Corporation is not a party to any litigation, proceeding or administrative investigation and to the best knowledge of the Seller none is pending against the Corporation or its properties.

i. Properties. The Corporation has good and merchantable title to all of its properties and assets which are those properties and assets set out in Exhibit "C" attached hereto and made a part hereof. At closing, such properties and assets will be subject to no mortgage, pledge, lien, conditional sales agreement, security agreement, encumbrance or charge, secured or unsecured, except for real estate taxes and tangible personal property taxes which shall be prorated as of the date of closing, or those specifically set out in Exhibit "B".

j. Compliance with Applicable Laws. None of the Corporation's actions are prohibited by or have violated or will violate any law in effect on the date of this Agreement or on the date of closing. None of the actions of the Corporation shall conflict with or result in any breach of any of the provisions of, or constitute a default under, or result in the creation of any lien, security interest, charge or encumbrance upon the capital stock of the Corporation, or upon any of the assets of the Corporation, under the provisions of the Certificate of Incorporation or Bylaws or any indenture, mortgage, lease, loan agreement or other agreement to which the Corporation and/or the Seller is a party or by which the capital stock or properties and assets of the Corporation are bound to effect it.

The Corporation is in compliance with all applicable laws, including, but not limited to, corporate laws, zoning regulations, restaurant and beverage laws and regulations, if applicable, city, and/or county and state occupational laws and regulations, internal revenue laws, and any and all other laws which may effect the operation or liability of the Buyers herein.

    k. **Documents for Review.** The Corporation's documents enumerated in Exhibit "D", attached hereto and made a part hereof, are true, authentic, and correct copies of the originals, or, if appropriate, the originals themselves, and no alterations or modifications thereof have been made.

4. REPRESENTATIONS AND WARRANTIES OF SELLER AND PURCHASER. Seller and Purchaser hereby represent and warrant that there has been no act or omission by Seller, Purchaser or the Corporation which would give rise to any valid claim against any of the parties hereto for a brokerage commission, finder's fee, or other like payment in connection with the transactions contemplated hereby.

5. TRANSACTIONS PRIOR TO THE CLOSING. Seller hereby covenants the following:

    a. **Conduct of Corporation's Business Until Closing.** Except as Purchaser may otherwise consent in writing prior to the Closing Date, Seller will not enter into any transaction, take any action or fail to take any action which would result in, or could reasonably be expected to result in or cause, any of the representations and warranties of Seller contained in this Agreement, to be not true on the Closing Date.

    b. **Resignations.** Seller will deliver to Purchaser prior to the Closing Date the resignation of each director and officer of the Corporation, each such resignation to be effective on the Closing Date.

    c. **Satisfactions.** Seller will deliver to Purchaser on the Closing Date a satisfaction from any mortgage and lien holder of the Corporation's property, satisfactory in form and substance to the Purchaser and his counsel indicating that the then outstanding unpaid principal balance of any promissory note secured thereby has been paid in full prior to or simultaneously with the Closing.

    d. **Advice of Changes.** Between the date hereof and the Closing Date, Seller will promptly advise Purchaser in writing of any fact which, if existing or known at the date hereof, would have been required to be set forth herein or disclosed pursuant to this Agreement, or which would represent a material fact the disclosure of which would be relevant to the Purchaser.

6. **EXPENSES.** Each of the parties hereto shall pay its own expense in connection with this Agreement and the transactions contemplated hereby, including the fees and expenses of its counsel and its certified public accountants and other experts.

7. **GENERAL.**

a. Survival of Representations and Warranties. Each of the parties to this Agreement covenants and agrees that the Seller's representations, warranties, covenants and statements and agreements contained in this Agreement and the exhibits hereto, and in any documents delivered by Seller to Purchaser in connection herewith, shall survive the Closing Date and terminate on the second anniversary of such date. Except as set forth in this Agreement, the exhibits hereto or in the documents and papers delivered by Seller to Purchaser in connection herewith, there are no other agreements, representations, warranties or covenants by or among the parties hereto with respect to the subject matter hereof.

b. Waivers. No action taken pursuant to this Agreement, including any investigation by or on behalf of any party shall be deemed to constitute a waiver by the party taking such action or compliance with any representation, warranty, covenant or agreement contained herein, therein and in any documents delivered in connection herewith or therewith. The waiver by any party hereto of a breach of any provision of this Agreement shall not operate or be construed as a waiver of any subsequent breach.

c. Notices. All notices, requests, demands and other communications which are required or may be given under this Agreement shall be in writing and shall be deemed to have been duly given if delivered or mailed, first class mail, postage prepaid:
  To Seller:
  To Purchaser:
  or to such other address as such party shall have specified by notice in writing to the other party.

d. Entire Agreement. This Agreement (including the exhibits hereto and all documents and papers delivered by Seller pursuant hereto and any written amendments hereof executed by the parties hereto) constitutes the entire Agreement and supersedes all prior agreements and understandings, oral and written, between the parties hereto with respect to the subject matter hereof.

e. Sections and Other Headings. The section and other headings contained in this Agreement are for reference purposes only and shall not affect the meaning or interpretation of this Agreement.

f. Governing Law. This agreement, and all transactions contemplated hereby, shall be governed by, construed and enforced in accordance with the laws of the State of _____. The parties herein waive trial by jury and agree to submit to the personal jurisdiction and venue of a court of subject matter jurisdiction located in_____County, State of   . In the event that litigation results from or arises out of this Agreement or the performance thereof, the parties agree to reimburse the prevailing party's reasonable attorney's fees, court costs, and all other expenses, whether or not taxable by the court as costs, in addition to any other relief to which the prevailing party may be entitled. In such event, no action shall be entertained by said court or any court of competent jurisdiction if filed more than one year subsequent to the date the cause(s) of action actually accrued regardless of whether damages were otherwise as of said time calculable.

g. Conditions Precedent. The Conditions Precedent to the enforceability of this Agreement are outlined in Exhibit "E", attached hereto and made a part hereof. In the event that said Conditions Precedent are not fulfilled by the appropriate dates thereof, this Agreement shall be deemed null and void and any deposits paid shall be returned to the Purchaser forthwith.

h. Treasury Stock. It is understood and agreed by the Purchaser that none of the consideration furnished by Purchaser hereunder ($_____) shall be for treasury stock and such consideration, subject to the terms hereof, shall be the sole property of Seller.

I. Contractual Procedures. Unless specifically disallowed by law, should litigation arise hereunder, service of process therefore may be obtained through certified mail, return receipt requested; the parties hereto waiving any and all rights they may have to object to the method by which service was perfected.

IN WITNESS WHEREOF, this Agreement has been executed by each of the individual parties hereto and signed by an officer thereunto duly authorized and attested under the corporate seal by the Secretary of the corporate party hereto, all on the date first above written.

Signed, sealed and delivered in the presence of:

(CORPORATE SEAL)

_____   By:_____
Witness   It's President
                                         Attest: _____
_____
Witness
It's Secretary

_____   _____
Witness   Seller

_____
Witness

_____   _____
Witness   Buyer

_____
Witness

EXHIBIT "A"
AMOUNT AND PAYMENT OF PURCHASE PRICE

a. Consideration. As total consideration for the purchase and sale of the Corporation's Stock, pursuant to this Agreement, the Purchaser shall pay to the Seller the sum of _____ Dollars ($_____), such total consideration to be referred to in this Agreement as the "Purchase Price".

b. Payment. The Purchase Price shall be paid as follows: I. Check of Purchaser in the sum of _____ Dollars ($_____), to be delivered to Seller upon the execution of this Agreement.

>   ii. Check of Purchaser in the sum of _____ Dollars ($_____), to be delivered to Seller upon Seller's examination and approval of the books and records of the Corporation.

>   iii. Check of Purchaser in the sum of _____ Dollars ($_____), to be delivered to Seller's attorney as escrow agent at closing to be held by said agent for a period of sixty (60) days to insure that the Corporation's liabilities have been fully satisfied and liquidated.

>   iv. Check of Purchaser in the sum of _____ Dollars ($_____), to be delivered to Seller at Closing.

c. In the event that the Purchaser, after a complete review of the Corporation's books, records, financial statements, sales tax receipts, bank statements, check books, and any other document required by Purchaser to verify the standing, status or performance of the Corporation, does not approve said purchase, then, in that event, all deposits paid to that date shall be returned to Purchaser with no further liability, responsibility or obligation.

EXHIBIT "B"
LIABILITIES OF CORPORATION

EXHIBIT "C"
PROPERTIES AND ASSETS OF CORPORATION

EXHIBIT "D" DOCUMENTS FOR REVIEW
i.   Corporate Articles of Incorporation
ii.   Corporate Bylaws
iii.   Corporate Minutes and Resolutions
iv.   Financial and Operating Statements
v.   Sales Tax Returns
vi.   Alcoholic Beverage Returns (If applicable)
vii.   Income Tax Returns

```
viii. Accounts Payable Ledgers
ix.   Accounts Receivable Ledgers
x.    Leasehold Agreement(s) (If applicable)
xi.   Warranty Deeds (If applicable)
xii.  Bills of Sale (If applicable)


EXHIBIT "E"
CONDITIONS PRECEDENT
```

Stock Purchase Agreement

(Source: www.lectlaw.com/forms/f049.htm)

```
JOINT VENTURE AGREEMENT FOR _____,

A _____ (state) JOINT VENTURE

THIS JOINT VENTURE AGREEMENT (herein after referred to as the
"Agreement" ) is entered into this _____ day of _____, 20___,
by and among _____, a _____ corporation,
and _____, a _____ corporation, (herein
after collectively referred to as the "Joint Venturers") for the
purpose of performing: _____.

W I T N E S S E T H:

WHEREAS, the parties are desirous of forming a joint venture (the
"Venture"), under the laws of the State of _____ by execution of this
Agreement for the purposes set forth herein and are desirous of fixing
and defining between themselves their respective responsibilities,
interests, and liabilities in connection with the performance of the
before mentioned construction project; and

NOW, THEREFORE, in consideration of the mutual covenants and promises
herein contained, the Parties herein agree to constitute themselves as
joint venturers, henceforth, "Venturers" for the purposes before
mentioned, and intending to be legally bound hereby, the parties hereto,
after first being duly sworn, do covenant, agree and certify as
follows:

ARTICLE I. DEFINITIONS:

1.1 "Affiliate" shall refer to (i) any person directly or indirectly
controlling, controlled by or under common control with another person,
(ii) any person owning or controlling 10% or more of the outstanding
voting securities of such other person, (iii) any officer, director or
other partner of such person and (iv) if such other person is an
officer, director, joint venturer or partner, any business or entity
for which such person acts in any such capacity.

1.2 "Venturers" shall refer to _____ Inc., and
_____, and any successor(s) as may be designated
and admitted to the Venture.
```

1.3 "Internal Revenue Code", "Code" or "I.R.C." shall refer to the current and applicable Internal Revenue Code.

1.4 "Net Profits and Net Losses" means the taxable income and loss of the Venture, except as follows:

1.5 The "book" value of an asset shall be substituted for its adjusted tax basis if the two differ, but otherwise Net Profits and Net Losses shall be determined in accordance with federal income tax principles.

1.6 "Project" shall refer to that certain City of Atlanta, Georgia construction project known as

1.7 "Treasury Regulations" shall refer to those regulations promulgated by the Department of the Treasury with respect to certain provision of Internal Revenue Code.

1.8 "Percentage of Participation" shall refer to that figure set forth in Article at section.

ARTICLE II
FORMATION, NAME, AND PRINCIPLE PLACE OF BUSINESS

2.1 FORMATION

(a) The Venturers do hereby form a joint venture pursuant to the laws of the State of _____ in order for the Venture to carry on the purposes for which provision is made herein.

(b) The Ventures shall execute such certificates as may be required by the laws of the State of _____ or of any other state in order for the Venture to operate its business and shall do all other acts and things requisite for the continuation of the Venture as a joint venture pursuant to applicable law.

2.2 NAME. The Name and style under which the Venture shall be conducted is:

2.3 PRINCIPAL PLACE OF BUSINESS. The Venture shall maintain its principal place of business at: _____. The Venture may re-locate its office from time to time or have additional offices as the Venturers may determine.

ARTICLE III
PURPOSE OF THE JOINT VENTURE

The business of the Venture shall be to perform: _____
project having the Contract # ___, being entitled , and being in a dollar amount of $_____., in accordance with the contract documents for the Project and all such other business incidental to the general purposes herein set forth.

ARTICLE IV
TERM

The term of the Venture shall commence as of the date hereof and shall
be terminated and dissolved upon the earliest to occur of: (i)
completion of the Project and receipt of all sums due the Venture by
the Owner, _____ pursuant thereto and payment of all
laborers and those employed by the Venture in connection with the
project; (ii) December 31, 2000; (iii) the unanimous agreement of the
Ventures; or (iv) the order of a court of competent jurisdiction.

ARTICLE V
PERCENTAGE OF PARTICIPATION

5.1 Except as otherwise provided in sections 6.0 and 9.0 hereof, the
interest of the Parties in any gross profits and their respective
shares in any losses and/or liabilities that may result from the filing
of a joint bid and/or the performance of the Construction Contract, and
their interests in all property and equipment acquired and all money
received in connection with the performance of the Construction
Contract shall be as follows:

Name Joint Venture Partner Percentage

5.2 The Parties agree that in the event any losses arises out of or
results from the performance of the Project, each Venturer shall assume
and pay the share of the losses that is equal to the percentage of
participation.

5.3 If for any reason, a Venturer sustains any liabilities or is
required to pay any losses arising out of or directly connected with
the construction of the Project, or the execution of any surety bonds
or indemnity agreements in connection therewith, which are in excess of
its Percentage of Participation, in the Joint Venture, the other
Venturer shall promptly reimburse such Venturer this excess, so that
each and every member of the Joint Venturer will then have paid its
proportionate share of such losses to the full extent of its Percentage
of Participation.

5.4 The Venturers agree to indemnify each other and to hold the other
harmless from, any and all losses of the Joint Venture that are in
excess of such other Venturer's Percentage of Participation. Provided
that the provisions of this subsection shall be limited to losses that
are directly connected with or arise out of the performance of the
Project and/or the execution of any bonds or indemnity agreements in
connection therewith and shall not be relate to or include any
incidental, indirect or consequential losses that may be sustained or
suffered by a Party.

5.5 The Parties shall from time to time execute such bonds and
indemnity agreements, including applications there and other documents
that may be necessary in connection with the performance of the Project.
Provided however, that the liability of each of the Parties under any
agreements to indemnify a surety company or surety companies shall be
limited to the percentage of the total liability assumed by all the
Parties under such indemnity agreements that is equal to the Party's
Percentage of Participation.

5.6 INITIAL CONTRIBUTION OF THE VENTURE.

(a) The Venturers shall contribute the Property to the Venture and their Capital Account shall each be credited with the appropriate value of such contribution in accordance with their Venture interests.

(b) Except as otherwise required by law or this Agreement, the Venturers shall not be required to make any further capital contributions to the Venture.

5.7 VENTURE INTERESTS

Upon execution of this Agreement, the Venturers shall each own the following interests in the Venture:

Joint Venture Partner: Percentage

(a) _____

(b) _____

5.8 RETURN OF CAPITAL CONTRIBUTIONS.

(a) No Venturer shall have the right to withdraw his capital contributions or demand or receive the return of his capital contributions or any part thereof, except as otherwise provided in this Agreement.

(b) The Venturers shall not be personally liable for the return of capital contributions or any part thereof, except as otherwise provided in this Agreement.

(c) The Venture shall not pay interest on capital contributions of any Venturer.

5.9 ALLOCATIONS OF NET PROFITS AND LOSSES

Subject to the provisions of this Article, the Net Profits and losses of the Venture (including any net "book" gains of the Venture resulting from a Capital Event) shall be allocated to the Venturers in the following priority:

A. NET PROFITS:

(1) First, to those Venturers with negative Capital Accounts, between them in proportion to the ratio of their negative Capital Account balances, until no Venturer has a negative Capital Account.

(2) Thereafter, to the Venturers, pro-rata, based on their respective Venture interests as set forth in Section 5.2 hereof.

B. NET LOSSES:

(1) Subject to the provisions of this Article VI, Net Losses of the Venture (including any net "book" loss of the Venture resulting from a Capital Event) shall be allocated to the Venturers, pro rata, based upon their respective Venture interests as set forth herein.

(2) For purposes of this, Capital Accounts shall be adjusted hypothetically as provided for in Sections 1.704-1(b)(2)(ii)(d) and 1.704- 1(b)(4)(iv)(f) of the Treasury Regulations. These adjustments shall include the qualified income offset as set forth in this Agreement.

C DISTRIBUTIONS. Distributable Cash of the Venture shall be distributed to the Venturers, pro rata, based on their respective Venture interests as set forth herein.

ARTICLE VI:
POLICY COMMITTEE

6.1 The management of the Joint Venture shall be conducted pursuant to policy established by the Parties acting through a "Policy Committee" which is hereby established.

6.2 Except as provided in sections 6.0 and 9.0, each Party shall have a voice in the Policy Committee equal to its Percentage of Participation. For such purpose each Party is assigned the following number of votes and hereby designates the following representatives to exercise such votes:

PARTY VOTES REPRESENTATIVES

6.2 Each Venturer may, at any time, substitute an alternative in place of any of its above-named representatives by serving written notice to all the other Parties. Each Venturer's representative or alternative representative on the Policy Committee is hereby granted and shall hereafter possess authority to act for such Venturer on all matters of interest to it with respect to its participation in the joint venture.

6.3 The Policy Committee shall determine the policy for the management of the joint venturer by majority vote and, as used in this Agreement, a "majority vote" is defined to be any figure greater than one-half of the authorized votes.

6.4 The Policy Committee shall have the following powers:

(a) To determine the time and place of holding its meetings and the procedures for conducting Committee Affairs.

(b) To determine and act upon the various matters, expressly or impliedly contained in other section of this Agreement, which require decision by the Policy Committee.

(c) To determine and act upon any other matters of joint interest to, or requiring prompt action by the Joint Venture.

(d) To determine rental rates not specifically set out in the Additional Provisions of this Agreement for equipment owned by the Venturers and made available for use on this project. Any equipment owned by third parties will be invoiced to the joint venture at actual rental costs.

(e) To determine insurance reserves and reserves for other potential liabilities that may result from or arise out of the Project work.

(f) To consider all claims and disputes of any kind between the joint venture and the Owner, subcontractors and/or third Parties and to authorize negotiation, arbitration, litigation, and/or any other process for their resolution and to authorize the settlement thereof.

6.5 Notwithstanding any other provisions to the contrary herein, insurance coverage and limits shall be subject to approval of all the parties.

6.6 The Policy Committee shall generally perform its duties at a meeting at which all designated representatives of the Parties are present, but where circumstances warrant, telephone communication between all party representatives or their alternatives is authorized.

6.7 Except as otherwise provided in the Additional Provisions herein, the salaries and expenses of each of the representatives on the Committee shall be borne by the Party whom the representative has been designated to represent and shall not be an expense to the joint venture.

ARTICLE VII
DELEGATION OF AUTHORITY

7.1 The Venturers agree to a split of authority betweens themselves as follows:

a. _____ shall be the Administrative Managing Partner responsible for all bookkeeping and payroll of the Joint Venture.

b. _____ shall be the Project Managing Partner in charge of the Project Work.

7.2 The Project Managing Partner shall appoint the General Manager through whom it shall direct charge and supervision of all matters necessary and connected with the performance of the Construction Contract, with the exception of that performed by the Administrative Managing Partner.

7.3 Authority to act for and bind the Venturers in connection with any and all of the performance of the Project may be delegated in writing by unanimous vote of the Venturers to any designated individual(s).

ARTICLE VIII
JOINT VENTURE BANK ACCOUNTS

8.1 All Working Capital or other funds received by the Joint Venture in connection with the performance of the project shall be deposited in a Checking Account, set up especially for the Joint Venture, and requiring the joint signatures of the parties for any withdrawals. Said accounts shall be kept separate and apart from any other accounts of the Venturers.

8.2 Withdrawal of funds from the Joint Venture's Joint Checking Account may be made in such amount and by such persons as authorized by the Policy Committee.

ARTICLE IX
ACCOUNTING AND AUDITING

9.1 Separate books of accounts shall be kept by the Administrative Managing Partner of the transactions of the Joint Venture. Any Venturer may inspect such books upon reasonable notice and at any reasonable time.

9.2 Periodic audits may be made upon said books at such time as authorized by the Policy Committee by persons designated by the same and copies of said audit shall be furnished to all Venturers.

9.3 Upon completion of the Project, a final audit shall be made and copies of such audit shall be furnished to each of the parties.

9.4 It is understood and agreed that the method of accounting used by the Administrative Managing Partner and for state and federal income tax purposes shall be the cash based method and that the accounting year shall be the calendar year.

9.5 The Administrative Managing Partner shall receive additional compensation in the amount of 3% of the total Project amount for the use of its data processing system and accounting, payroll and tabulating work. Work performed by the Administrative Managing Partner's in-house counsel or executive secretary on behalf of the Joint Venture shall be charged separately to the Joint Venture's account at a rate agreed upon by the Venturers.

ARTICLE X
RESOLUTION OF DISPUTES

10.1 All disputes arising out of this Joint Venture Agreement between the Venturers that is not resolvable by good faith negotiations by the same, shall be filed in the Atlanta division of the GAMA, Inc., and shall be settled by arbitration under the rules of the GAMA, Inc. In so agreeing the parties expressly waive their right, if any, to a trial by jury of these claims and further agree that the award of the arbitrator shall be final and binding upon them as though rendered by a court of law and enforceable in any court having jurisdiction over the same.

ARTICLE XII
OTHER PROVISIONS

11.1 This agreement constitutes the entire agreement of the parties and may not be altered, unless the same is agreed upon in writing signed and acknowledged by the parties.

11.2 This agreement is binding upon the heirs, court appointed representatives, assigns, and successors of the parties.

11.3 This agreement shall be governed by the laws of the state of_____.

So agreed and executed this ____, day of _____, 20__.

```
_____
JOINT VENTURE PARTNER #1

_____
JOINT VENTURE PARTNER #2
```

Joint Venture Agreement: Use this form if you're entering into a joint venture and want some legal protection. It is advised you run this by an attorney.

(Source: www.lectlaw.com/forms/f083.htm)

BILL OF SALE OF BUSINESS

For good and sufficient consideration, receipt of which is hereby acknowledged, the undersigned ("Seller") hereby sells, transfers and conveys to ("Buyer"):

1. All and singular, the goods and chattels, property and effects, listed in Schedule "A" annexed hereto, which is incorporated herein and made a part hereof; and

2. The whole of the good will of the _____ business formerly operated by the undersigned that is the subject of this sale.

The undersigned warrants that said goods and chattels are free and clear of all encumbrances, that it has full right and title to sell the same, and that it will warrant and defend the same against the claims and demands of all persons.

The undersigned hereby warrants and covenants that I shall not within _____ years of the date of this instrument engage in the business of _____ within _____.

Dated:

_____   _____
Witness   (Seller)

Bill of Sale of Business

(Source: www.lectlaw.com/forms/f159.htm)

AGREEMENT TO SELL BUSINESS

Agreement made this _____day of _____, 20__ by and between [name]and [name](doing business as [name].) of [address] (hereinafter referred to as "Seller") and [name] (hereinafter referred to as the "Buyer").

Whereas the Seller desires to sell and the Buyer desires to buy the business now being operated at [address] and known as [business name] and all assets thereof as contained in Schedule "A" attached hereto, the parties hereto agree and covenant as follows:

1. The total purchase price for all fixtures, furnishings and equipment is $_____ Dollars payable as follows:

(a) $_____ paid in cash; certified or bank checks, as a deposit upon execution of this Agreement, to be held by [name].

(b) $_____ additional to be paid in cash, certified or bank checks, at the time of passing papers.

(c) $_____ to be paid by a note of the Buyer to the Seller, bearing interest at the rate of _____ percent per annum with an option of the Buyer to prepay the entire outstanding obligation without penalty. Said note shall be secured by a chattel mortgage and financing statement covering the property to be sold hereunder, together with any and all other property acquired during the term of said note and placed in or within the premises known as [describe fully].

2. The property to be sold hereunder shall be conveyed by a standard form Bill of Sale, duly executed by the Seller.

3. The Seller promises and agrees to convey good, clear, and marketable title to all the property to be sold hereunder, the same to be free and clear of all liens and encumbrances. Full possession of said property will be delivered in the same condition that it is now, reasonable wear and tear expected.

4. Consummation of the sale, with payment by the Buyer of the balance of the down payment and the delivery by the Seller of a Bill of Sale, will take place on or before _____, 20__.

5. The Seller may use the purchase money, or any portion thereof, to clear any encumbrances on the property transferred and in the event that documents reflecting discharge of said encumbrances are not available at the time of sale, the money needed to effectuate such discharges shall be held by the attorneys of the Buyer and Seller in escrow pending the discharges.

6. Until the delivery of the Bill of Sale, the Seller shall maintain insurance on said property in the amount that is presently insured.

7. Operating expenses of [business name] including but not limited to rent, taxes, payroll and water shall be apportioned as of the date of the passing of papers and the net amount thereof shall be added to or deducted from, as the case may be, the proceeds due from the Buyer at the time of delivery of the Bill of Sale.

8. If the Buyer fails to fulfill his obligations herein, all deposits made hereunder by the Buyer shall be retained by the Seller as liquidated damages.

9. The Seller promises and agrees not to engage in the same type of business as the one being sold for_____ years from the time of passing, within a [# of blocks/miles] radius of [location].

10. A Broker's fee for professional services in the amount of _____($____) Dollars is due from the Seller to_____, provided and on the conditions that papers pass.

11. The Seller agrees that this Agreement is contingent upon the following conditions:

(a) Buyer obtaining a Lease on the said premises or that the existing Lease be assigned in writing to the Buyer.

(b) Buyer obtaining the approval from the proper authorities (Town and State) of the transfer of all necessary licenses to the Buyer.

(c) The premises shall be in the same condition, reasonable wear and tear expected, on the date of passing as they are currently in.

12. All of the terms, representations and warranties shall survive the closing. This Agreement shall bind and inure to the benefit of the Seller and Buyer and their respective heirs, executors, administrators, successors and assigns.

13. If this Agreement shall contain any term or provision which shall be invalid or against public policy or if the application of same is invalid or against public policy, then, the remainder of this Agreement shall not be affected thereby and shall remain in full force and effect.

IN WITNESS WHEREOF, the parties hereto have caused this instrument to be executed in triplicate on the day and year first above written.

SELLER: _____   BUYER: _____

SELLER: _____   BROKER: _____

Agreement to Sell Business: This is used when you are selling your business.

(Source: www.lectlaw.com/forms/f158.htm)

PARTNERSHIP AGREEMENT

(NAME), and (NAME), the below signed hereby enter into this Partnership Agreement on behalf of themselves, their heirs, successors and assigns, and set forth following terms and conditions as constituting the Partnership Agreement in its entirety:

1. The partnership shall go by the following name: (NAME).

2. The partnership's principle place of business shall be (DESCRIBE).

3. The first day that the partnership shall begin business is: (DATE) and it will continue until the partners agree to terminated it or until forced cease its operations by law.

4. The partnership's operations shall be primarily in the following field or area: (DESCRIBE)

5. The partnership shall be capitalized as follows: For each $ (AMOUNT) (dollars) each partner shall receive (#) shares with contribution being made as follows:

Partner A contributes $(AMOUNT). and shall receive (#) shares, the same being (#)% of the total shares available.

Partner B contributes $(AMOUNT). and shall receive (#)shares, the same being (#)% of the total shares available.

6. Losses and gains on contributed capital and other property shall be assigned as follows: (DESCRIBE)

The IRS's general allocation rule shall apply, and gains and losses shall be allocated according to the % of total capital contributed by each partner as set out in paragraph 5 above.

7. Profits and losses shall be allocated according to the same percentage allocation set forth in paragraph 6 above.

8. Salary, if any, for the services rendered shall be determined by unanimous approval of the partners.

9. Control and management of the partnership shall be spit equally amongst the partners.

10. Each partner shall maintain both an individual drawing account and an individual capital account. Into the capital account shall be placed that partner's initial capitalization and any increases thereto. The drawing accounts shall be used for withdrawal of amounts, the size of which is limited to $(AMOUNT) on any one day.

11. Adequate accounting records shall be made and maintained. Any partner or his/her agent, may review any and all accounting or other records at anytime.

12. The partners designate the following as the Partnership's business and checking accounts into which all the funds of the Partnership shall be placed and maintained: (DESCRIBE)

13. Accounting records and books shall be kept on a (select one) 1. cash basis 2. accrual basis and the fiscal year shall begin on the (#) day of (MONTH) and shall end (#) day of (MONTH).

14. At the close of the fiscal year there shall be an annual audit conducted by the following accounting firm: (DESCRIBE)

15. The partnership shall dissolve upon the retirement, death or incapacity of any partner unless the remaining partner elects the option of buying out that partner's share. If so elected, the partnership shall be valued by submission to arbitration with GAMA, Inc., according to reasonable accounting and valuation principles, and as set forth in paragraph 17 below. The finding of the arbitrator as to the value of the partnership shall be final and binding upon the partners, their heirs, successors, and assigns. Upon the issuance of this finding, the remaining partner shall have (TIME) to buy out the previous partner's share. Should more than one remaining partner desire to buy this share, the share shall be split evenly between the same.

16. Upon termination or dissolution of the Partnership, the Partnership will be promptly liquidated, with all debts being paid first, prior to any distribution of the remaining funds. Distribution shall be made according to the percentage of ownership as set out in paragraph 5 above.

17. Any controversy or claim arising out of or relating to this Agreement, or the breach thereof, shall be settled by arbitration in accordance with the Commercial Arbitration Rules of the American Arbitration Association, and judgment upon the award rendered by the arbitrator(s) may be entered in any court having jurisdiction thereof.

So agreed, this (#) day of (MONTH), 20___.

_____
(NAME)

_____
(NAME)

Partnership Agreement: This is a basic document and I recommend you run these (and all) documents that are vital to your business through an attorney. This partnership agreement forms an official partnership between two or more parties or entities.

(Source: www.lectlaw.com/forms/f086.htm)

EMPLOYMENT AGREEMENT

This Agreement made and entered into this _____ day of _____,
20__, by and between _____ ("employer"), and _____
("employee"). The parties recite that:

A. Employer is engaged in _____ and maintains business premises at
_____.

B. Employee is willing to be employed by employer, and employer is
willing to employ employee, on the terms and conditions hereinafter set
forth. For the reasons set forth above, and in consideration of the
mutual covenants and promises of the parties hereto, employer and
employee covenant and agree as follows:

1. AGREEMENT TO EMPLOY AND BE EMPLOYED
Employer hereby employs employee as _____ at the above-mentioned
premises, and employee hereby accepts and agrees to such employment.

2. DESCRIPTION OF EMPLOYEE'S DUTIES
Subject to the supervision and pursuant to the orders, advice, and
direction of employer, employee shall perform such duties as are
customarily performed by one holding such position in other businesses
or enterprises of the same or similar nature as that engaged in by
employer. Employee shall additionally render such other and unrelated
services and duties as may be assigned to him from time to time by
employer.

3. MANNER OF PERFORMANCE OF EMPLOYEE'S DUTIES
Employee shall at all times faithfully, industriously, and to the best
of his ability, experience, and talent, perform all duties that may be
required of and from him pursuant to the express and implicit terms
hereof, to the reasonable satisfaction of employer. Such duties shall
be rendered at the abovementioned premises and at such other place or
places as employer shall in good faith require or as the interests,
needs, business, and opportunities of employer shall require or make
advisable.

4. DURATION OF EMPLOYMENT
The term of employment shall be _____ years, commencing on _____,
20___, and terminating _____, 20_____,subject, however, to prior
termination as otherwise provided herein.

5. COMPENSATION; REIMBURSEMENT
Employer shall pay employee and employee agrees to accept from
employer, in full payment for employee's services hereunder,
compensation at the rate of _____ Dollars ($_____) per annum,
payable _____. In addition to the foregoing, employer will
reimburse employee for any and all necessary, customary, and usual
expenses incurred by him while traveling for and on behalf of the
employer pursuant to employer's directions.

6. EMPLOYEE'S LOYALTY TO EMPLOYER'S INTERESTS
Employee shall devote all of his time, attention, knowledge, and skill
solely and exclusively to the business and interests of employer, and
employer shall be entitled to all benefits, emoluments, profits, or
other issues arising from or incident to any and all work, services,

and advice of employee. Employee expressly agrees that during the term hereof he will not be interested, directly or indirectly, in any form, fashion, or manner, as partner, officer, director, stockholder, advisor, employee, or in any other form or capacity, in any other business similar to employer's business or any allied trade, except that nothing herein contained shall be deemed to prevent or limit the right of employee to invest any of his surplus funds in the capital stock or other securities of any corporation whose stock or securities are publicly owned or are regularly traded on any public exchange, nor shall anything herein contained by deemed to prevent employee from investing or limit employee's right to invest his surplus funds in real estate.

7. NONDISCLOSURE OF INFORMATION CONCERNING BUSINESS

Employee will not at any time, in any fashion, form, or manner, either directly or indirectly divulge, disclose, or communicate to any person, firm, or corporation in any manner whatsoever any information of any kind, nature, or description concerning any matters affecting or relating to the business of employer, including, without limitation, the names of any its customers, the prices it obtains or has obtained, or at which it sells or has sold its products, or any other information concerning the business of employer, its manner of operation, or its plans, processes, or other date of any kind, nature, or description without regard to whether any or all of the foregoing matters would be deemed confidential, material, or important. The parties hereby stipulate that, as between them, the foregoing matters are important, material, and confidential, and gravely affect the effective and successful conduct of the business of employer, and its good will, and that any breach of the terms of this section is a material breach of this agreement.

8. OPTION TO TERMINATE ON PERMANENT DISABILITY OF EMPLOYEE

Not withstanding anything in this agreement to the contrary, employer is hereby given the option to terminate this agreement in the event that during the term hereof employee shall become permanently disabled, as the term "permanently disabled" is hereinafter fixed and defined. Such option shall be exercised by employer giving notice to employee by registered mail, addressed to him in care of employer at the above stated address, or at such other address as employee shall designate in writing, of its intention to terminate this agreement on the last day of the month during which such notice is mailed. On the giving of such notice this agreement and the term hereof shall cease and come to an end on the last day of the month in which the notice is mailed, with the same force and effect as if such last day of the month were the date originally set forth as the termination date. For purposes of this agreement, employee shall be deemed to have become permanently disabled if, during any year of the term hereof, because of ill health, physical or mental disability, or for other causes beyond his control, he shall have been continuously unable or unwilling or have failed to perform his duties hereunder for thirty (30) consecutive days, or if, during any year of the term hereof, he shall have been unable or unwilling or have failed to perform his duties for a total period of thirty (30) days, whether consecutive or not. For the purposes hereof, the term "any year of the term hereof" is defined to mean any period of 12 calendar months commencing on the first day of _____ and terminating on the last day of _____ of the following year during the term hereof.

9. DISCONTINUANCE OF BUSINESS AS TERMINATION OF EMPLOYMENT
Anything herein contained to the contrary notwithstanding, in the event that employer shall discontinue operations at the premises mentioned above, then this agreement shall cease and terminate as of the last day of the month in which operations cease with the same force and effect as if such last day of the month were originally set forth as the termination date hereof.

10. EMPLOYEE'S COMMITMENTS BINDING ON EMPLOYER ONLY ON WRITTEN CONSENT
Employee shall not have the right to make any contracts or other commitments for or on behalf of employer without the written consent of employer.

11. CONTRACT TERMS TO BE EXCLUSIVE
This written agreement contains the sole and entire agreement between the parties, and supersedes any and all other agreements between them. The parties acknowledge and agree that neither of them has made any representation with respect to the subject matter of this agreement or any representations inducing the execution and delivery hereof except such representations as are specifically set forth herein, and each party acknowledges that he or it has relied on his or its own judgment in entering into the agreement. The parties further acknowledge that any statements or representations that may have heretofore been made by either of them to the other are void and of no effect and that neither of them has relied thereon in connection with his or its dealings with the other.

12. WAIVER OR MODIFICATION INEFFECTIVE UNLESS IN WRITING
No waiver or modification of this agreement or of any covenant, condition, or limitation herein contained shall be valid unless in writing and duly executed by the party to be charged therewith. Furthermore, no evidence of any waiver or modification shall be offered or received in evidence in any proceeding, arbitration, or litigation between the parties arising out of or affecting this agreement, or the rights or obligations of any party hereunder, unless such waiver or modification is in writing, duly executed as aforesaid. The provisions of this paragraph may not be waived except as herein set forth.

13. CONTRACT GOVERNED BY LAW
This agreement and performance hereunder shall be construed in accordance with the laws of the State of _____.

14. BINDING EFFECT OF AGREEMENT
This agreement shall be binding on and inure to the benefit of the respective parties and their respective heirs, legal representatives, successors, and assigns.

Executed on the date first above written.

_____, Employer

_____, Employee

Employment Agreement

(Source: www.lectlaw.com/forms/f111.htm)

APPLICATION FOR EMPLOYMENT
For Personnel use only

Employment Form

Last Name: _____

First: _____ MI: ___

Date of Application: _____

Street Address: _____

City: _____ State: _____ ZIP: _____

Type(s) of Work Desired:

_____

Social Security number: _____

Home telephone: _____

Work telephone: _____

How Were You Referred To Us? (Circle only one.)

A By Your College
B Advertisement
C Employment Agency
D By an Employee
   If So, Give Name: _____
E Open house
F Walk-in
G Other

Please Read Carefully And Complete By Printing In Ink Or Typing.

An Equal Opportunity Employer
We are an equal opportunity employer, and we do not and will not
discriminate on the basis of race, religion, national origin, sex, age,
handicap, marital status, or status as a disabled veteran. Information
provided on this application will not be used for any discriminatory
purpose.

Provide All Information Requested.

Your complete application form will be maintained in our active files
for six (6) months from the date of application. You may submit a new
application at any time.

EMPLOYMENT RECORD

Starting with present or most recent, list all previous employers.
Include self-employment and summer and part-time jobs. If more space is
required, please continue on a separate sheet. You may attach a resume,
but complete this application as well.

Last Or Present Company:

_____

Type of Business:

_____

Type or Classification of Job:

_____

Street Address:_____

City: _____ State: _____ ZIP: _____

Phone number: _____

Brief Description of Job Duties:

_____

Supervisor's Name: _____

Phone number: _____

Base salary: _____

Dates worked: From _____ To _____

Reason for leaving:

_____

Last or Present Company:

_____

Type of Business:

_____

Type or Classification of Job:

_____

City: _____ State: _____ ZIP: _____

Phone number: _____

Brief Description of Job Duties:

_____

Supervisor's Name:

_____

Phone number: _____

Base salary: _____

Dates worked: From _____ To _____

Reason for Leaving:

_____

EDUCATIONAL HISTORY

High School:

School Name: _____

Location (city, state): _____

Major Course or Subject: _____

Dates Attended: From _____ To _____

Graduated: Yes _____ No _____

Degree: _____

Technical/Trade (after high school)

School Name: _____

Location (city, state): _____

Major Course or Subject: _____

Dates Attended: From _____ To _____

Graduated: Yes _____ No _____

Degree: _____

College (list all attended)

School Name: _____

Location (city, state): _____

Major Course or Subject: _____

Dates Attended: From _____ To _____

Graduated: Yes _____ No _____

Degree: _____

School Name: _____

Location (city, state): _____

Major Course or Subject: _____

Dates Attended: From _____ To _____

Graduated: Yes _____ No _____

Degree: _____

Other education/training

School Name: _____

Location (city, state): _____

Major Course or Subject: _____

Dates Attended: From _____ To _____

Graduated: Yes _____ No _____

Degree: _____

School name: _____

Location (city, state): _____

Major Course or Subject: _____

Dates Attended: From _____ To _____

Graduated: Yes _____ No _____

Degree: _____

OUTSIDE ACTIVITIES

(Exclude those indicating race, color, religion, sex, national origin, age, or handicap.) Professional memberships, certificates, or licenses held:

_____

_____

_____

Past and Present Civic or Cultural Activities (include offices held):

_____

_____

Principal Hobbies

_____

_____

SPECIAL SKILLS

To be Completed by Applicant for Office/Clerical Work

Typing: Yes _____ Words per Minute: _____ No _____

Dictation: Yes _____ Words per minute: _____ No _____

To be Completed By Applicant for Shop/Plant Work

Type of Machines Operated:

_____

_____

Years Experience: _____

Computer Skills

Hardware:

_____

Software:

_____

Please list Other Skills and/or Equipment/Language Experience You Have Acquired:

_____

List Other Shop/Production Skills:

_____

_____

Served Apprenticeship:

Yes _____ Type: _____

No _____

MILITARY RECORD

Branch of Service

_____

From _____ To _____

Present Military Affiliation:

None_____ Reserve (active)_____ Reserve (inactive)_____

Kinds of Training and Duty While in Service:

_____

_____

PROFESSIONAL/WORK REFERENCES

List two past supervisors and one person who is not related to you who have knowledge of your qualifications for the position for which you are applying.

Name: _____

Title/Relationship: _____

Street Address:_____

City: _____ State: _____ ZIP: _____

Phone no. (include area code)_____

Occupation: _____

May We Contact Your Present Employer?

Yes _____ No _____

Wage or Salary Required: _____

Date Available: _____

I hereby certify that the answers and other information on this application are true and correct and that I understand any misrepresentation or omission of facts on my part will be justification for separation from the company's service, if employed. I understand that my employment may be contingent upon receipt of an alien registration number, verification of birth, and any other pertinent information bearing upon my employment, and that my continued employment depends upon the will of the company or myself.

_____
Signature

Date: _____

If any of your educational or employment records are under other than the above name, please provide other names.

_____

_____

Employment Application

(Source: www.lectlaw.com/forms/f153.htm)

EMPLOYEE NONCOMPETE AGREEMENT (Specific Locations)

In consideration of my being employed by _____ (Company), I, the undersigned, hereby agree that upon the termination of my employment and notwithstanding the cause of termination, I shall not compete with the business of the Company or its successors or assigns, to wit: _____ and shall not directly or indirectly, as an owner, officer, director, employee, consultant, or stockholder, engage in the business of _____ or a business substantially similar or competitive to the business of the Company.

This noncompete agreement shall extend only for a radius of _____ miles from the present location of the Company, and shall be in full force and effect for _____ years, commencing with the date of employment termination.

Signed and sealed this _____ day of _____, 20__.

_____
Employee

Employee Noncompete Agreement

(Source: www.lectlaw.com/forms/f019.htm)

SALES REPRESENTATIVE AGREEMENT

THIS AGREEMENT by and between _____, whose address is _____, hereinafter referred to as "Company", and _____, whose address is _____, hereinafter referred to as "Sales Representative".

WHEREAS, Company is engaged in the marketing and sale of _____; and

WHEREAS, Sales Representative desires to sell Company's services in accordance with the terms and conditions of this Agreement.

NOW, THEREFORE, it is agreed as follows:

1. Company hereby appoints Sales Representative as an authorized non-exclusive independent representative to sell and promote all services provided by Company in the following geographical area: _____, hereinafter referred to as "Territory".

2. Sales Representative shall devote such time, energy and skill on a regular and consistent basis as is necessary to sell and promote the sale of Company's services in the Territory during the term of this Agreement. Sales Representative's sales and promotional efforts shall be directed toward the following:

The aforementioned customers are intended only to be examples of the nature and type of market to which Company desires that its services be sold and should not be construed as a limitation upon the contracts that can be made by Sales Representative under this Agreement within the designated market. In addition to the foregoing, Sales Representative shall assist Company and shall perform any and all services required or requested in connection with Company's business, including, but not limited to, such services of an advisory nature as may be requested from time to time by Company. Sales Representative shall periodically, or at any time upon Company's request, submit appropriate documentation of any and all sales and promotional efforts performed and to be performed for Company pursuant to this Agreement.

3. For each contract for the performance of Company's services as arranged by Sales Representative under this Agreement, Sales Representative shall be entitled to a commission as follows:

a. (___%) percent of contract billing during the first year; b. (___%) percent of contract billing during the second year; c. (___%) percent of contract billing during the third year, and for any year thereafter.

The commission rates and time periods set forth in this paragraph shall commence as of the date of the first invoice on the contract; provided, however that no commission will be due and payable to Sales Representative until _____ (___) days from receipt of payment of Company from any customer on the contract for any underlying invoice. Commissions will be paid on fees for services rendered by shall not include freight, supplies, and other charges incidental to the performance of said services. For purposes of this Agreement, "Contract" shall mean any agreement and/or order of Company's services sold or arranged by Sales Representative. Any and all commissions payable to Company to Sales Representative under this Agreement shall terminate on the __ day of the _____ full month after termination of this Agreement and Company shall then be discharged and released of any further obligation to pay commissions to Sales Representative under this Agreement.

4. During the term of this Agreement or within ____year(s) after its termination, Sales Representative, or any agents or representatives under Sales Representative's control, shall not compete with Company, directly or indirectly, for Sales Representative or on behalf of any other person, firm, partnership, corporation or other entity in the sale or promotion of services the same as or similar to Company's services within the Territory. Under no circumstances and at no time shall Sales Representative disclose to any person any of the secrets, methods or systems used by Company in its business. All customer lists, brochures, reports, and other such information of any nature made available to Sales Representative by virtue of Sales Representative's association with Company shall be held in strict confidence during the term of this Agreement and after its termination.

5. This Agreement shall not create a partnership, joint venture, agency, employer/employee or similar relationship between Company and Sales Representative. Sales Representative shall be an independent contractor. Company shall not be required to withhold any amounts for state or federal income tax or for FICA taxes from sums becoming due to Sales Representative under this Agreement. Sales Representative shall not be considered an employee of Company and shall not be entitled to participate in any plan, arrangement or distribution by Company pertaining to or in connection with any pension, stock, bonus, profit sharing or other benefit extended to Company's employees. Sales Representative shall be free to utilize his time, energy and skill in such manner as he deems advisable to the extent that he is not otherwise obligated under this Agreement.

6. Sales Representative shall bear any and all costs or expenses incurred by Sales Representative to perform his obligation under this Agreement, including, but not limited to, vehicle insurance, travel expenses and telephone expenses.

7. The rights and duties of Sales Representative under this Agreement are personal and may not be assigned or delegated without prior written consent of Company.

8. Sales Representative is not authorized to extend any warranty or guarantee or to make representations or claims with respect to Company's services without express written authorization from Company.

9. Sales Representative shall indemnify and hold Company harmless of and from any and all claims or liability arising as a result of negligent, intentional or other acts of Sales Representative or his agent or representatives.

10. Company shall indemnify and hold Sales Representative harmless of and from any and all liability attributable solely to the negligent, intentional or other acts of Company or its employees.

11. This agreement, and all transactions contemplated hereby, shall be governed by, construed and enforced in accordance with the laws of the State of _____. The Parties herein waive trial by jury and agree to submit to the personal jurisdiction and venue of a court of subject matter jurisdiction located in_____County, State of____ . In the event that litigation results from or arises out of this Agreement or the performance thereof, the Parties agree to reimburse the prevailing party's reasonable attorney's fees, court costs, and all other expenses, whether or not taxable by the court as costs, in addition to any other relief to which the prevailing party may be entitled. In such event, no action shall be entertained by said court or any court of competent jurisdiction if filed more than one year subsequent to the date the cause(s) of action actually accrued regardless of whether damages were otherwise as of said time calculable.

12. Any notice under this Agreement shall be deemed given on the third business day following the mailing of any such notice, postage paid, to the address set forth above.

13. This Agreement contains the entire agreement between the parties and any representation, promise or condition not incorporated herein shall not be binding upon either party.

IN WITNESS WHEREOF, the parties have hereunto executed this Agreement on the _____ day of ____ , 20__ , to become effective as of ____ , 20__ .

"COMPANY"

By: _____

Witness   President
_____

Witness
_____

Witness
_____

"SALES REPRESENTATIVE"
_____

Witness

Sales Rep Agreement

(Source: www.lectlaw.com/forms/f051.htm)

CONSULTING AGREEMENT

AGREEMENT made this_____day of _____, 20___, by and between
_____, whose address is _____, hereinafter
referred to as the "Consultant", and_____, whose principal
place of business is located at _____, hereinafter referred to
as "Company".

WHEREAS, the Company desires to engage the services of the Consultant
to perform for the Company consulting services regarding the functions
for the operation of_____as an independent contractor and not as
an employee; and

WHEREAS, Consultant desires to consult with the Board of Directors,
the officers of the Company, and the administrative staff, and to
undertake for the Company consultation as to the direction of certain
functions in said management of;

NOW, THEREFORE, it is agreed as follows:

1. **Term.** The respective duties and obligations of the contracting
parties shall be for a period of _____ commencing on _____, 20__,
and may be terminated by either party giving thirty (30) days'
written notice to the other party at the addresses stated above or at
an address chosen subsequent to the execution of this agreement and
duly communicated to the party giving notice.

2. **Consultations.** Consultant shall be available to consult with the
Board of Directors, the officers of the Company, and the heads of the
administrative staff, at reasonable times, concerning matters
pertaining to the organization of the administrative staff, the
fiscal policies of the Company, the relationship of the Company with
its employees or with any organization representing its employees,
and, in general, the important problems of concern in the business
affairs of the Company. Consultant shall not represent the Company,
its Board of Directors, its officers or any other members of the
Company in any transactions or communications nor shall Consultant
make claim to do so.

3. **Liability.** With regard to the services to be performed by
the Consultant pursuant to the terms of this agreement, the
Consultant shall not be liable to the Company, or to anyone who may
claim any right due to any relationship with the Corporation, for any
acts or omissions in the performance of services on the part of the
Consultant or on the part of the agents or employees of the
Consultant, except when said acts or omissions of the Consultant are
due to willful misconduct or gross negligence. The Company shall
hold the Consultant free and harmless from any obligations, costs,
claims, judgments, attorneys' fees, and attachments arising from or
growing out of the services rendered to the Company pursuant to the
terms of this agreement or in any way connected with the rendering of
services, except when the same shall arise due to the willful
misconduct or gross negligence of the Consultant and the Consultant
is adjudged to be guilty of willful misconduct or gross negligence by
a court of competent jurisdiction.

4. Compensation. The Consultant shall receive at least monthly from the Company for the performance of the services to rendered to the Company pursuant to the terms of the agreement $_____ per hour for work performed by the Consultant; however, in no event shall the compensation paid to the Consultant by the Company be less than $_____ per month nor more than $_____ per month. In addition, the Company shall reimburse the Consultant per diem for any reasonable out of pocket expenses incurred by the Consultant pursuant to the terms of this agreement. The Consultant shall submit itemized statements of hours of services performed and expenses incurred during any particular month by the fifth (5th) day of the next succeeding month. The amount shall be paid to the Consultant by the fifteenth (15th) day of the latter month.

5. Retainer. A minimum retainer of_____Dollars ($_____) will be paid Consultant by Company in advance of any consultations and will be applied by client in advance of any consultations on account of the fee for such consultations.

6. Arbitration. Any controversy or claim arising out of or relating to this contract, or the breach thereof, shall be settled by arbitration in accordance of the rules of the American Arbitration Association, and judgment upon the award rendered by the arbitrator(s) shall be entered in any court having jurisdiction thereof. For that purpose, the parties hereto consent to the jurisdiction and venue of an appropriate court located in _____ County, State of_____ . In the event that litigation results from or arises out of this Agreement or the performance thereof, the parties agree to reimburse the prevailing party's reasonable attorney's fees, court costs, and all other expenses, whether or not taxable by the court as costs, in addition to any other relief to which the prevailing party may be entitled. In such event, no action shall be entertained by said court or any court of competent jurisdiction if filed more than one year subsequent to the date the cause(s) of action actually accrued regardless of whether damages were otherwise as of said time calculable.

IN WITNESS WHEREOF, the parties have hereunto executed this Agreement on the_____ day of _____ , 20__ .

"Company"

Witness   Company Name
By: _____   Witness _____

"Consultant"

Witness   Firm's Name (if applicable)
By: _____   Witness _____

Consulting Agreement

(Source: www.lectlaw.com/forms/f052.htm)

BUSINESS CONSULTANT AGREEMENT

This agreement dated _____, is made By and Between _____, whose address is _____, ("Company"), AND _____, whose address is _____, ("Consultant.")

1. **Consultation Services.** The company hereby employs the consultant to perform the following services in accordance with the terms and conditions set forth in this agreement: The consultant will consult with the officers and employees of the company concerning matters relating to the management and organization of the company, their financial policies, the terms and conditions of employment, and generally any matter arising out of the business affairs of the company.

2. **Terms of Agreement.** This agreement will begin _____ and will end _____. Either party may cancel this agreement on thirty (30) days notice to the other party in writing, by certified mail or personal delivery.

3. **Time Devoted by Consultant.** It is anticipated the consultant will spend approximately _____ in fulfilling its obligations under this contract. The particular amount of time may vary from day to day or week to week. However, the consultant shall devote a minimum of _____ per month to its duties in accordance with this agreement.

4. **Place Where Services Will Be Rendered.** The consultant will perform most services in accordance with this contract at a location of consultant's discretion. In addition the consultant will perform services on the telephone and at such other places as necessary to perform these services in accordance with this agreement.

5. **Payment to Consultant.** The consultant will be paid at the rate of $_____ per _____ for work performed in accordance with this agreement. However, the consultant will be paid at least $_____ per month regardless of the amount of time spent in accordance with this agreement. The consultant will submit an itemized statement setting forth the time spent and services rendered, and the company will pay the consultant the amounts due as indicated by statements submitted by the consultant within ten (10) days of receipt.

6. **Independent Contractor.** Both the company and the consultant agree that the consultant will act as an independent contractor in the performance of its duties under this contract. Accordingly, the consultant shall be responsible for payment of all taxes including Federal, State and local taxes arising out of the consultant's activities in accordance with this contract, including by way of illustration but not limitation, Federal and State income tax, Social Security tax, Unemployment Insurance taxes, and any other taxes or business license fee as required.

7. **Confidential Information.** The consultant agrees that any information received by the consultant during any furtherance of the consultant's obligations in accordance with this contract, which concerns the personal, financial or other affairs of the company will be treated by the consultant in full confidence and will not be revealed to any other persons, firms or organizations.

8. **Employment of Others.** The company may from time to time request that the consultant arrange for the services of others. All costs to the consultant for those services will be paid by the company but in no event shall the consultant employ others without the prior authorization of the company.

By: _____

By: _____

Independent Contractor Agreement

(Source: www.lectlaw.com/forms/f050.htm)

SUBCONTRACT

On ___ day of _____, 20 ____, _____,
henceforth "Contractor" and _____,
henceforth "Subcontractor", HEREBY ENTER into the following
subcontract:

WITNESSETH:

WHEREAS Contractor has entered into, or will hereafter enter into,
a general construction contract, henceforth "The Prime Contract"
with: _____ (Owner or General Contractor), to perform in
accordance with various contract documents and specifications certain
work prepared by: _____, henceforth "Architect", and/or to
furnish labor, materials, supplies, labor and/or goods required to
construct the following named and described construction project:

_____, henceforth "The Project", located
in _____county, at _____ address, and WHEREAS Contractor
desires to retain Subcontractor to perform certain contract work in
accordance with various contract documents and specifications and/or to
furnish labor, materials, supplies, labor and/or goods for The Project;

NOW THEREFORE Contractor and Subcontractor agree as follows:

ARTICLE I.
SUBCONTRACT WORK

1.1 Subcontractor shall be employed as an independent contractor
and shall provide and furnish all labor, materials, tools,
supplies, equipment, services, facilities, supervision, and
administration necessary for the proper and complete performance
and acceptance of the following portions of the work, hereinafter
"the Subcontract Work", for the Project, together with such other
portions of the drawings, specifications and addendum as related
thereto:

SEE EXHIBIT A: Scope, Conditions, And List of Attachments

ARTICLE II.
SUBCONTRACTOR PRICE

2.1 In consideration of Subcontractor's performance of this
Subcontract, and at the times and subject to the terms and
conditions hereinafter set forth, Contractor shall pay to
Subcontractor the total sum of _____ dollars ($000,000.00),
hereinafter "subcontract price." Said subcontract price is
dependant upon the conditions set forth in Exhibit A being met.
Should said conditions not be met, the subcontract amount shall be
modified accordingly.

ARTICLE III.
SPECIAL CONDITIONS

The Special Conditions to Subcontract (Articles I through XXI) are incorporated in this Subcontract as though fully set forth herein. Subcontractor hereby acknowledges receipt of the Special Conditions.

ARTICLE IV
COMMUNICATION AND NOTICE

4.1 All communications between Subcontractor and General Contractor, Owner or Architect shall be via Contractor.

4.2 Subcontractor shall furnish Contractor with periodic progress reports as required by Contractor, including status of material, equipment, manpower and submittal.

4.3 Subcontractor shall be deemed to have received notice of a fact, request, order, or demand when its Superintendent is notified, either orally or in writing, or three (3) days after written notice is sent by registered or certified mail addressed to Subcontractor's last known place of business, whichever is sooner.

4.4 Contractor shall be deemed to have received notice of a fact, request, or demand three (3) days after written notice is sent by registered or certified mail addressed to the following address:

(Contractor's address)

ARTICLE V
GOVERNING LAW AND RULES OF CONSTRUCTION

5.1 The validity, interpretation, and performance of this Subcontract shall be governed by the laws of the jurisdiction where The Project is located.

5.2 Titles, captions, or headings to any provision, article, etc., shall not limit the full contents of the same. These articles have the full force and effect as if no titles existed.

5.3 If any term or provision of this Subcontract is determined to be invalid, it shall not affect the validity and enforcement of the remaining terms and provisions of this Subcontract.

5.4 This contract shall be binding upon and inure to the benefit of the respective successors, assigns, representatives, and heirs of the parties herein.

ARTICLE VI
AMENDMENT

6.1 This Subcontract shall only be amended or modified by written document executed by authorized representatives of Contractor and Subcontractor. This Subcontract supersedes all prior representations made by Contractor.

ARTICLE VII
ARBITRATION

7.1 Any and all disputes or claims between the Contractor and the Subcontractor arising out of this Subcontract shall be resolved by submission of the same to   for resolution by binding arbitration according to _____ Rules of Arbitration. In so agreeing the parties expressly waive their right to a jury trial, if any, on these issues and further agree that the award of the arbitrator shall be final and binding upon them as though rendered by a court of law and shall be enforceable in any court having jurisdiction over the same.

THIS SUBCONTRACT IS ACKNOWLEDGED AND EXECUTED AS OF THE DATE SET FORTH ABOVE:

_____   _____

SUBCONTRACTOR   **CONTRACTOR**

By: _____   By: _____

Titles: _____   Title: _____

Subcontractor Agreement

(Source: www.lectlaw.com/forms/f088.htm)

INDEPENDENT CONTRACTOR AGREEMENT

THIS AGREEMENT is made and entered into this____day of ___ , 20__ , by and between _____ , with offices at_____ , in the City_____ of _____ , and the State of_____ , hereinafter referred to as the "Contractor", and _____ , whose address is _____ , in the City of _____ , and the State of_____ , hereinafter referred to as the "Subcontractor".

WITNESSETH:

WHEREAS, the Contractor is engaged in the business of_____ , and the Subcontractor is engaged in the business of _____ ; and

WHEREAS, the Contractor desires to enter into this Agreement with the Subcontractor, providing, among other things, for Subcontractor's services to the Contractor; and

WHEREAS, the Subcontractor desires to enter into this Agreement with respect to his services to the Contractor, upon the terms and conditions hereinafter set forth.

NOW, THEREFORE, the parties agree as follows:

1. The Contractor shall retain the Subcontractor and the Subcontractor shall assist the Contractor upon the terms and conditions hereinafter set forth.

2. Term. The term of this Agreement shall commence on the _____day of _____ , 20__ , and terminate on the_____ day of _____ , 20__ , unless terminated prior to that date as set out hereinafter.

3. Duties of Subcontractor. During the period of this Agreement, the Subcontractor shall have the full and complete obligation and responsibility for the performance of the duties and/or work described in the attached Exhibit "A" for the Contractor and the Subcontractor shall be obligated to the Contractor for the performance of all such duties and/or work. During the period hereof, the Subcontractor shall assist the Contractor and shall perform any and all services required or requested in connection with the Contractor's business. Within the limitations herein provided, the Subcontractor will render such services of an advisory nature as may be requested from time to time by the Contractor.

4. Time Requirements. The Subcontractor shall devote, during the term of this Agreement, such of his time, energy, and skill as is necessary in the performance of his duties hereunder and shall periodically, or at any time, upon the request of the Contractor, submit data as to the time requirements of work performed and to be performed by him for the Contractor in connection with this Agreement.

5. Fees to Subcontractor. The Contractor shall pay the Subcontractor on a "per project" basis for services in connection with this Agreement, the exact amount for each project to be agreed upon in writing by the Contractor and the Subcontractor, prior to any work being performed, or, in the alternative, per the attached Exhibit "B".

6.   Relation of the Parties. The Subcontractor is retained by the Contractor only for the purposes and to the extent set forth in this Agreement and the Subcontractor's relationship to the Contractor shall, during the term of this Agreement, be that of an Independent Contractor. The Contractor shall not withhold, from sums becoming payable to the Subcontractor hereunder, any amounts for State or Federal Income Tax, or for FICA (Social Security) Taxes, during the term of this Agreement. The Subcontractor shall be free to dispose of such portions of his entire time, energy and skill as he is not obligated to devote hereunder to the Contractor in such manner as he deems advisable. The Subcontractor shall not be considered as having an employee status or as being entitled to participate in any plans, arrangements or distributions by the Contractor pertaining to or in connection with any pension, stock, bonus, profit sharing or other benefit extended to the Contractor's employees.

7.   Worker's Compensation. If required by the laws of this State, the Contractor shall maintain in full force and effect a policy of worker's compensation insurance covering the Subcontractor during the term of this Agreement and the Subcontractor's account shall be debited by the pro-ration of premiums thereon attributable to the Subcontractor.

8.   Professional Responsibility. Nothing in this Agreement shall be construed to interfere with or otherwise affect the rendering of services by the Subcontractor in accordance with his independent and professional judgment. The Subcontractor shall perform his services substantially in accordance with generally accepted practices and principles of his trade. This Agreement shall be subject to the rules and regulations of any and all organizations and associations to which the Subcontractor may from time to time belong and to the laws and regulations governing the practice of the Subcontractor's trade in this State.

9.   Indemnity to Subcontractor. The Contractor indemnifies the Subcontractor against any loss or liability which the Subcontractor may sustain by reason of any contract entered into by the Contractor with any principal, but this indemnity shall not extend to any loss which the Subcontractor may incur by reason of the work performed by the Subcontractor hereunder.

10. Termination. This Agreement may be terminated at any time, with or without cause, by either party upon thirty (30) days written notice.

11. Notice. Any notice required to be given hereunder shall be deemed given on the third (3rd) business day following mailing of any such notice, postage paid, to the address set out herein above.

12. Income Tax Designation. In the event that the Internal Revenue Service should determine that the subcontractor is, according to I.R.S. guidelines, an employee subject to withholding and social security contributions, the subcontractor shall acknowledge, as the subcontractor acknowledges herein, that all payments to the subcontractor are gross payments, and the subcontractor is responsible for all income taxes and social security payments thereon.

IN WITNESS WHEREOF, the parties have hereunto set their hands and seals the day and year first above written.

Signed, sealed and delivered in the presence of:

"CONTRACTOR"

_____ Witness
_____ Witness

"SUBCONTRACTOR"

_____ Witness
_____ Witness

EXHIBIT "A"
Duties and/or Work to be Performed by Subcontractor

EXHIBIT "B"
Alternate Fee Arrangement

Independent Contractor Agreement
(Source: www.lectlaw.com/forms/f050.htm)

ACKNOWLEDGMENT OF WORK RULES

Employee name: _____

Employee number: _____

Department: _____

Social Security number: _____

I have read and understand the company work rules. I acknowledge that I am expected to conform to those rules and that I am subject to termination for failure to conform to the said rules. It is understood that any modification to the work rules must be in writing and signed by [individual with the authority to modify work rules]. In addition, I acknowledge that I have a duty to report to [supervisor] any violations of the work rules by other employees.

Acknowledged by: _____

Date: _____

Acknowledgement of Work Rules
(Source: www.lectlaw.com/forms/f185.htm)

Spreadsheets

By far some of the best spreadsheets out there are available on the web at www. exinfm.com. One particular spreadsheet at www.exinfm.com/excel%20files/ Workbook1-2.xls has numerous workbooks at the bottom that include everything from balance sheets to income statements and from horizontal analyses to key financials.

Balance Sheet for X Y Z Corporation USA

millions of dollars

	Ref	Description	Annual Period 1996	Annual Period 1997	Annual Period 1998	Annual Period 1999	Annual Period 2000
Current Assets	3-1	Cash and Cash Equivalents	990	950	901	998	870
	3-2	Short Term Marketable Securities	10	15	12	6	11
	3-3	Accounts Receivable	1,020	1,550	1,830	2,250	3,040
	3-4	Inventory	1,005	1,360	1,650	1,900	2,060
	3-5	Other Current Assets	870	1,150	1,370	1,650	1,530
	3-6	Total Current Assets	3,895	5,025	5,763	6,804	7,511
NonCurrent Assets	3-7	Fixed Assets	14,006	17,605	21,826	26,950	28,100
	3-8	Accumulated Depreciation	(1,280)	(1,700)	(2,100)	(2,550)	(3,010)
	3-9	Net Fixed Assets	12,726	15,905	19,726	24,400	25,090
	3-10	Longterm Investments	360	320	120	590	905
	3-11	Investments in Other Companies	65	0	0	250	412
	3-12	Intangibles and Other Assets	100	110	105	135	195
		Total Noncurrent Assets	13,251	16,335	19,951	25,375	26,602
	3-13	Total Assets	17,146	21,360	25,714	32,179	34,113
Current Liab	3-14	Accounts Payable	2,050	3,150	3,290	3,870	4,800
	3-15	Short Term Borrowings	1,200	1,830	2,580	3,100	3,550
	3-16	Short Term Portion of LT Debt	12	15	25	30	36
	3-17	Other Current Liabilities	1,050	1,250	1,480	1,590	1,301
	3-18	Total Current Liabilities	4,312	6,245	7,375	8,590	9,687
	3-19	Longterm Debt / Borrowings	1,160	1,750	2,600	3,600	3,950
	3-20	Other Longterm Liabilities	650	750	701	890	995
		Total Noncurrent Liabilities	1,810	2,500	3,301	4,490	4,945
	3-21	Total Liabilities	6,122	8,745	10,676	13,080	14,632
Equity	3-22	Preferred Equity	0	0	0	0	0
	3-23	Common Equity	2,044	2,005	2,069	2,090	2,120
	3-24	Additional Paid in Capital	5,013	4,900	5,159	5,626	5,628
	3-25	Retained Earnings	5,097	7,050	9,840	15,050	20,005
	3-26	Adj for Foreign Currency Transl	275	120	(550)	(2,147)	(6,722)
	3-27	Treasury Stock	(1,405)	(1,460)	(1,480)	(1,520)	(1,550)
	3-28	Total Shareholder Equity	11,024	12,615	15,038	19,099	19,481
		Total Liabilities & Equity	17,146	21,360	25,714	32,179	34,113
	3-29	Check: Assets = Liab + Equity ?	0	0	0	0	0
		Comment =>	Balances	Balances	Balances	Balances	Balances
Additional Information	3-30	NonDdepreciable Fixed Assets	0	0	0	0	0
	3-31	Deferred Taxes	112	101	90	98	109
	3-32	Goodwill Write Off	0	0	0	0	0
	3-33	# of Common Shares o/s	1,320	1,290	1,302	1,345	1,322
	3-34	Par Value of Common Stock	$10.00	$10.00	$10.00	$10.00	$10.00
	3-35	No of Preferred Shares o/s	0	0	0	0	0
	3-36	Par Value of Preferred Stock					
	3-37	Market Price of Common Stock	$22.65	$28.90	$37.05	$33.60	$29.40
	3-38	Market Price of Preferred Stock	$0.00	$0.00	$0.00	$0.00	$0.00
	3-39	Preferred Dividends in Arrears	0	0	0	0	0
	3-40	Liquidating value of Preferred Stk	0	0	0	0	0
	3-41	Book Value per Share	$8.35	$9.78	$11.55	$14.20	$14.74
	3-42	Dividends per Common Share	$1.01	$1.49	$1.89	$1.75	$1.76
	3-43	Dividend Payout Ratio	45.47%	38.61%	39.44%	29.76%	30.24%
	3-44	Cash Dividends to Preferred Stock	0	0	0	0	0
	3-45	Cash Dividends to Common Stock	1,330	1,918	2,461	2,354	2,329
	3-46	Total Dividends Paid	1,330	1,918	2,461	2,354	2,329

Sample Balance Sheet

(Source: www.exinfm.com/excel%20files/Workbook1-2.xls. Permission given by Matt H. Evans.)

Income Statement for X Y Z Corporation USA

millions of dollars

	Ref	Description	Annual Period 1996	Annual Period 1997	Annual Period 1998	Annual Period 1999	Annual Period 2000
Operating	4-1	Net Sales	12,060	16,700	21,170	24,700	27,400
	4-2	Other Operating Revenues	16	19	26	37	48
	4-3	**Total Revenues**	**12,076**	**16,719**	**21,196**	**24,737**	**27,448**
	4-4	Cost of Goods Sold	(4,950)	(7,050)	(8,233)	(9,050)	(10,150)
	4-5	Other Operating Expenses	(11)	(13)	(17)	(22)	(28)
	4-6	**Total Direct Expenses**	**(4,961)**	**(7,063)**	**(8,250)**	**(9,072)**	**(10,178)**
	4-7	Selling, General & Administrative	(3,300)	(3,880)	(4,637)	(5,670)	(7,120)
	4-8	**Operating Income**	**3,815**	**5,776**	**8,309**	**9,995**	**10,150**
NonOperating	4-9	Interest Expenses	(117)	(122)	(216)	(282)	(304)
	4-10	Foreign Exchange (Loss) Gain	0	0	0	0	0
	4-11	Associated Company (Loss) Gain	0	0	(22)	0	0
	4-12	Other Nonoperating (Loss) Gain	0	17	0	0	0
	4-13	Income Tax Expense	(790)	(1,005)	(2,050)	(2,105)	(2,660)
	4-14	Reserve Charges	0	0	0	0	0
	4-15	**Income Before Extra Ord Items**	**2,908**	**4,666**	**6,021**	**7,608**	**7,186**
	4-16	Extra Ordinary Items (Loss) Gain	0	0	0	0	0
	4-17	Tax Effects of Extraordinary Items	0	0	0	0	0
	4-18	Minority Interests	17	302	219	303	515
	4-19	**Net Income**	**2,925**	**4,968**	**6,240**	**7,911**	**7,701**
Other	4-20	Primary EPS	$2.22	$3.85	$4.79	$5.88	$5.83
		Earnings Before Int & Taxes	3,832	6,095	8,506	10,298	10,665
	4-22	Depreciation & Amortization	(310)	(420)	(400)	(450)	(460)
	4-23	Research & Devel Expenses	0	0	0	0	0
	4-23	Capitalized Interest Expense	(16)	(19)	(33)	(39)	(30)
	4-24	Interest Income	4	6	11	19	27
	4-25	Total Nonoperating Expenses	(907)	(1,110)	(2,288)	(2,387)	(2,964)
	4-26	Total Extra Ordinary Items	17	302	219	303	515
	4-27	Tax Rate	21.36%	17.78%	25.33%	21.67%	27.02%

Sample Income Statement

(Source: www.exinfm.com/excel%20files/Workbook1-2.xls. Permission given by Matt H. Evans.)

Cash Flow Statement for X Y Z Corporation USA

Description	millions of dollars				
	Annual Period 1996	Annual Period 1997	Annual Period 1998	Annual Period 1999	Annual Period 2000
Net Income	2,925	4,968	6,240	7,911	7,701
Depreciation and Amortization	310	420	400	450	460
(Increase) Decrease Defer Taxes	(2)	11	11	(8)	(11)
(Gain) Loss on Sale of Assets	(55)	0	45	0	0
(Increase) Decrease Current Assets	(162)	(1,130)	(738)	(1,041)	(707)
Increase (Decrease) Current Liab	206	1,933	1,130	1,215	1,097
Cash Flow from Operations	**3,222**	**6,202**	**7,088**	**8,527**	**8,540**
Capital Expenditures	(1,455)	(2,750)	(3,880)	(5,220)	(4,108)
Acquisition in Other Co's	(135)	0	0	0	0
Proceeds from Sales of Assets	112	35	0	150	182
Purchases of Investments	(712)	(1,979)	(1,801)	(2,314)	(2,609)
Sale of Investment	162	129	330	221	50
Other Investment Activities	33	(166)	61	(12)	0
Cash Provided (Used) from Investmts	**(1,995)**	**(4,731)**	**(5,290)**	**(7,175)**	**(6,485)**
Proceeds from Borrowings	1,070	1,044	1,460	1,880	1,105
Payments on Borrowings	(1,112)	(650)	(898)	(801)	(961)
Dividends Paid to Shareholders	(1,330)	(1,918)	(2,461)	(2,354)	(2,329)
Proceeds from Minority Interest	5	12	7	7	8
Issue Stock / Exercise Options	195	1	45	13	6
Purchase / Retire Common Stock	0	0	0	0	0
Other Financing Activities	(75)	0	0	0	(12)
Cash Provided (Used) from Financing	**(1,247)**	**(1,511)**	**(1,847)**	**(1,255)**	**(2,183)**
Increase (Decrease) to Cash	**(20)**	**(40)**	**(49)**	**97**	**(128)**

Sample Cash Flow Statement

(Source: www.exinfm.com/excel%20files/Workbook1-2.xls. Permission given by Matt H. Evans.)

Key Financial Data for
X Y Z Corporation USA

		millions of dollars				
Ref	Description	Annual Period 1996	Annual Period 1997	Annual Period 1998	Annual Period 1999	Annual Period 2000
	EBITDA:					
4-15	Income before Extra Ord Items	2,908	4,666	6,021	7,608	7,186
4-9	Interest Expense	117	122	216	282	304
4-23	Capitalized Interest Expense	16	19	33	39	30
4-13	Income Tax Expense	790	1,005	2,050	2,105	2,660
4-14	Reserve Charges	0	0	0	0	0
4-22	Depreciation and Amortization	310	420	400	450	460
6-1	**EBITDA**	**4,141**	**6,232**	**8,720**	**10,484**	**10,640**
	EBITDA Margin	**34%**	**37%**	**41%**	**42%**	**39%**
	Free Cash Flow:					
5-7	Operating Cash Flow	3,222	6,202	7,088	8,527	8,540
5-14	Investment Cash Flows	(1,995)	(4,731)	(5,290)	(7,175)	(6,485)
3-43	Preferred Dividends Paid (fixed)	0	0	0	0	0
5-16	Redemption of Fixed Obligations	(1,112)	(650)	(898)	(801)	(961)
6-2	Other Critical Outlays	(35)	(45)	(42)	(30)	(25)
6-3	**Free Cash Flow**	**80**	**776**	**858**	**521**	**1,069**
	Working Capital:					
3-6	Current Assets	3,895	5,025	5,763	6,804	7,511
3-18	Current Liabilities	4,312	6,245	7,375	8,590	9,687
6-4	**Working Capital**	**(417)**	**(1,220)**	**(1,612)**	**(1,786)**	**(2,176)**
	Liquid Capital:					
3-1	Cash and Cash Equivalents	990	950	901	998	870
3-2	Marketable Securities	10	15	12	6	11
3-3	Accounts Receivable	1,020	1,550	1,830	2,250	3,040
6-5	Notes Receivable	0	0	0	0	0
3-18	Total Current Liabilities	(4,312)	(6,245)	(7,375)	(8,590)	(9,687)
3-19	Long Term Debt	(1,160)	(1,750)	(2,600)	(3,600)	(3,950)
3-22	Preferred Equity	0	0	0	0	0
6-6	**Liquid Capital**	**(3,452)**	**(5,480)**	**(7,232)**	**(8,936)**	**(9,716)**

The following valuation indicators are very simple and basic; they are used as quick, rough estmates.

	Market Capitalization:					
6-7	Market Cap - Common Stk	$29,898	$37,281	$48,239	$45,192	$38,867
6-8	Market Cap - Preferred Stk	$0.00	$0.00	$0.00	$0.00	$0.00
6-9	**Total Market Capitalization**	**$29,898**	**$37,281**	**$48,239**	**$45,192**	**$38,867**

Cash Flow / Liquidity Indicators

			5.00%	10.00%	15.00%	30.00%	40.00%	100.00%
		Present Value:						
	6-10	Normalized Cash Flow Weight %s	5.00%	10.00%	15.00%	30.00%	40.00%	100.00%
	6-11	Normalized Cash Flow					794	
	6-12	Number of Future Periods					15	
	6-13	Required Rate of Return					11.00%	
	6-14	Present Value of Free Cash Flow					$5,711	
	6-15	Present Value of Selling Price	$315,000 <= estimated selling price				$65,836	
	6-16	**Present Value of Business**					**$71,547**	
		Revenue Multiplier:						
	4-3	Recent Gross Revenues					27,448	
	6-17	Average Competitive Rev Multiplier					3.14	
		Value based on Revenue Multiple					**$86,187**	
		Capitalization of Earnings:						
	6-18	Normalized Net Income Weights %	5.00%	5.00%	25.00%	30.00%	35.00%	100.00%
	6-19	Normalized Net Income					6,681	
	6-20	Capitalization Rate					12.00%	
	6-21	Nominal Growth Rate					3.50%	
	6-22	Net Capitalization Rate					8.50%	
	6-23	**Value based on Earnings**					**$78,605**	
	6-24	Operating Leverage		1.31	1.49	1.21	0.14	
	6-25	Financial Leverage		1.46	0.61	1.12	(0.65)	
	6-26	Total Leverage		1.92	0.91	1.36	(0.09)	
	6-27	*Check Totals*	*0.00*	*1.92*	*0.91*	*1.36*	*(0.09)*	
		NOPAT / Operating Indicators:						
	6-28	Net Interest Expense After Tax	(95)	(105)	(169)	(236)	(242)	
	6-29	Interest Bearing Liabilities	2,372	3,595	5,205	6,730	7,536	
	6-30	NOPAT	3,020	5,073	6,409	8,147	7,943	
	6-31	Operating Working Capital	(205)	(340)	80	340	529	
	6-32	Net Longterm Assets	12,601	15,585	19,250	24,485	25,607	
	6-33	Net Debt	1,372	2,630	4,292	5,726	6,655	
	6-34	Net Assets	12,396	15,245	19,330	24,825	26,136	
	6-35	Net Capital	12,396	15,245	19,330	24,825	26,136	
	6-36	Operating ROA	24%	33%	33%	33%	30%	
	6-37	Operating WC Turnover	(59)	(49)	265	73	52	

Left side vertical labels: **Valuation Indicators**, **Leverage**, **Operating Indicators**

Sample Balance Sheet

(Source: www.exinfm.com/excel%20files/Workbook1-2.xls. Permission given by Matt H. Evans.)

Ratio Analysis for
X Y Z Corporation USA

Title of Ratio	Annual Period 1996	Annual Period 1997	Annual Period 1998	Annual Period 1999	Annual Period 2000
Acid Test Ratio	0.47	0.40	0.37	0.38	0.40
Current Ratio	0.90	0.80	0.78	0.79	0.78
Operating Cash Flow to Net Income	1.10	1.25	1.14	1.08	1.11
Liquidity Index:					
Cash - Days Removed	0	0	0	0	0
Cash Balance	990	950	901	998	870
Cash Balance Total	0	0	0	0	0
Marketable Sec - Days Removed	11	12	16	15	14
Marketable Securities Balance	10	15	12	6	11
Marketable Securities Total	110	180	192	90	154
Receivables - Days Removed	34	30	31	32	36
Receivable Balance	1,020	1,550	1,830	2,250	3,040
Receivable Balance Total	34,257	46,158	56,217	72,213	110,751
Inventory - Days Removed	79	61	67	72	71
Inventory Balance	1,005	1,360	1,650	1,900	2,060
Inventory Balance Total	79,745	83,261	110,092	136,018	146,676
Other - Days Removed	16	22	26	21	19
Other Current Assets Balance	870	1,150	1,370	1,650	1,530
Other Current Assets Total	13,920	25,300	35,620	34,650	29,070
Liquidity Index (Days)	**33**	**31**	**35**	**36**	**38**
Z Score:					
1.2 x (working capital / total assets)	(0.03)	(0.07)	(0.08)	(0.07)	(0.08)
1.4 x (retained earn / total assets)	0.42	0.46	0.54	0.65	0.82
3.3 x (EBIT / total assets)	0.74	0.94	1.09	1.06	1.03
.6 x (market value equity / b.v. debt)	15.46	12.78	11.13	7.53	5.90
.999 x (sales / total assets)	0.70	0.78	0.82	0.77	0.80
Z Score	**17.29**	**14.90**	**13.51**	**9.94**	**8.48**
Receivable Turnover:					
Credit Sales	11,520	15,750	20,080	23,200	26,500
Average Receivable Balance	1,060	1,285	1,690	2,040	2,645
Receivable Turnover	**10.9**	**12.3**	**11.9**	**11.4**	**10.0**
Days Required to Collect A/R	**34**	**30**	**31**	**32**	**36**
Inventory Turnover:					
Average Inventory Balance	1,046	1,183	1,505	1,775	1,980
Inventory Turnover	**4.6**	**6.0**	**5.5**	**5.1**	**5.1**
Days in Inventory	**79**	**61**	**67**	**72**	**71**
Total Asset Turnover	**0.7**	**0.8**	**0.8**	**0.8**	**0.8**

**Ratio Analysis for
X Y Z Corporation USA**

Title of Ratio	Annual Period 1996	Annual Period 1997	Annual Period 1998	Annual Period 1999	Annual Period 2000
Operating Assets Ratio	0.97	0.98	0.99	0.97	0.96
Gross Profit Margin	59%	58%	61%	63%	63%
Operating Margin	32%	35%	39%	40%	37%
Net Profit Margin	24%	30%	29%	32%	28%
Direct Cost to Operating Revenues	41%	42%	39%	37%	37%
Capitalization Rate / Asset Return:					
Net Operating Income	3,000	4,749	6,204	7,829	7,408
Total Investments / Operating Assets	16,621	20,930	25,489	31,204	32,601
Capitalization Rate / Return	**18.05%**	**22.69%**	**24.34%**	**25.09%**	**22.72%**
Return on Shareholder Equity	24%	33%	35%	33%	26%
Debt to Total Assets	0.36	0.41	0.42	0.41	0.43
Debt to Common Equity	0.50	0.63	0.63	0.57	0.53
Times Interest Earned	33	50	39	37	35
Price to Earnings (P/E)	10.2	7.5	7.7	5.7	5.0
Price to Book Value	2.7	3.0	3.2	2.4	2.0
Stock Yield	4.45%	5.14%	5.10%	5.21%	5.99%

Ratio Analysis

(Source: www.exinfm.com/excel%20files/Workbook1-2.xls. Permission given by Matt H. Evans.)

Final Budgets for X Y Z Corporation USA

Now that we have analyzed our historical data and placed it into a set of forecast, we can pull it all together with our assumptions for a final budget. Many of these assumptions should be included in our forecast for improved accuracy. However, we need to fine tune and finalize all assumptions so that we can produce a final finished budget for planning purposes.

Ref		Budget Period 2001	Assumptions & Comments
	Operating Plan		
16-1	Total Revenues	30,500	Based on review of Pro Forma Financials, Marketing, etc.
16-2	Cost of Goods Sold	(11,929)	Volume projections, production budgets, and vertical analysis
16-3	Operating Expenses	(7,424)	Average % of Sales per Vertical Analysis
16-4	Operating Income	11,146	
16-5	Interest Expenses	(310)	Based on anticipated levels of debt and past history
16-6	Income Taxes	(3,300)	Based on anticipated taxable income and effective rate
16-7	Other Non Operating Expenses	(200)	Provision for contingency was added on this line item
16-8	Earnings Before Extra Ord Items	7,336	
16-9	Extra Ordinary Items	650	Per our Simple Model Forecast
16-10	Net Income	7,986	
	Financial Plan		
	Budgeted Cash Flows		
16-11	Net Income	7,986	
16-12	Depreciation and Amortization	470	Review of Simple Model Forecast and Capital Expenditure Budget
16-13	(Increase) Decrease Defer Taxes	0	
16-14	(Gain) Loss on Sale of Assets	15	Per Simple Forecast Model

16-15	(Increase) Decrease Current Assets	(724)	Same formula as used in forecast models
16-16	(Increase) Decrease Current Liab	988	Same formula as used in forecast models
16-17	Operating Cash Flow	8,735	
	Investment Sources of Cash:		
16-18	Planned Sale of Assets	100	Per Simple Model Forecast
16-19	Planned Sale of Investments	2,200	Per Simple Model Forecast
16-20	Other Investment Sources to be used	0	
16-21	Total Investment Sources of Cash	2,300	
	Planned Investments:		
16-22	Capital Expenditures	(4,500)	Budgeted $ 4.5 million in Capital Expenditure Budget
16-23	Acquisitions in Other Co's	(350)	Per forecast, strategic plan, and other budgets
16-24	Purchases of Investments	(2,500)	Per forecast, strategic plan, and other budgets
16-25	Total Investment Applications of Cash	(7,350)	
	Cash Flow from Financing Activities		
16-26	Proceeds from Loans & Debt	1,450	Per Financing Requirements and other budgets
16-27	Proceeds from Minority Interest	15	Per historical financials and investment budget
16-28	Other Financing Activities	0	
16-29	Total Financing Sources of Cash	1,465	
	Cash Flow Applied for Financing:		
16-30	Payments on Loans and Debt	(1,250)	Per forecast and other budgets
16-31	Dividends Paid to Shareholders	(2,500)	Per Simple Model Forecast
16-32	Purchase / Retire Stock	(1,500)	Per strategic plan and other budgets
16-33	Other Financing Activities	0	
16-34	Total Financing Applications of Cash	(5,250)	
16-35	Total Change to Cash	(100)	
16-36	Beginning Cash Balance	870	
16-37	Forecasted Ending Balance	770	

Budgeted Balance Sheet

16-38	Cash and Cash Equivalents	770	Per above
16-39	Short Term Marketable Securities	10	Per historical financials
16-40	Accounts Receivable	3,050	Same formula as used in forecast models
16-41	Inventory	2,440	Same formula as used in forecast models
16-42	Other Current Assets	1,983	Same formula as used in forecast models
16-43	Total Current Assets	8,253	
16-44	Fixed Assets	32,600	Same formula as used in forecast models
16-45	Accumulated Depreciation	(3,480)	Same formula as used in forecast models
16-46	Net Fixed Assets	29,120	
16-47	Longterm Investments	1,205	Same formula as used in forecast models
16-48	Investments in Other Companies	1,000	Per review of forecast and strategic plans
16-49	Intangibles and Other Assets	230	Per review of forecast and historical balances
16-50	Total Non Current Assets	31,555	
16-51	Total Assets	39,808	
16-52	Accounts Payable	5,185	Same formula as used in forecast models
16-53	Short Term Borrowings	3,660	Same formula as used in forecast models
16-54	Short Term Portion of LT Debt	40	Per review of forecast and historical information
16-55	Other Current Liabilities	1,830	Same formula as used in forecast models
16-56	Total Current Liabilities	10,715	
16-57	Longterm Debt / Borrowings	4,150	Same formula as used in forecast models
16-58	Other Longterm Liabilities	1,100	Per review of historical information and expected growth rates.
16-59	Total Non Current Liabilities	5,250	
16-60	Total Liabilities	15,965	

16-61	Preferred Stock	0	Per Simple Model Forecast
16-62	Common Equity	2,200	Per Simple Model Forecast
16-63	Additional Paid in Capital	5,700	Per Simple Model Forecast
16-64	Retained Earnings	25,491	Same formula as used in forecast models
16-65	Adj for Foreign Currency Translation	(5,000)	Per Simple Model Forecast
16-66	Treasury Stock	(3,050)	Same formula as used in forecast models
16-67	Total Equity	25,341	
16-68	Total Liabilities and Equity	41,306	
16-69	External Financing Required	(1,499)	

Final Budgets

(Source: www.exinfm.com/excel%20files/Workbook1-2.xls. Permission given by Matt H. Evans.)

Resources

This appendix contains lots of resources for small- and medium-sized businesses; from governmental resources to tax resources; employment law to help on managing the day to day tasks of owning your own company.

Small Business Administration

The Small Business Administration (SBA) was created in 1953 as an independent agency of the federal government. It was formed to assist and counsel small businesses and assist those contributing to free enterprise and strengthening the economy. The SBA has a network of field offices and partnerships with public and private organizations, and serves Americans in the United States, Puerto Rico, the U.S. Virgin Islands, and Guam. The SBA website has tools, planners, and services online, as well as numerous local resources. Available on the web at www.sba.gov/index.html.

Internal Revenue Service Small Business Sources

Available on the web at www.irs.gov/businesses/small, the IRS's small business website focuses on everything from knowing if you need an Employee Identification Number to how and when to file taxes, how to incorporate, and when to file employee or contractor tax forms. A powerful, useful site for small business owners with lots of forms to download. Even if you use an accountant, this is a great site with loads of useful information that is essential for any business owner.

Legal Resources

Nolo.com: Nolo provides law forms and do-it-yourself legal kits and books for consumers and small businesses, on subjects including estate planning, business law, debt and credit, and so on. Also take a look at *The Employer's Legal Guide* (1997), by Stephen Fishman, published by Nolo Press. An in-depth and comprehensive discussion of employee vs. independent contractor legal issues is available online at Fenwick & West: Publications.

SmallBusiness.FindLaw.com: FindLaw's Small Business Center provides information and resources for small businesses, including employment law, human resources, an overview of legal issues faced by small businesses, and more.

LegalZoom.com: LegalZoom was founded by renowned attorney Robert Shapiro, whom you may remember from the O. J. Simpson trial. LegalZoom provides all sorts of valuable legal forms and services for both personal and business use.

California Chamber of Commerce: Offers a summary of legal issues related to hiring independent contractors. "Independent Contractors: A Manager's Guide and Audit Reference," published by the California Chamber of Commerce, PO Box 1736, Sacramento, CA 95812-1736, 916-444-6670. Their website is www.calchamber.com/Pages/Default.aspx.

You should also look at the Chamber of Commerce for other states; which you can find at www.uschamber.com/chambers/directory/default.htm.

'Lectric Law Library: Available at www.lectlaw.com—an incredibly useful, exhaustive list of forms for everything from real estate businesses to creating applications for employees. Some of the best online resources on the web, the LectLaw website has useful, easy-to-follow information in a very straightforward format.

Business Planning and Assessment

Value-Based Management Tools and SWOT Analysis: Available at www. valuebasedmanagement.net, this site offers fantastic tools for identifying the strengths and weaknesses of businesses. This site lists about every management model and method, from contingency theory to risk management and root cause analysis. A great overall resource for business owners.

Excel Spreadsheets: Matt H. Evans, CPA, CMA, CFM, offers resources, training, and many Excel spreadsheets available at www.exinfm.com/free_spreadsheets.html. This is an astounding resource that provides tools for everything from valuation models to cash flow analysis to financial charting to risk analysis.

Small Business Taxes and Management: A fabulous website created by the fine folks at www.smbiz.com, offering tools for everything from evaluating S corporation officers' salaries to avoiding scams to filing extensions for partnerships and trusts. Truly a fantastic, comprehensive resource.

isquare.com: Offers numerous articles about starting and operating a business, marketing a business, websites, business tips, stress tips, and tradeshows. They also have excellent technology archives and product reviews. Check out their terrific site!

Kwintessential: Want to know more about other cultures and the norms and customs of other nations? A helpful resource for many countries that you could potentially need information on can be found at Kwintessential Cross Culture Solutions's website, at www.kwintessential.co.uk/resources/country-profiles.html.

Billing and Payments

Regardless of what your business does or how it is structured, being able to accept payments through many means is very important. There are three recommended companies to look at, depending on your needs. Each one and their associated website is listed here.

Authorize.net: A simple service provider that will allow you to accept credit card payments online or on your web-enabled mobile device (like a BlackBerry), through mail order and telephone sales, and even within a retail establishment (meaning you can utilize their services even if you run a traditional brick-and-mortar store). This is the company that I use on my teachonlinetraining.com website; it has easy integration with lots of tools—even precreated custom training applications!

MerchantExpress.com: Merchant Accounts Express has been providing online merchant services since 1998; they offer quick and easy solutions for accepting credit card payments online. Merchant Accounts Express also handles physical acceptance of credit cards with point-of-sale (POS) terminals and service as well.

PayPal.com: Getting its start as the primary payment option for eBay and then later becoming an eBay-owned business, PayPal has been and remains sufficient for many business owners. It has basic invoicing capabilities, the ability to transfer funds to accounts and easily handle payments from any source, including checking accounts, and provides security and low fees—as well as cash back when you use it as a credit card.

References

Andrews, K. R., C. R. Christensen, W. D. Guth, and E. P. Learned. *Business Policy, Text and Cases*. McGraw Hill: 1969.

AOL Small Business Website. "Small Business Myths." smallbusiness.aol.com/features/small-business-myths (accessed August 24, 2008).

Babb, D. & A. Lazo. (2007) Real Estate v2.0. Kaplan Press.

BusinessWeek. "25 Companies Where Customers Come First." articles.moneycentral.msn.com/News/25CompaniesWhereCustomersComeFirst.aspx (accessed August 29, 2008).

California Chamber of Commerce. "Independent Contractors: A Manager's Guide and Audit Reference." n.p., n.d.

Chun, J. "To Tell the Truth." April 1998. findarticles.com/p/articles/mi_m0DTI/is_n4_v26/ai_20484748 (accessed August 24, 2008).

Cooper, J. "A Helping Hand from Foreign Demand." *BusinessWeek*, November 5, 2007. www.businessweek.com/magazine/content/07_45/b4057032.htm (accessed August 29, 2008).

Copernicus Marketing Consulting. "Identifying Profitable Customer Targets." www.copernicusmarketing.com/univers/target.shtml (accessed August 29, 2008).

Coyne, K. P. and Sujit Balakrishnan. "Bringing Discipline to Strategy." *The McKinsey Quarterly* 4 (1996).

Datko, K. "Reach a Human When You Call Customer Service." blogs. moneycentral.msn.com/smartspending/archive/2008/01/15/reach-a-human-when-you-call-customer-service.aspx (accessed August 29, 2008).

Ebben, J. "Developing Effective Vision and Mission Statements." www.inc.com/resources/startup/articles/20050201/missionstatement.html (accessed August 29, 2008).

EmployeeIssues.com. "Overtime pay." employeeissues.com/overtime_pay.htm (accessed August 29, 2008).

Evans, M. "Free Excel spreadsheets." www.exinfm.com/ free_spreadsheets.html (accessed August 29, 2008).

Financial Guide. "Glossary: G." www.financial-guide.net/ glossary.php?language=en#G (accessed August 24, 2008).

Fishman, S. "The Employer's Legal Guide." Nolo Press, 1997.

Google. "Google Checkout—Protect Yourself from Fraud with Google Checkout." checkout.google.com/seller/fraud.html (accessed August 28, 2008).

Grant, R. M. *Contemporary Strategy Analysis.* Oxford: Blackwell Publishing, 2005.

Hunger, J. David & Thomas L. Wheelen. *Essentials of Strategic Management.* New Jersey: Pearson Education, 2003.

Investopedia. "Double taxation." www.investopedia.com/terms/d/ double_taxation.asp (accessed August 24, 2008).

John, J. "Top Down Management vs. Bottom Up Management." February 10, 2008. www.kenneyjacob.com/2008/02/10/top-down-management-vs-bottom-up-management (accessed August 24, 2008).

LegalZoom. "Copyright FAQ." www.legalzoom.com/copyrights-faq/ copyright-name-title-slogan-logo.html (accessed August 24, 2008).

McGahan, A. *How Industries Evolve—Principles for Achieving and Sustaining Superior Performance.* Boston: Harvard Business School Press, 2004.

McGregor, J., F. F. Jespersen, M. Tucker, and D. Foust. "Customer Service Champs." *BusinessWeek*, 2007. www.businessweek.com/magazine/content/ 07_10/b4024001.htm (accessed August 29, 2008).

McRae, Shannon. "Debunking Small-Business myths." September 26, 2007. www.nfib.com/object/IO_34898.html (accessed June 26, 2008).

NetMBA. "Porter's Five Forces." www.quickmba.com/strategy/porter.shtml (accessed August 29, 2008).

———. "Scenario Planning." www.netmba.com/strategy/scenario (accessed August 29, 2008).

———. "SWOT Analysis." www.netmba.com/strategy/swot (accessed August 29, 2008).

Porter, M. E. *Competitive Advantage*. New York: The Free Press, 1985.

———. *Competitive Strategy*. New York: The Free Press, 1980.

———. "How Competitive Forces Shape Strategy." *Harvard Business Review*, March/April 1979.

Small Business Administration. "Note on Grants." sba.gov/services/financialassistance/grants/index.html (accessed August 24, 2008).

Small Business Boomers. "Small Business Myth Busters—Myth 1: Your Credit Rating." www.smallbusinessboomers.com/small-business-myth-busters-myth-1-your-credit-rating (accessed August 24, 2008).

Small Business Taxes and Management. "Corporate and Individual Tax Rates." www.smbiz.com/sbrl001.html (accessed August 24, 2008).

Social Security Administration. "FICA & SECA Tax Rates." www.ssa.gov/OACT/ProgData/taxRates.html (accessed August 29, 2008).

SurePayroll. "SurePayroll Insights Survey: Fewer Small Business Owners Can Afford to Offer Healthcare, but Split on Solution." April 16, 2008. www.surepayroll.com/spsite/press/releases/2008/release041608.asp (accessed August 24, 2008).

U.S. Bureau of Labor. "Employer Costs for Employee Compensation for the Regions: March 2008." June 17, 2008. www.bls.gov/ro7/ro7ecec.htm (accessed August 24, 2008).

U.S. Department of the Treasury, Internal Revenue Service. "Determination of Worker Status for Purposes of Federal Employment Taxes and Income Tax Withholding." November 2006. www.irs.gov/pub/irs-pdf/fss8.pdf (accessed August 24, 2008).

———. "Independent Contractor (Self-Employed or Employee?)." www.irs.gov/businesses/small/article/0,,id=99921,00.html (accessed August 24, 2008).

ValueBasedManagement.net. "SWOT Analysis." www.valuebasedmanagement.net/methods_swot_analysis.html (accessed August 29, 2008).

Virgin Money. "Business Loans." www.virginmoneyus.com/BusinessLoans/tabid/138/Default.aspx (accessed August 24, 2008).

Ward, S. "Top 7 Myths About Starting a Small Business." sbinfocanada.about.com/od/startup/a/businessmyths.htm (accessed August 24, 2008).

Weston, L. "7 Ways to Win the Customer-Service Game." articles.moneycentral.msn.com/SavingandDebt/ConsumerActionGuide/7waysToWinTheCustomerServicegame.aspx?page=1 (accessed August 29, 2008).

———. "Are You a Bad Customer?" articles.moneycentral.msn.com/SavingandDebt/ConsumerActionGuide/AreYouABadCustomer.aspx (accessed August 29, 2008).

———. "Hounded by Customer Service." articles.moneycentral.msn.com/SavingandDebt/ConsumerActionGuide/HoundedByCustomerService.aspx (accessed August 29, 2008).

Index

D

G

J-K

L